Creative Concepts for Artists

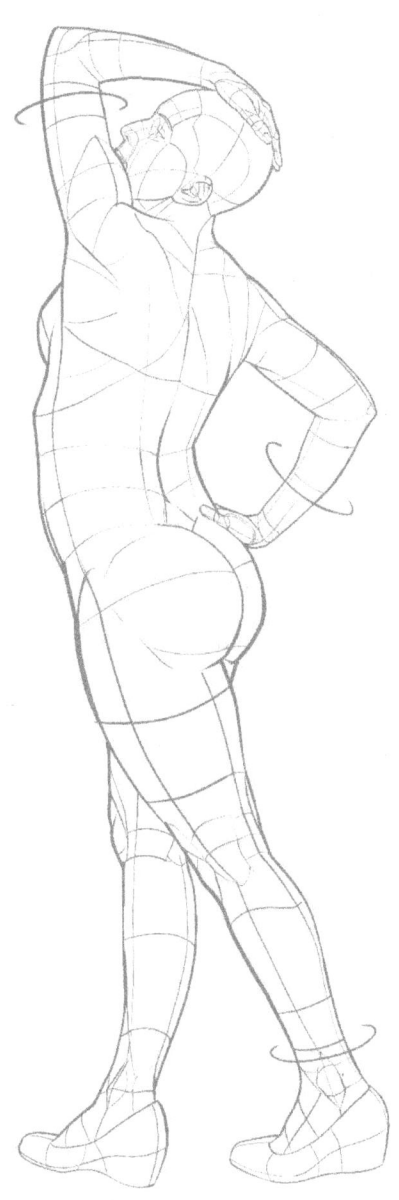

CREDITS

INSPIRATION: SAKKY FORD/SENSHISTOCK.COM

Thank you...

To the aritsts. This project was personal, until you convinced me to share it, and the books happened. You deserve the credit for planting the seed that grew into this...the 6th book of poses. I'll keep drawing them if you keep supporting them.

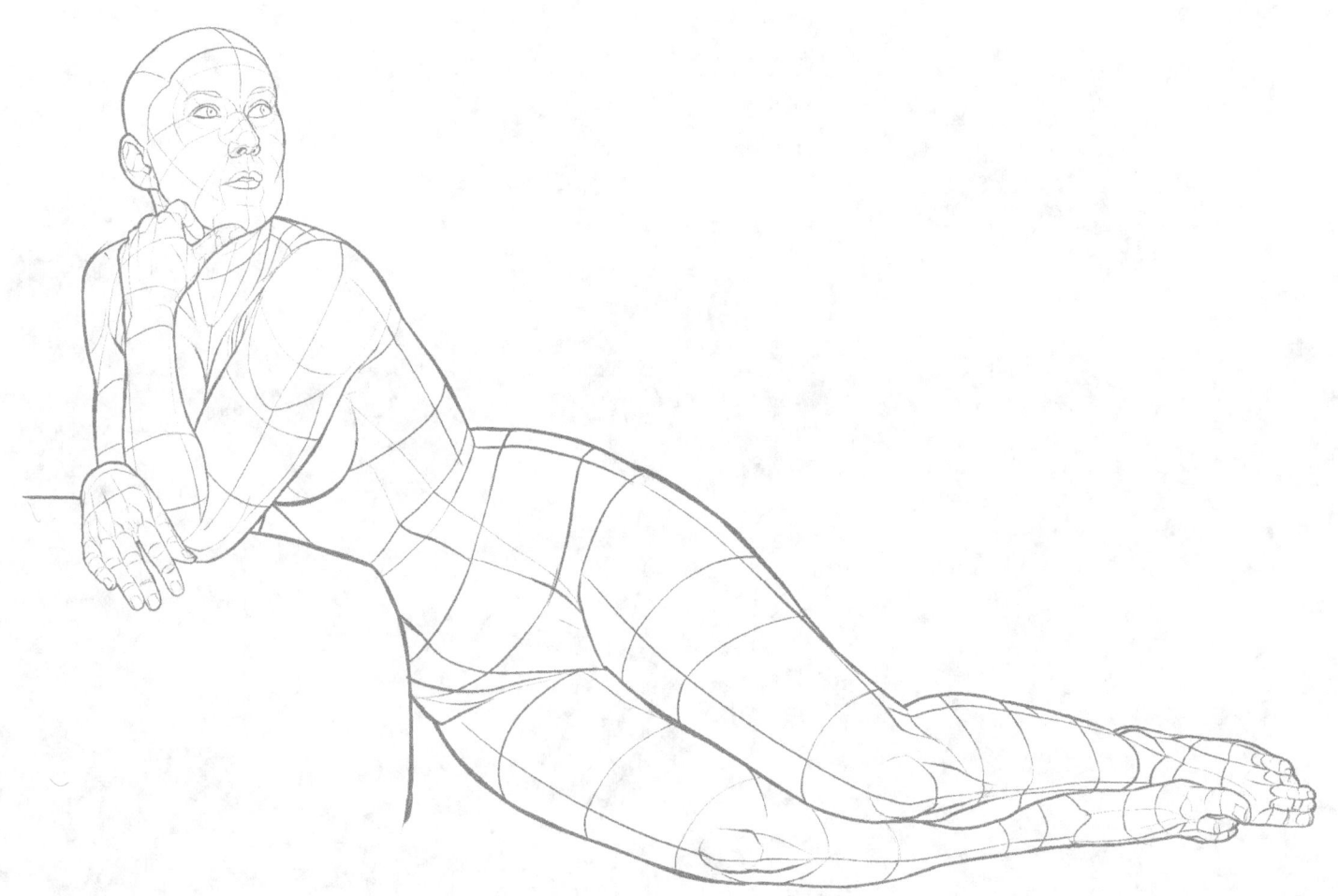

ISBN: 9798652990350
Imprint: Independently published
FIRST EDITION

Web: www.POSEmuse.com for more info

DISCLAIMER: All images in this publication are copyright 2020 by Justin Martin and POSEmuse. Use the poses to make new art, don't sell the poses. Contact Justin via email at justin@posemuse.com

Contents

Weilding Poses . . . . 5 - 36
Standing Poses . . . . .37 - 66
Sitting Poses . . . . 67 - 91
Leaning/Laying Poses . . . . 92 - 97
Kneeling/Crouching Poses.. . . . .98 - 112
Magic Poses . . . . 113 - 118
Leaping/Fying Poses . . . . 119 - 130

SenshiStock is a pose reference artist and photographer, probably the most generous artist in the field. I first found her poses on DeviantArt then on her website, www.SenshiStock.com, where she has created a feature that mimics a timed figure drawing class.

All for free.

The poses are real. The models are interesting. The variety of poses is creative and always inspiring.

This book is a collection of poses I have drawn using her photo reference. Some of the drawings have appeared in previous books, but over 100 of them are new, just for this project.

Weilding Poses

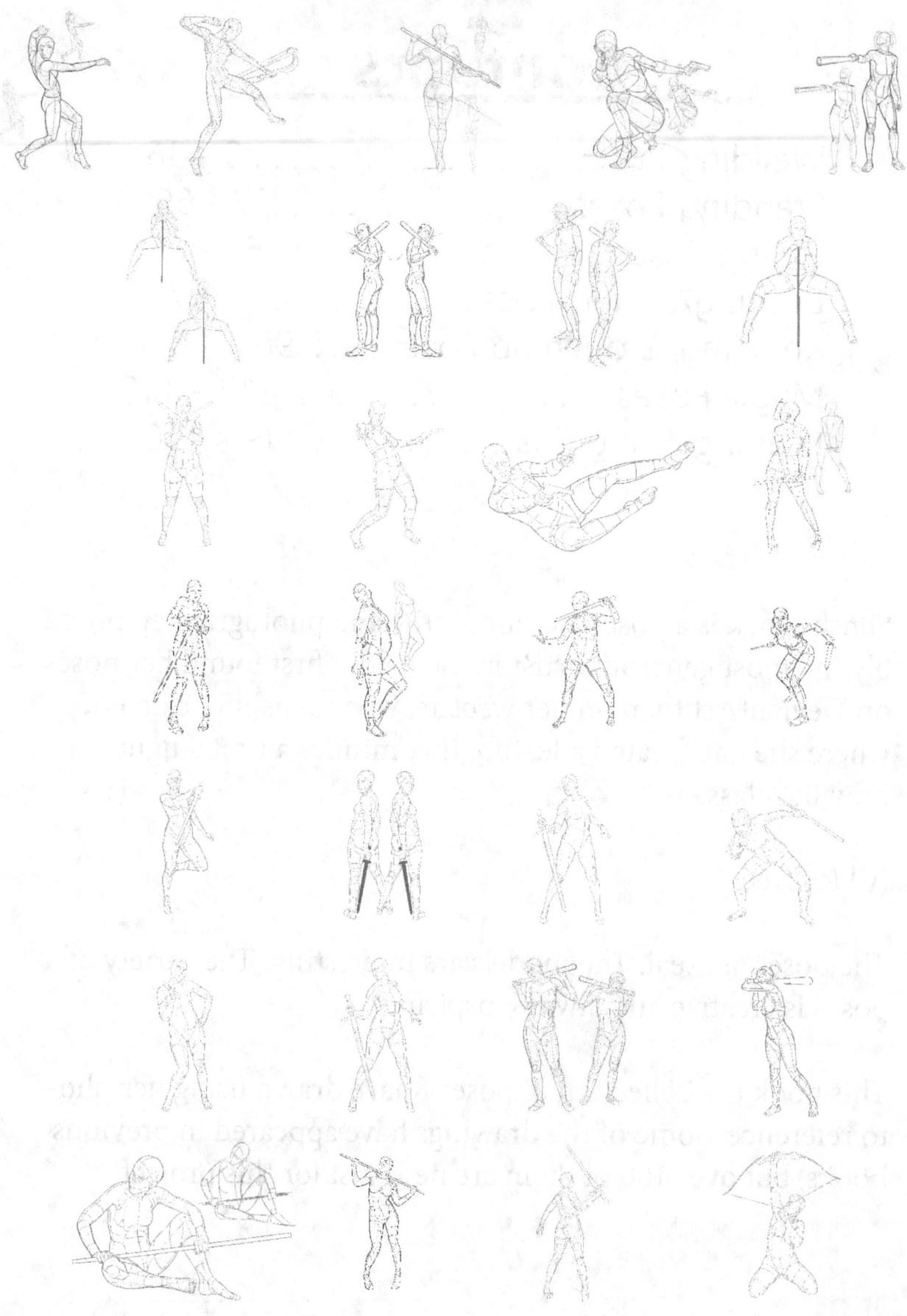

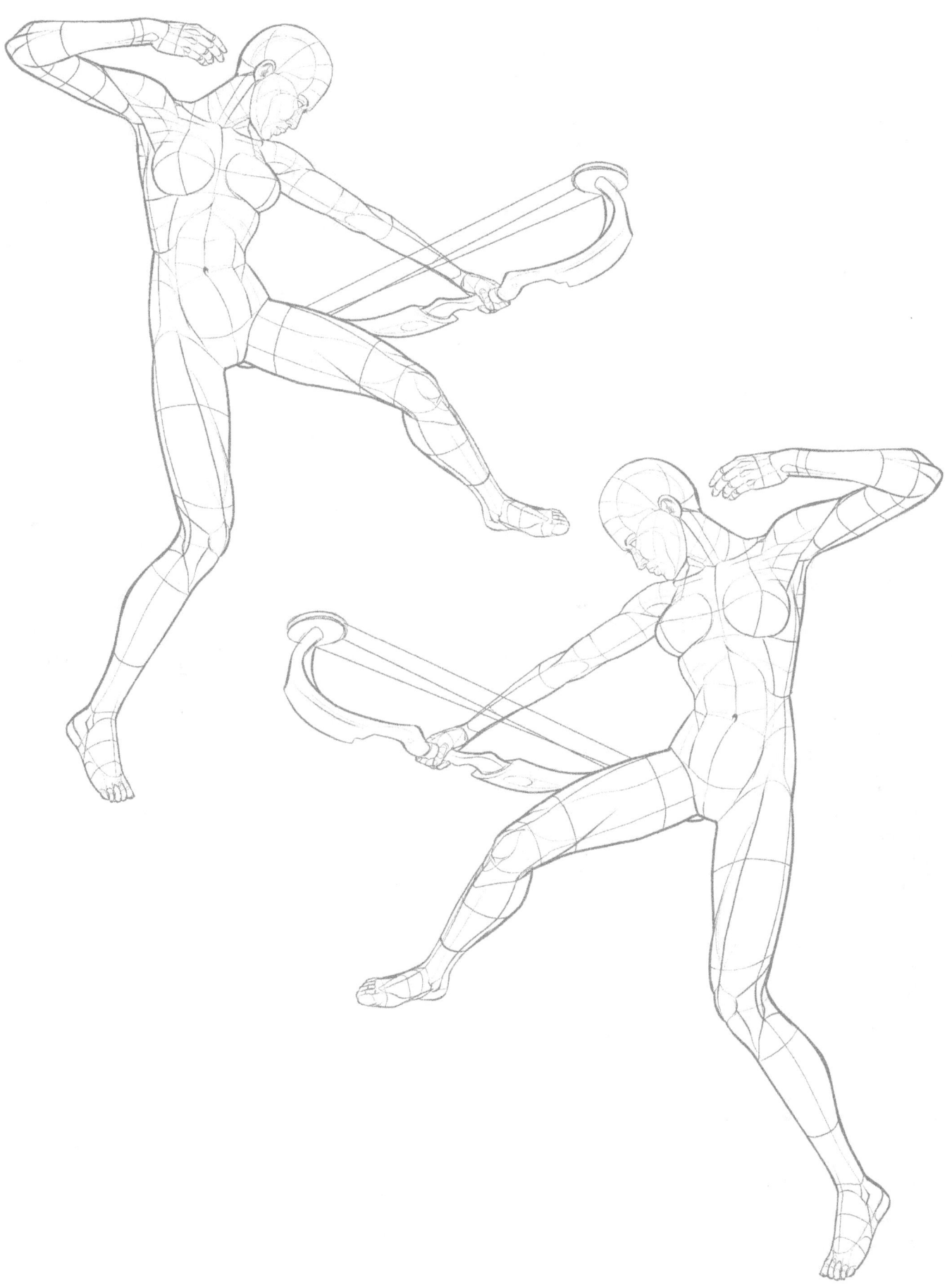

Weilding Poses | **5**

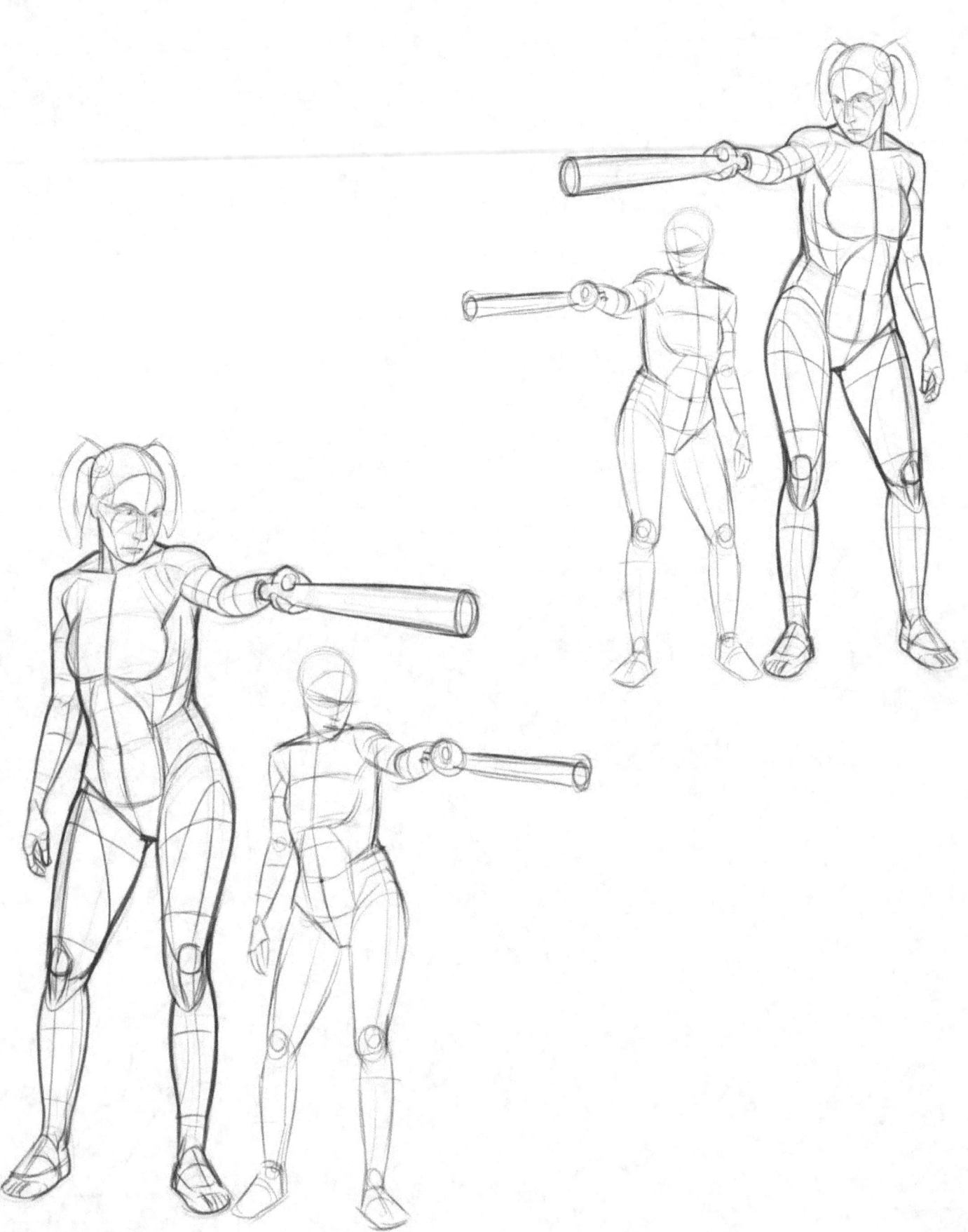

6 | Weilding Poses

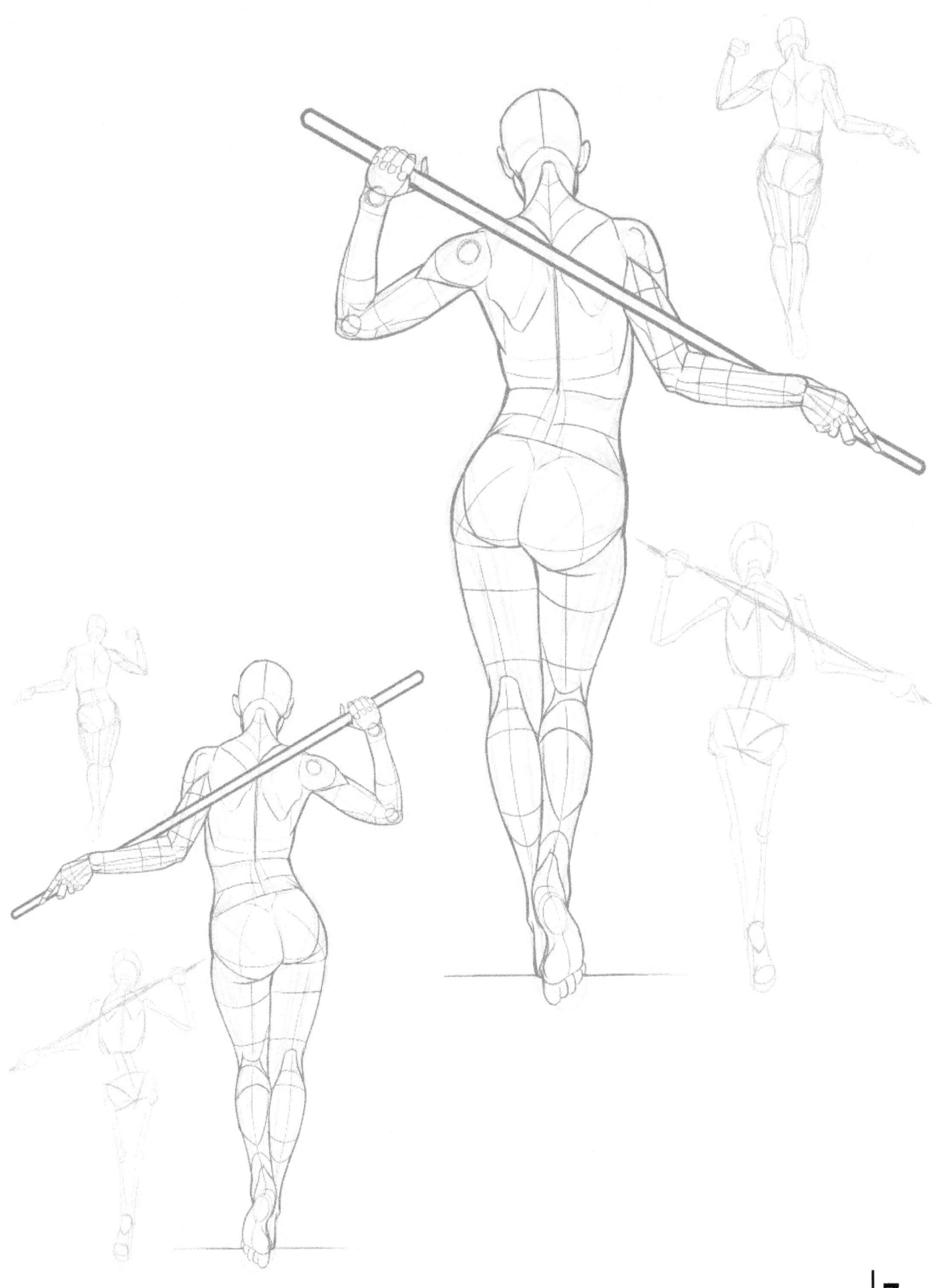

Weilding Poses | 7

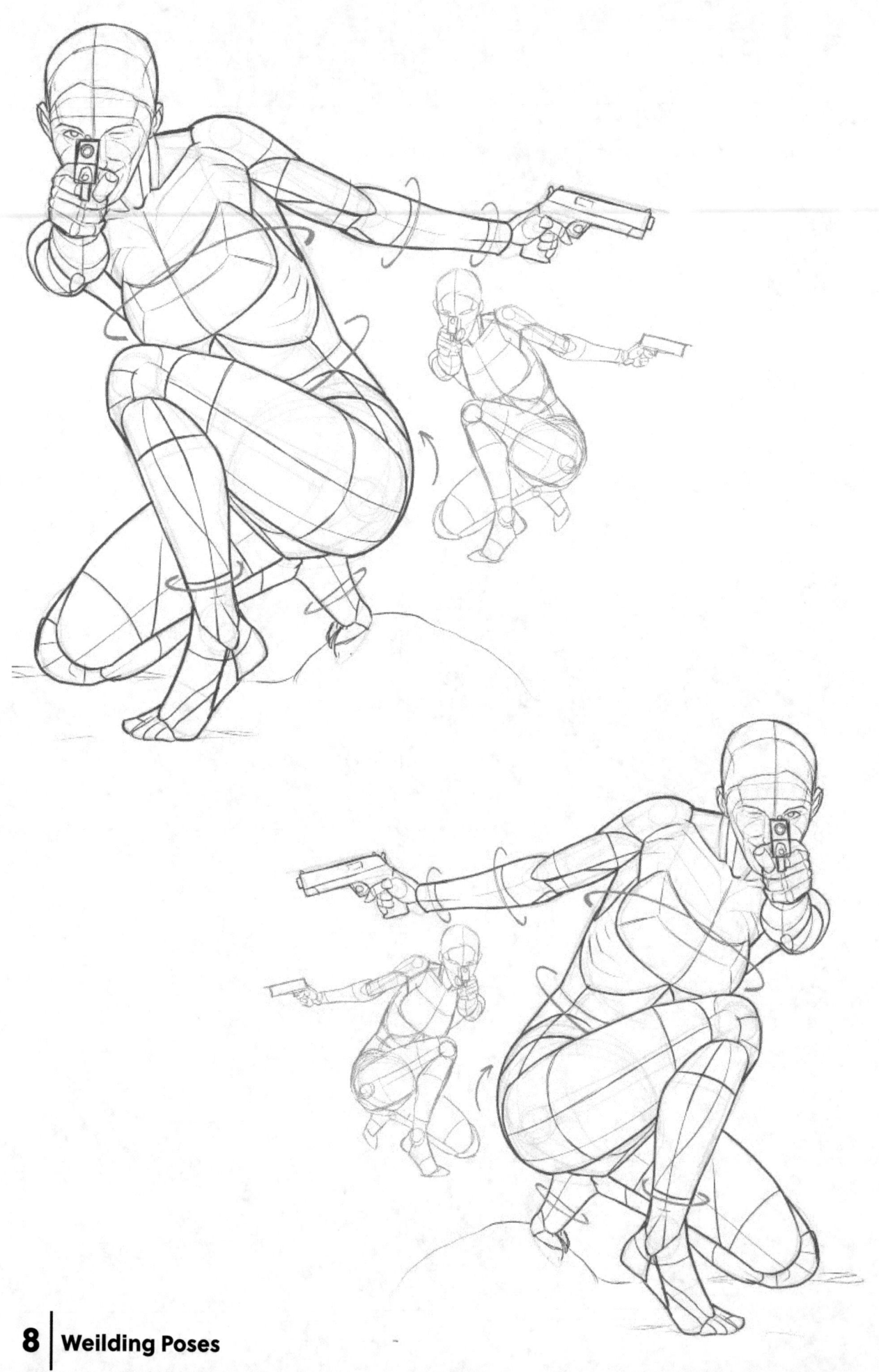

8 | Weilding Poses

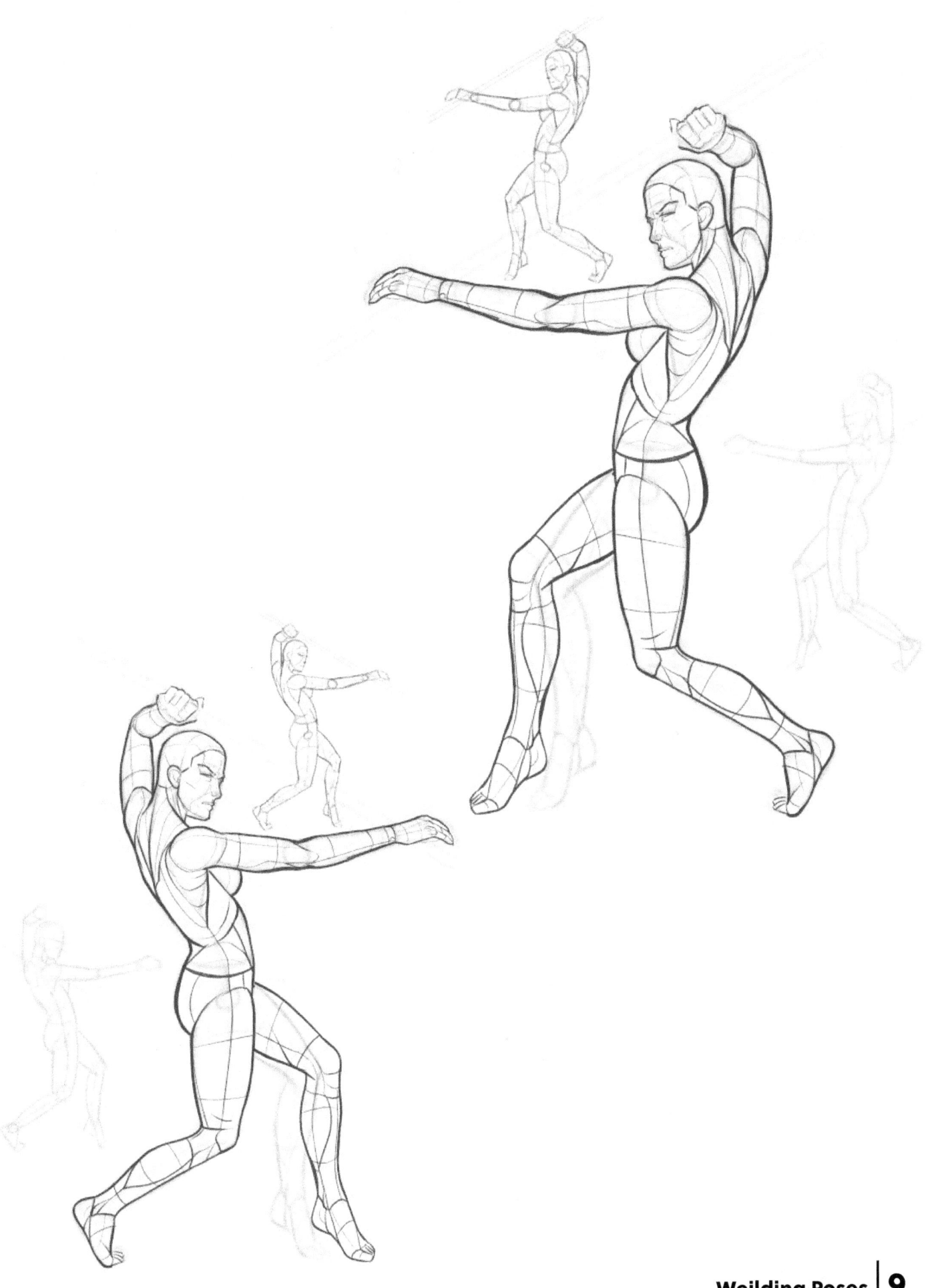

Weilding Poses | 9

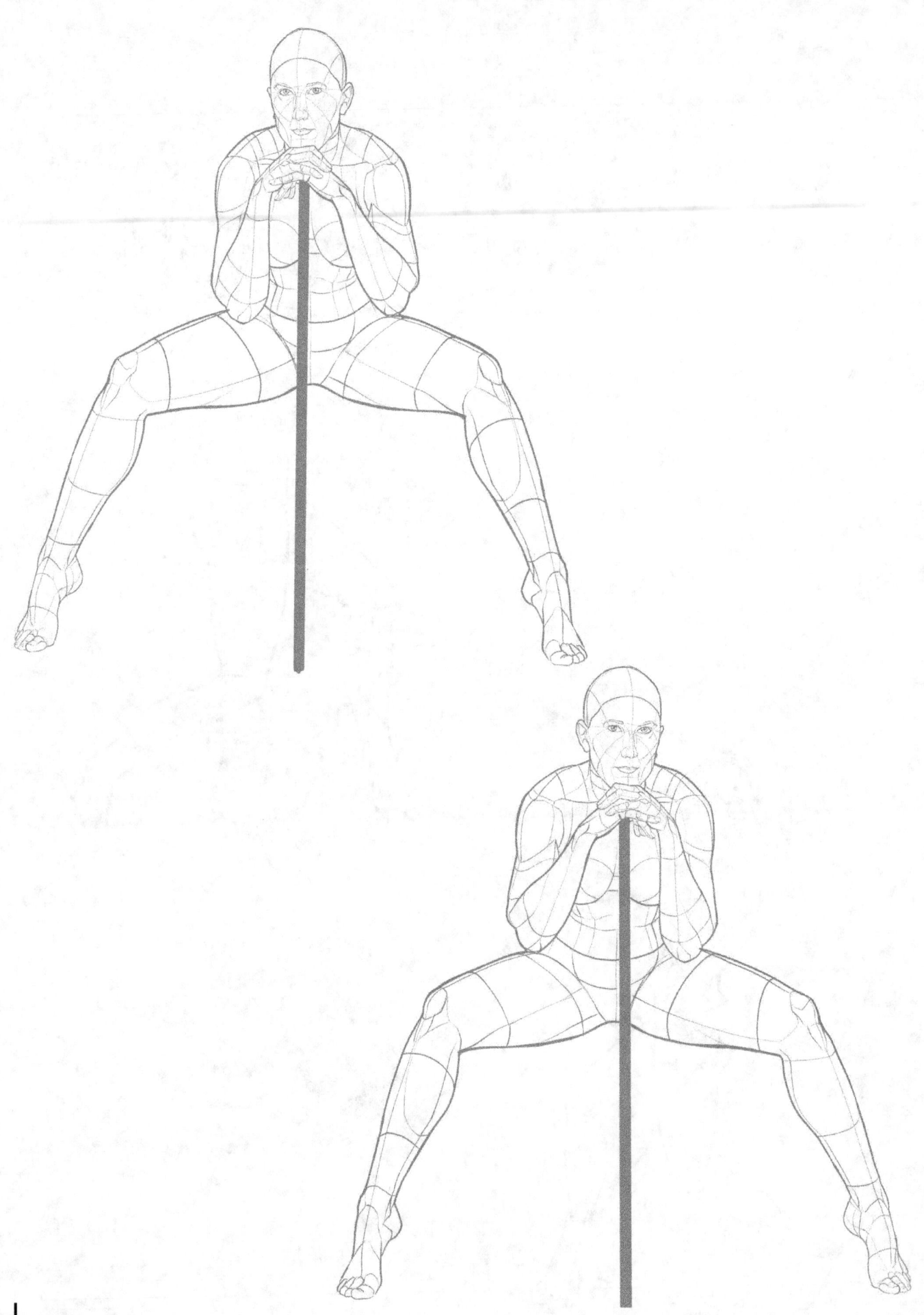

10 | Weilding Poses

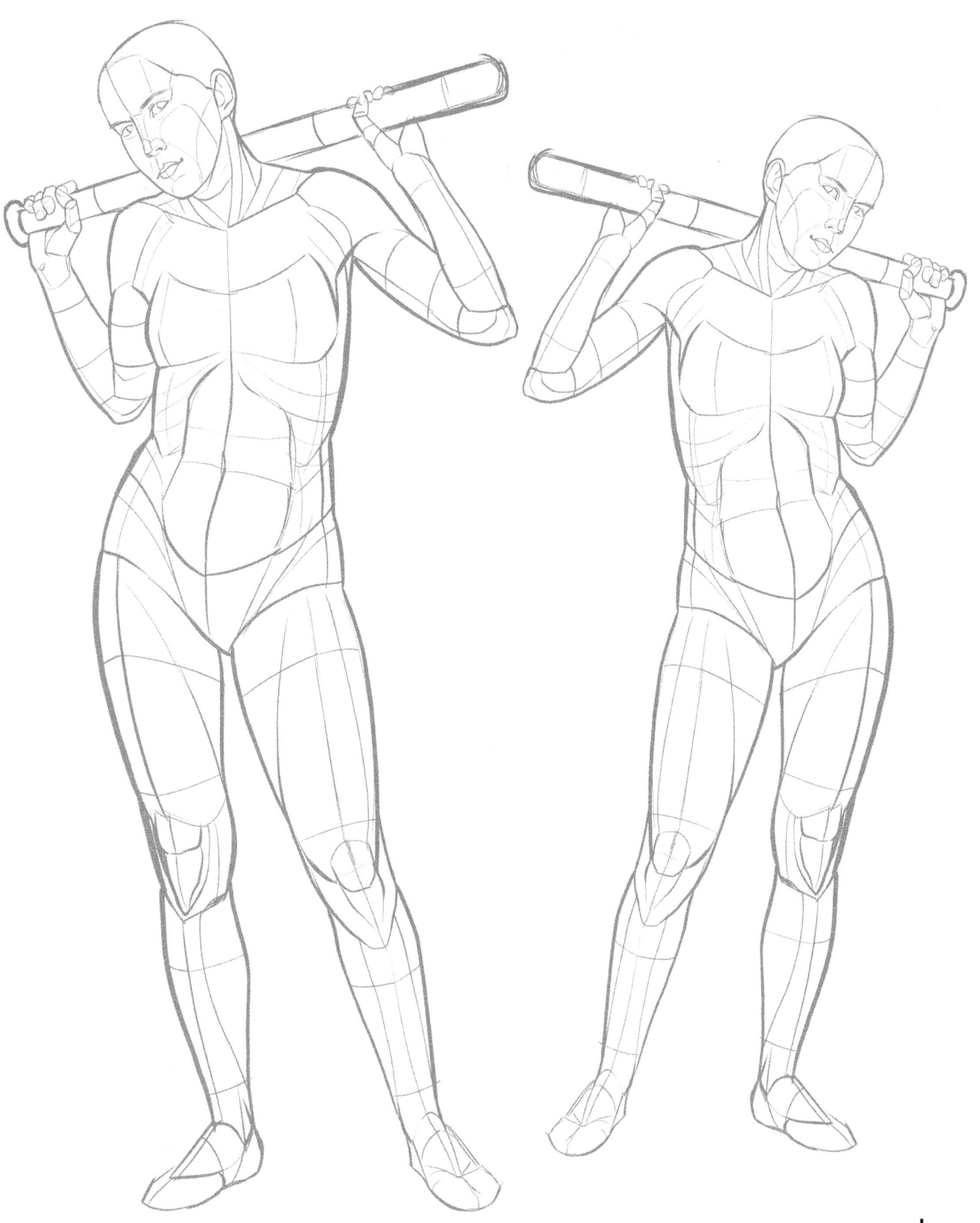

Weilding Poses | 11

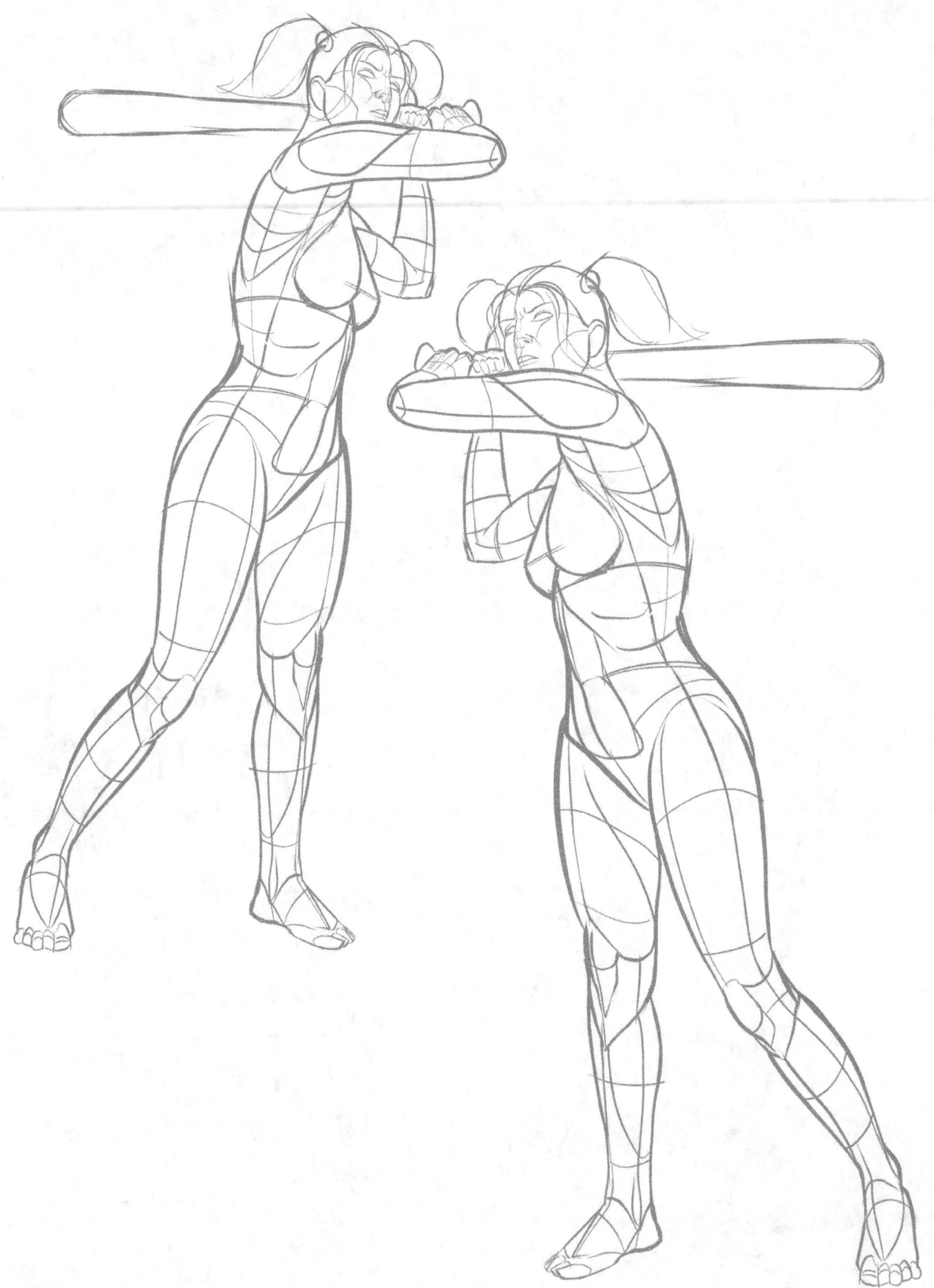

12 | Weilding Poses

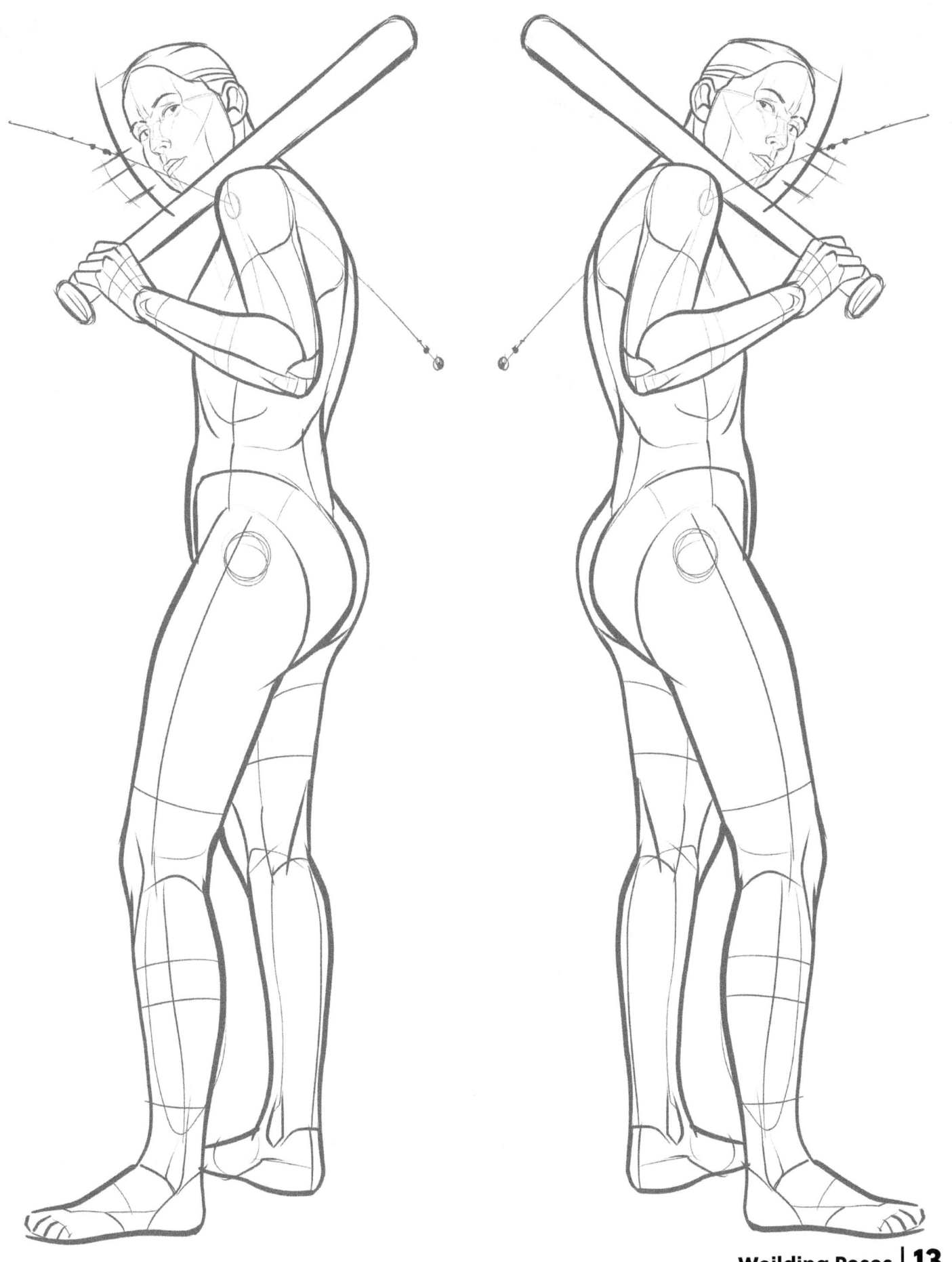

Weilding Poses

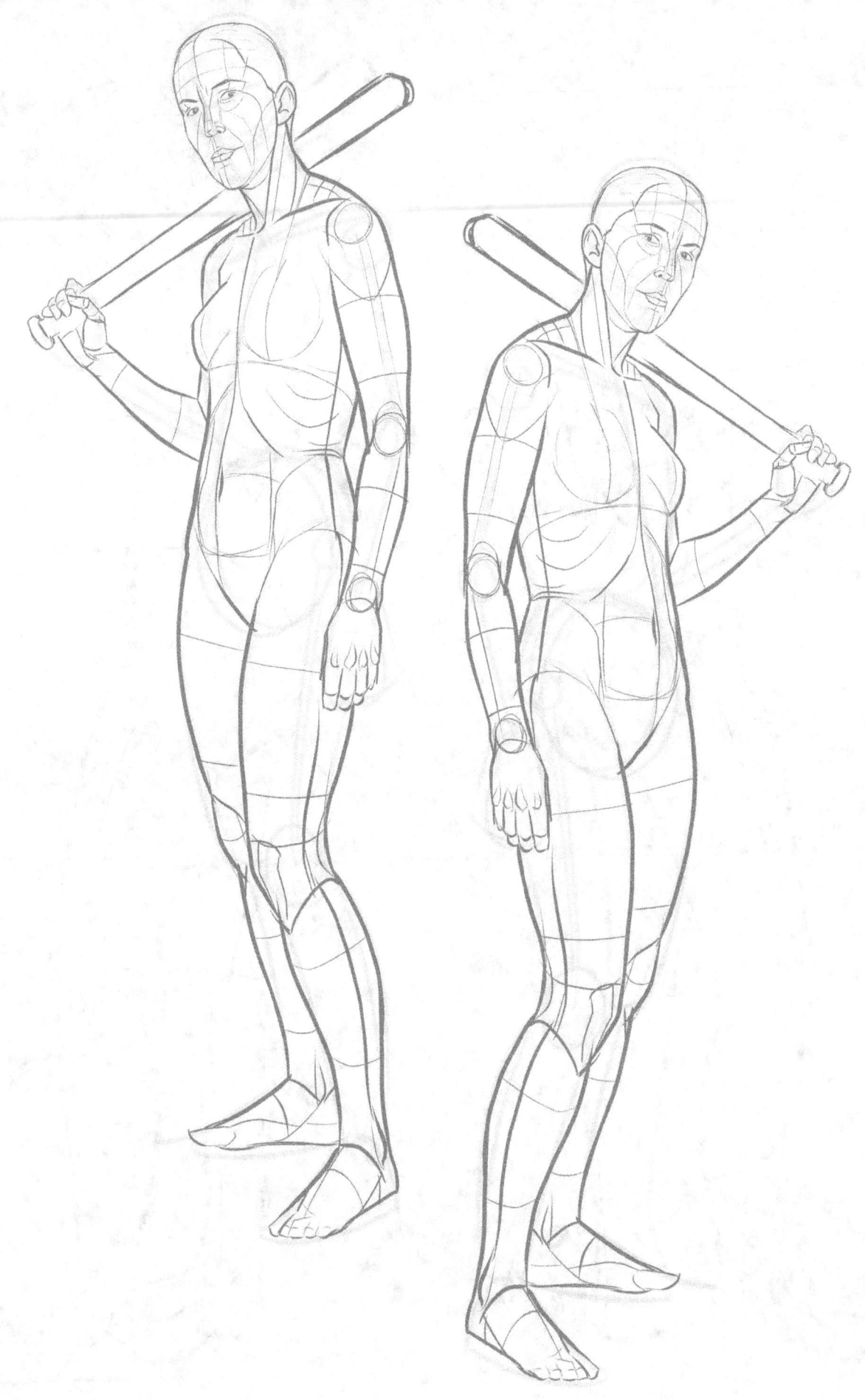

14 | **Weilding Poses**

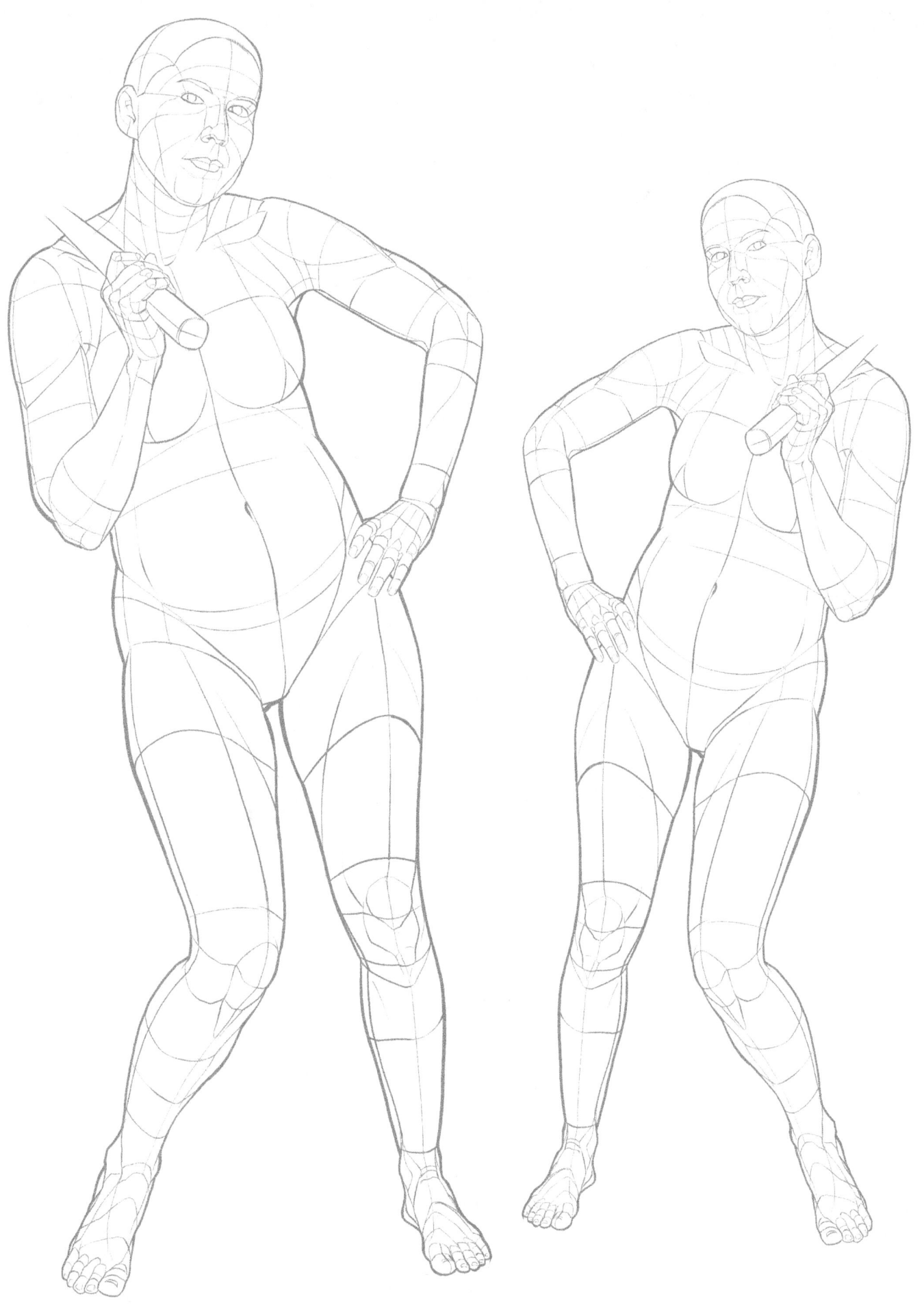

Weilding Poses | 15

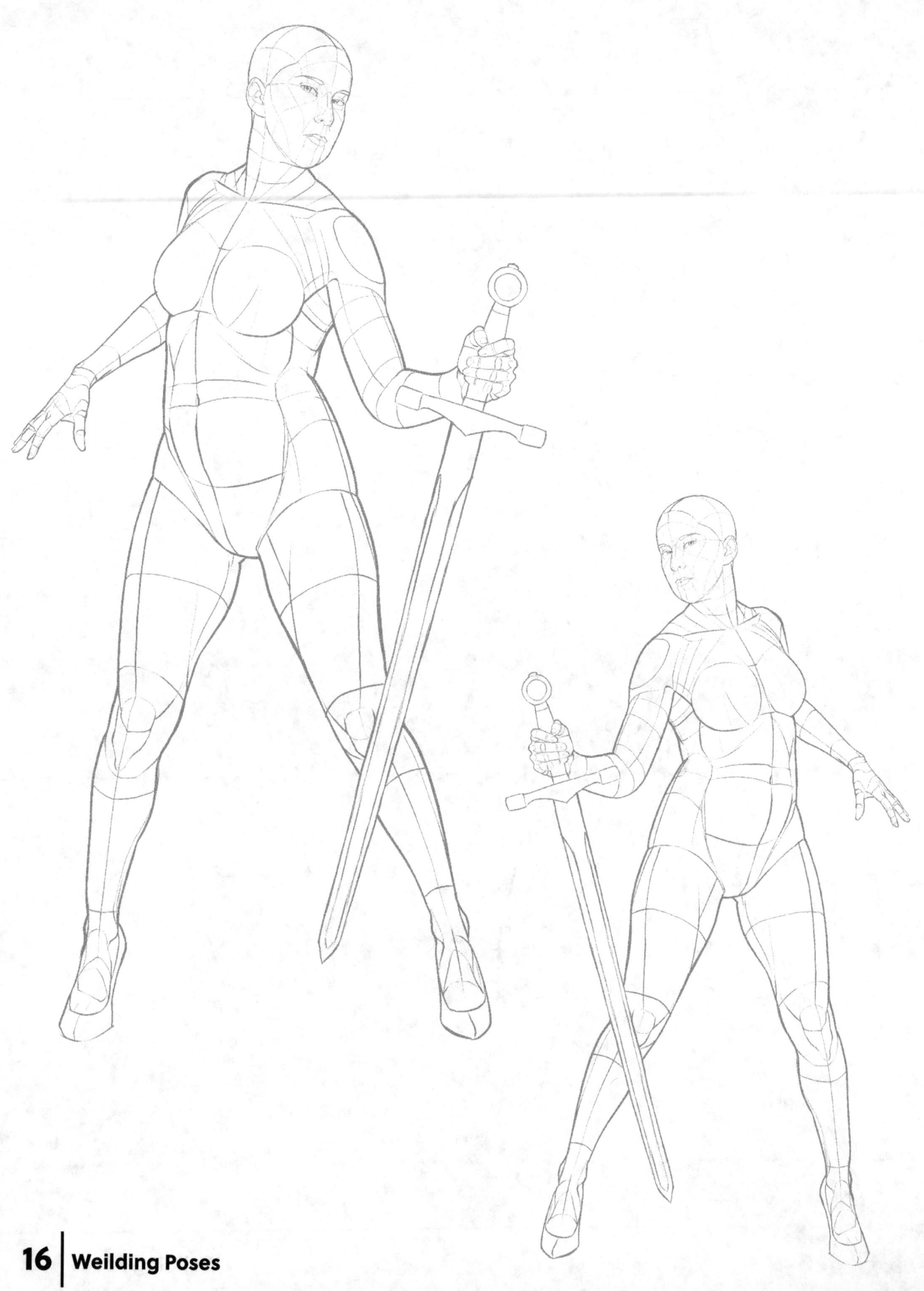

16 | Weilding Poses

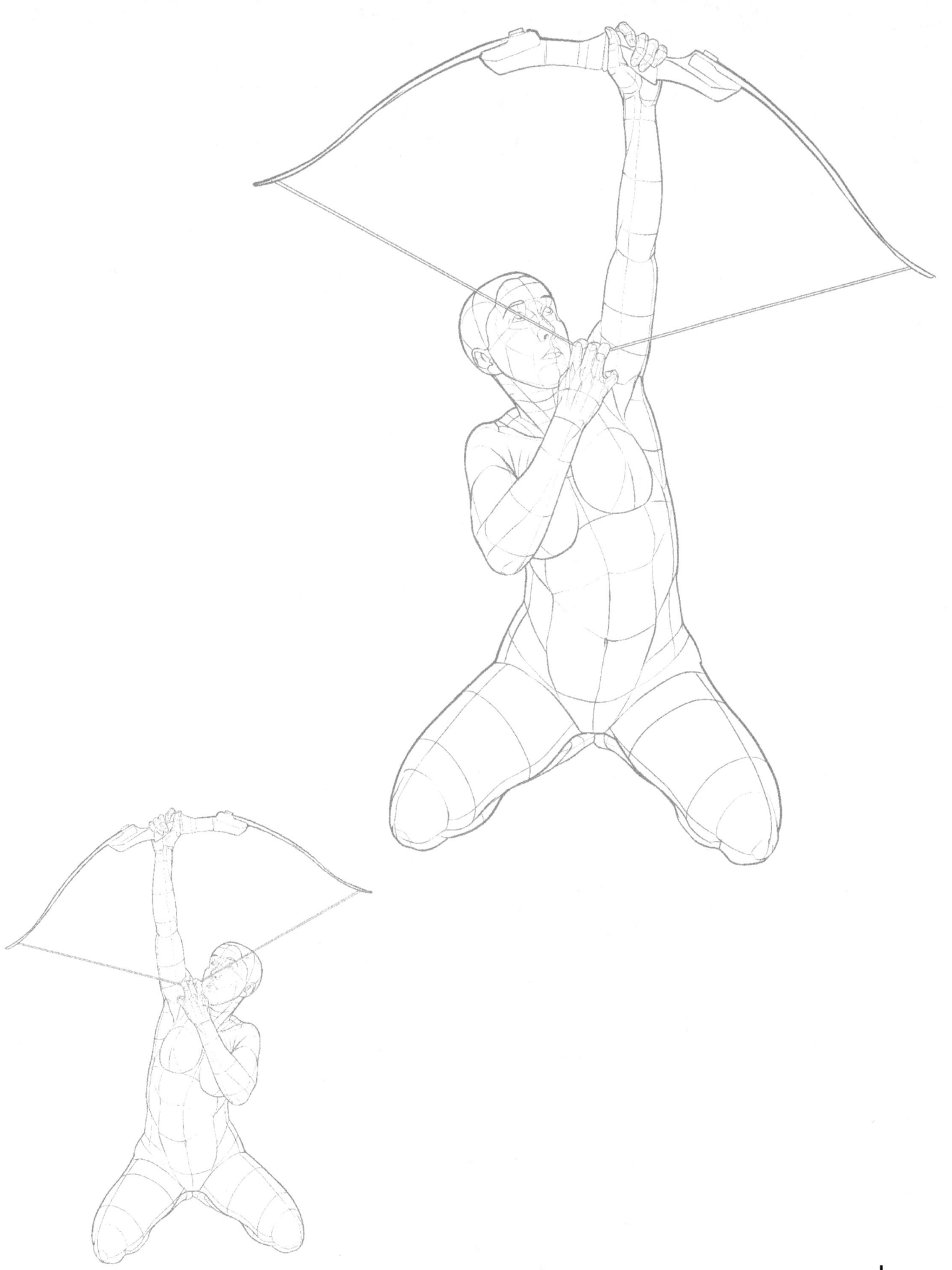

Weilding Poses | **17**

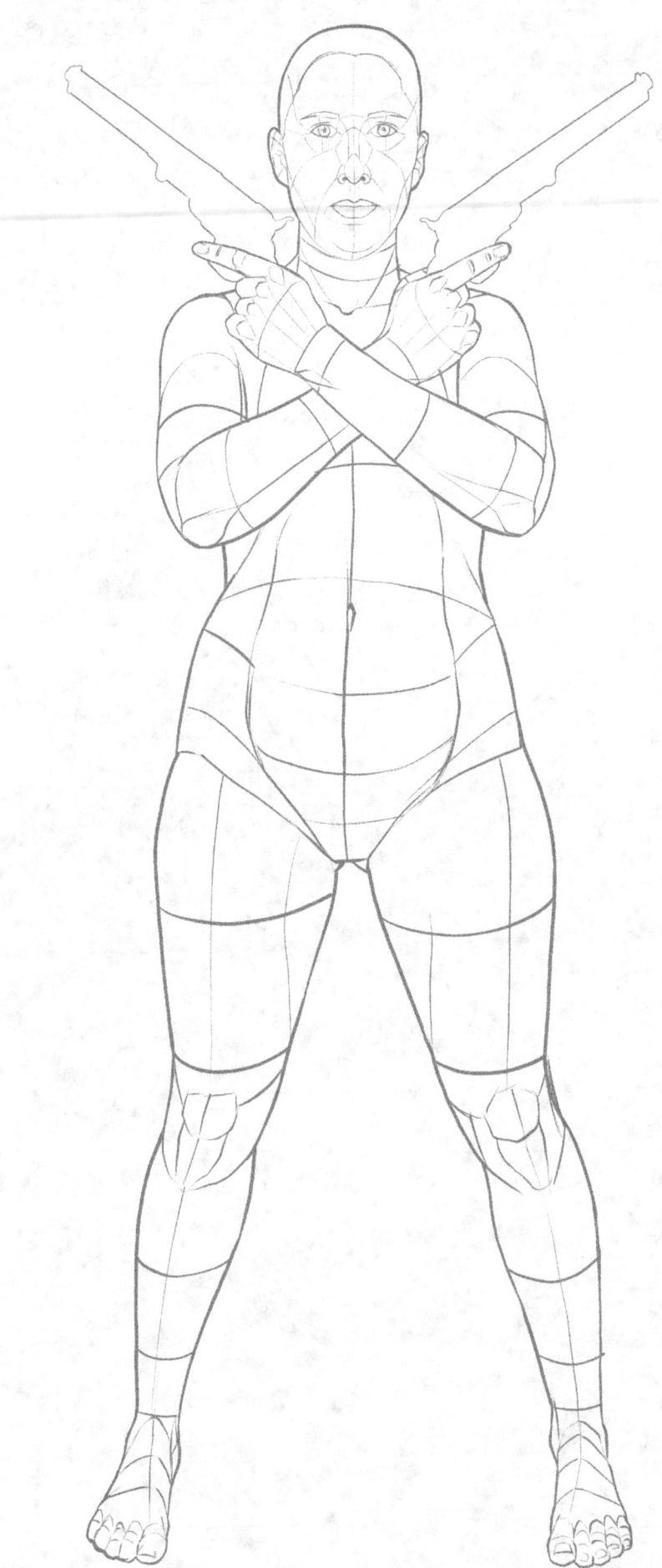

18 | Weilding Poses

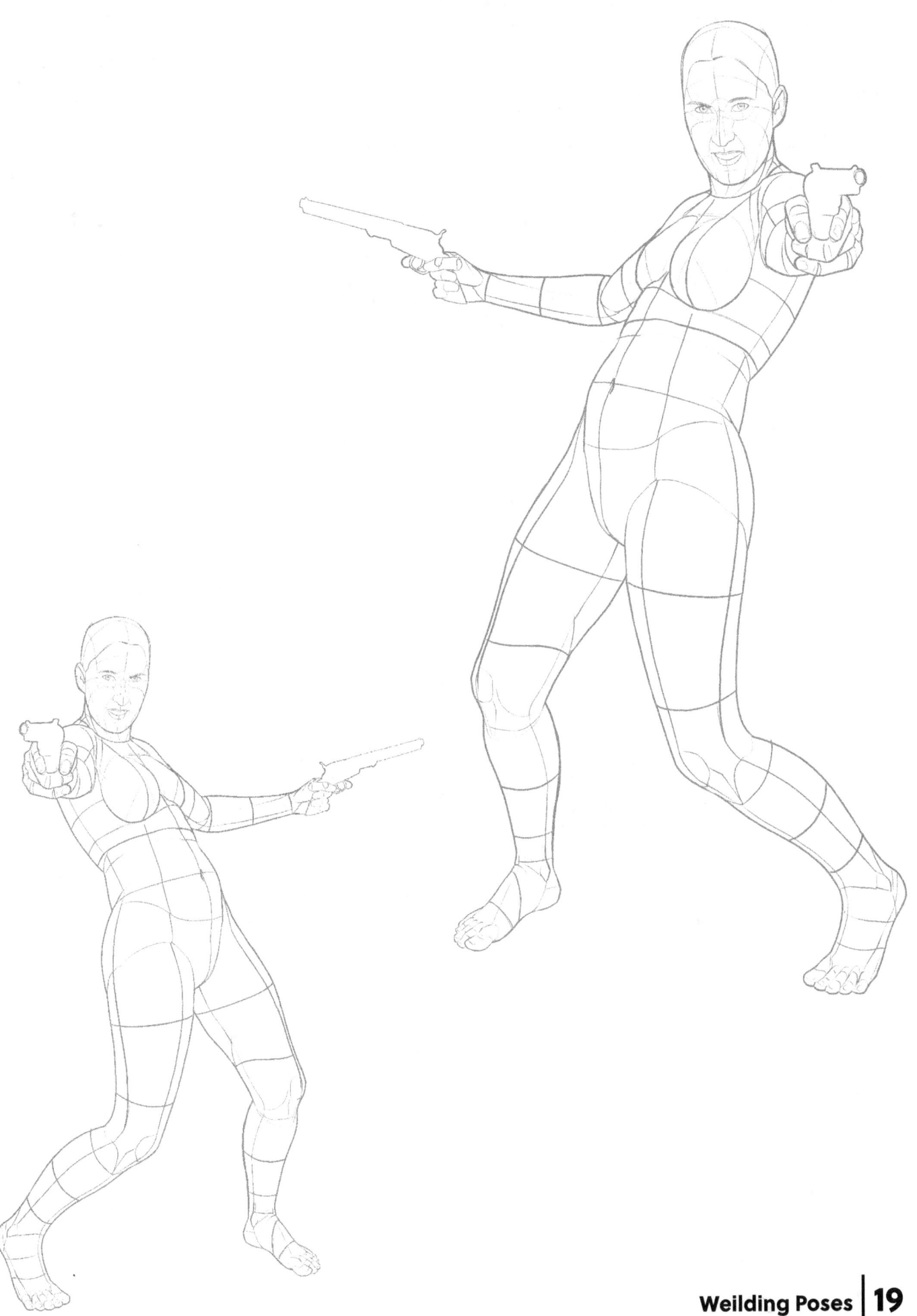

Weilding Poses | 19

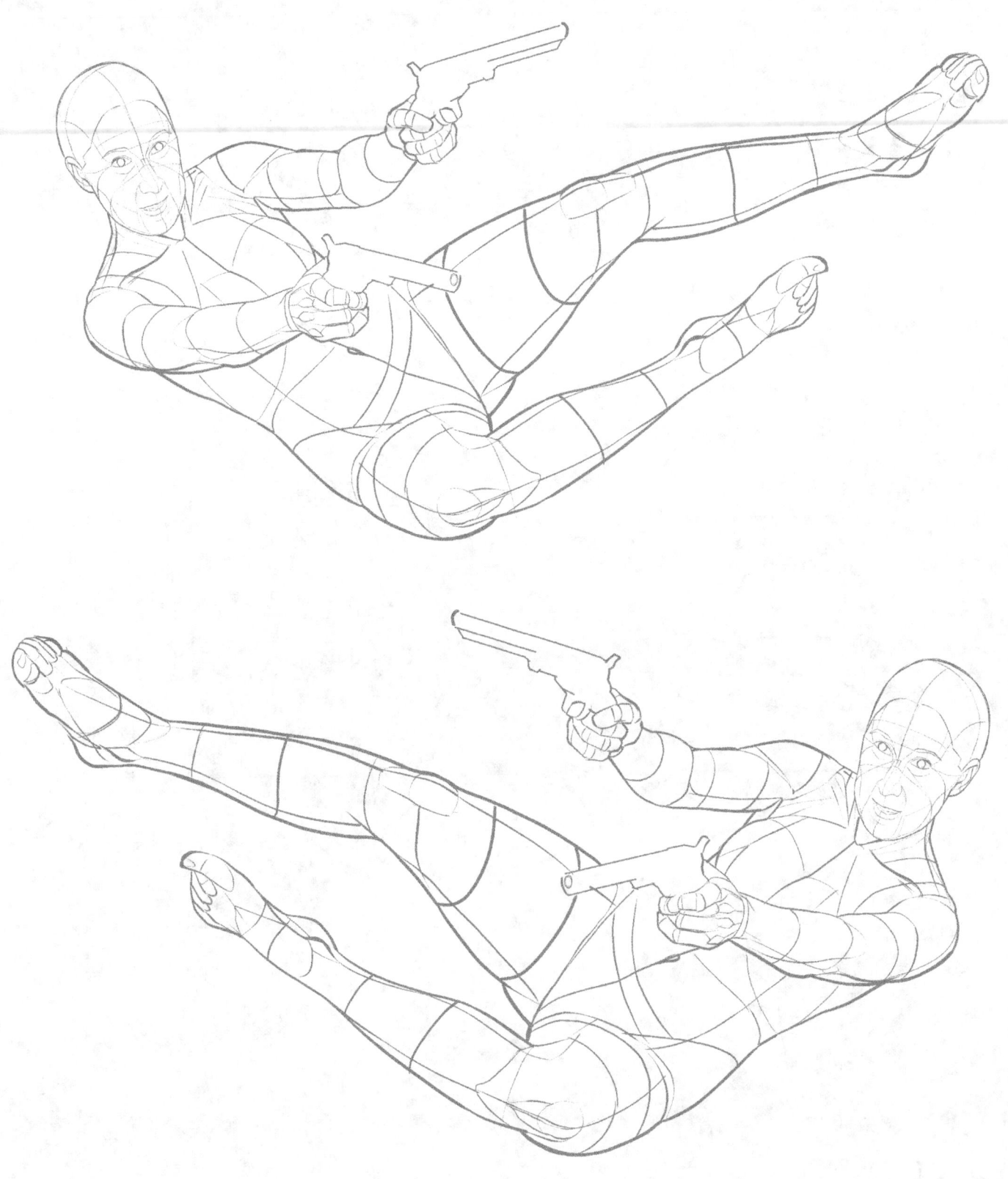

20 | Weilding Poses

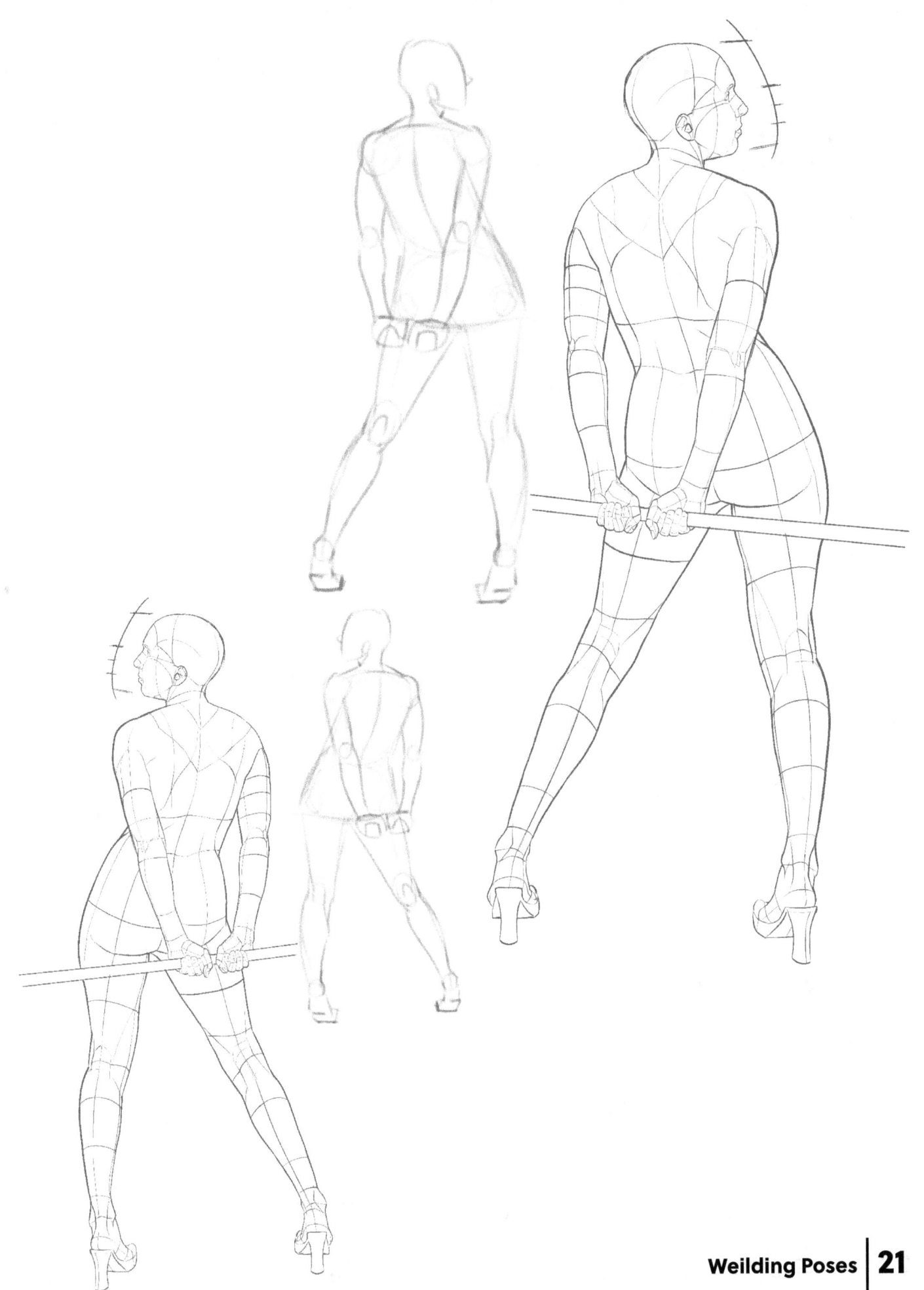

Weilding Poses | 21

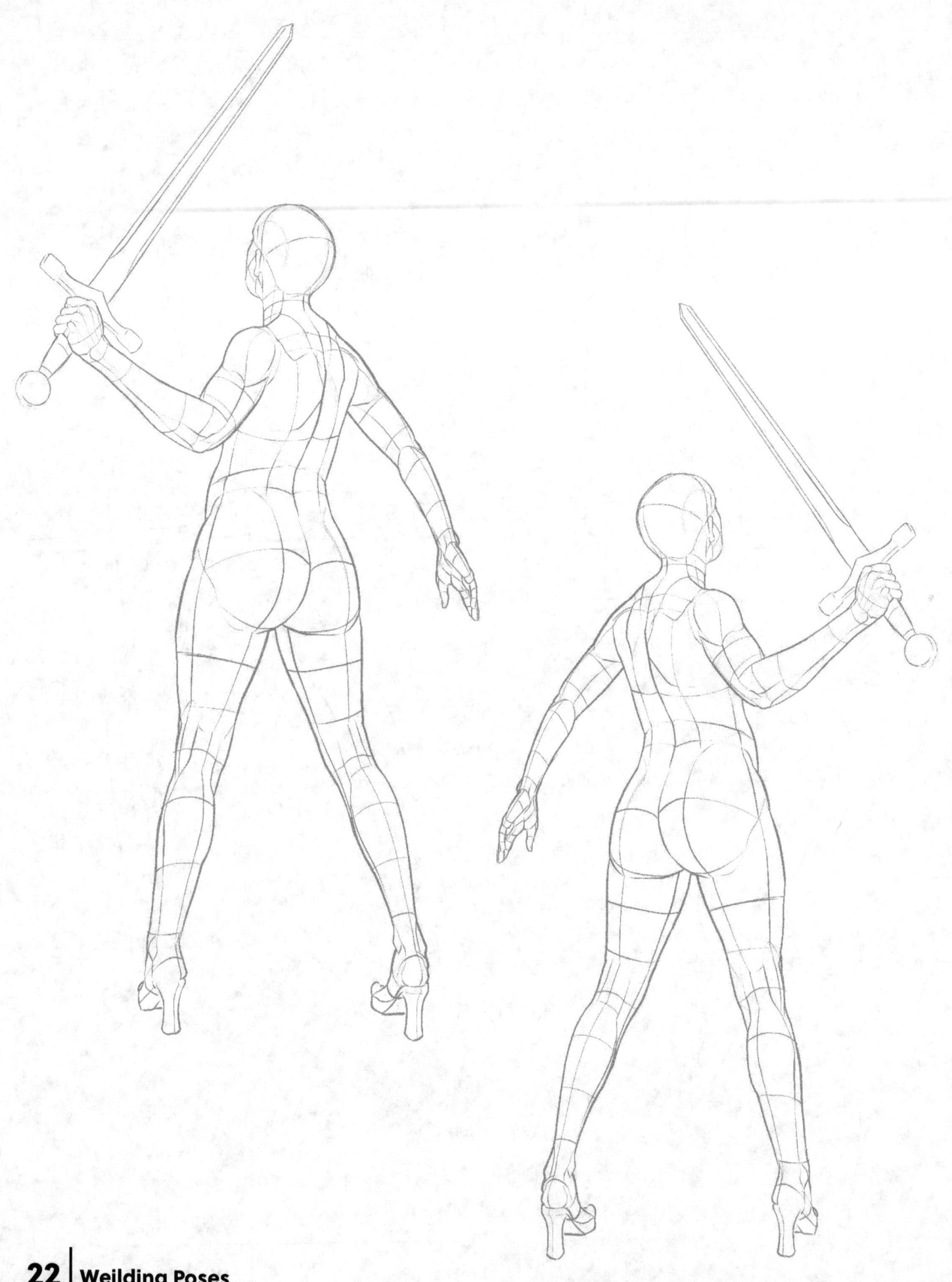

22 | **Weilding Poses**

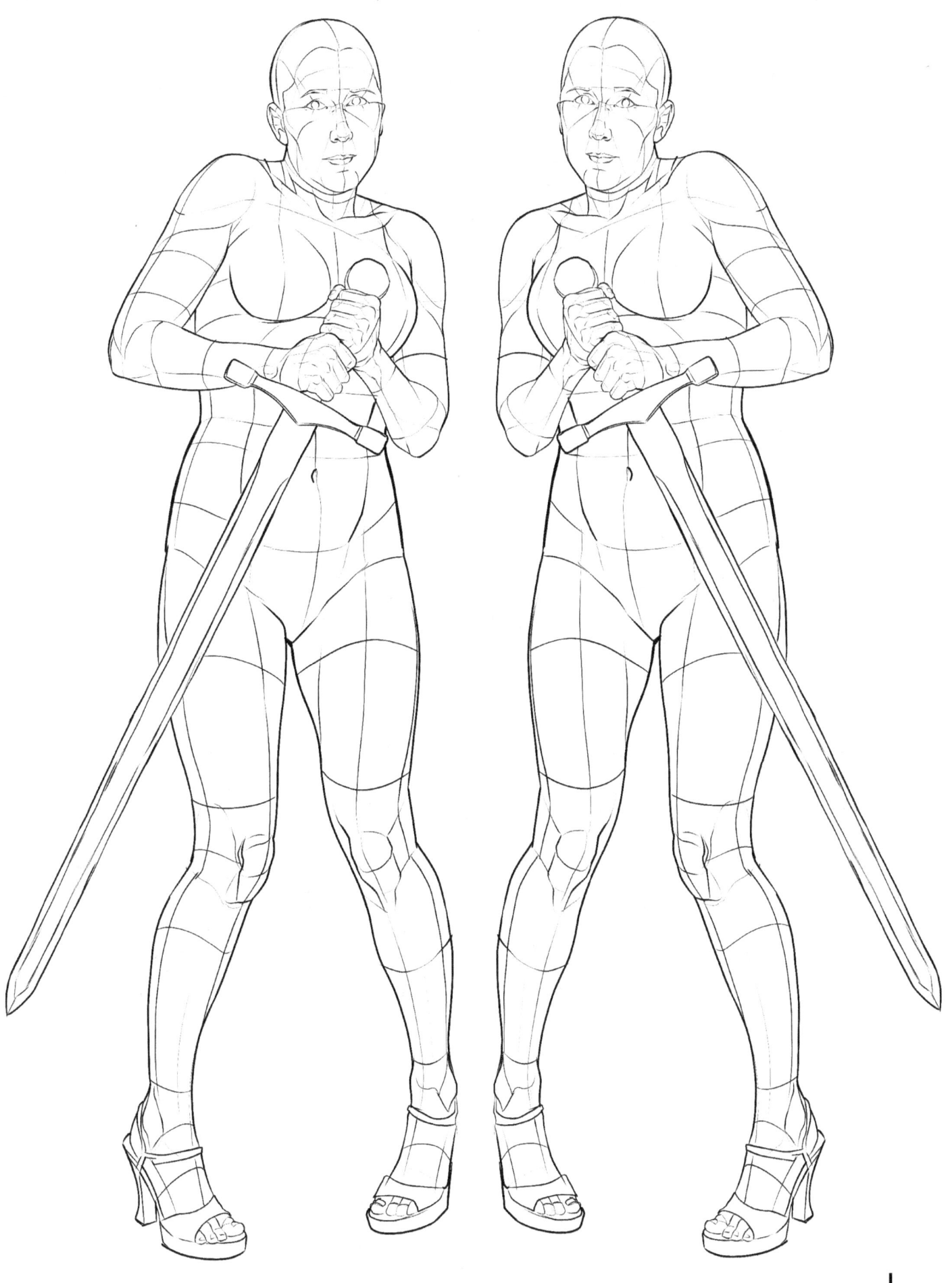

Weilding Poses | 23

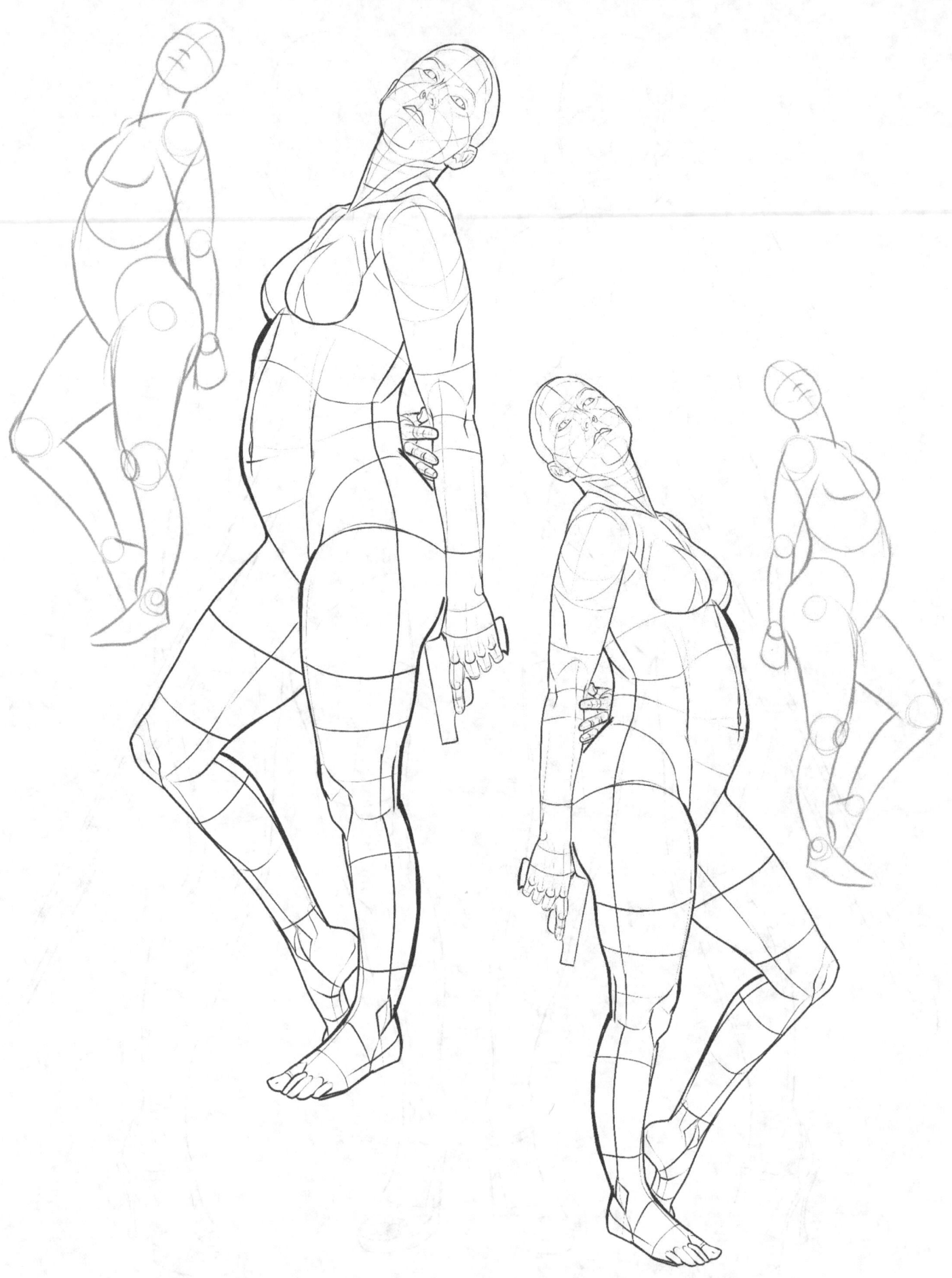

24 | **Weilding Poses**

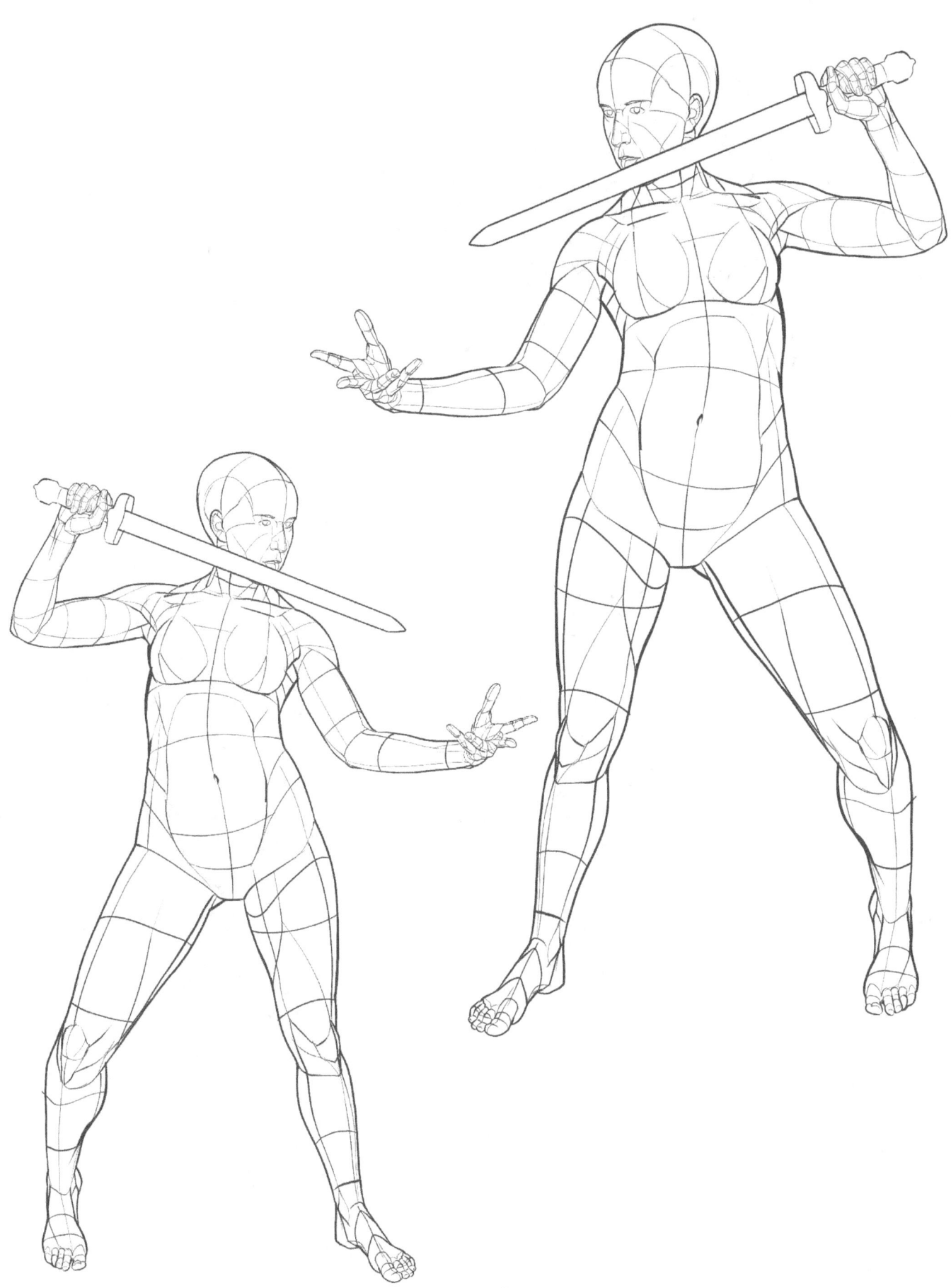

Weilding Poses | 25

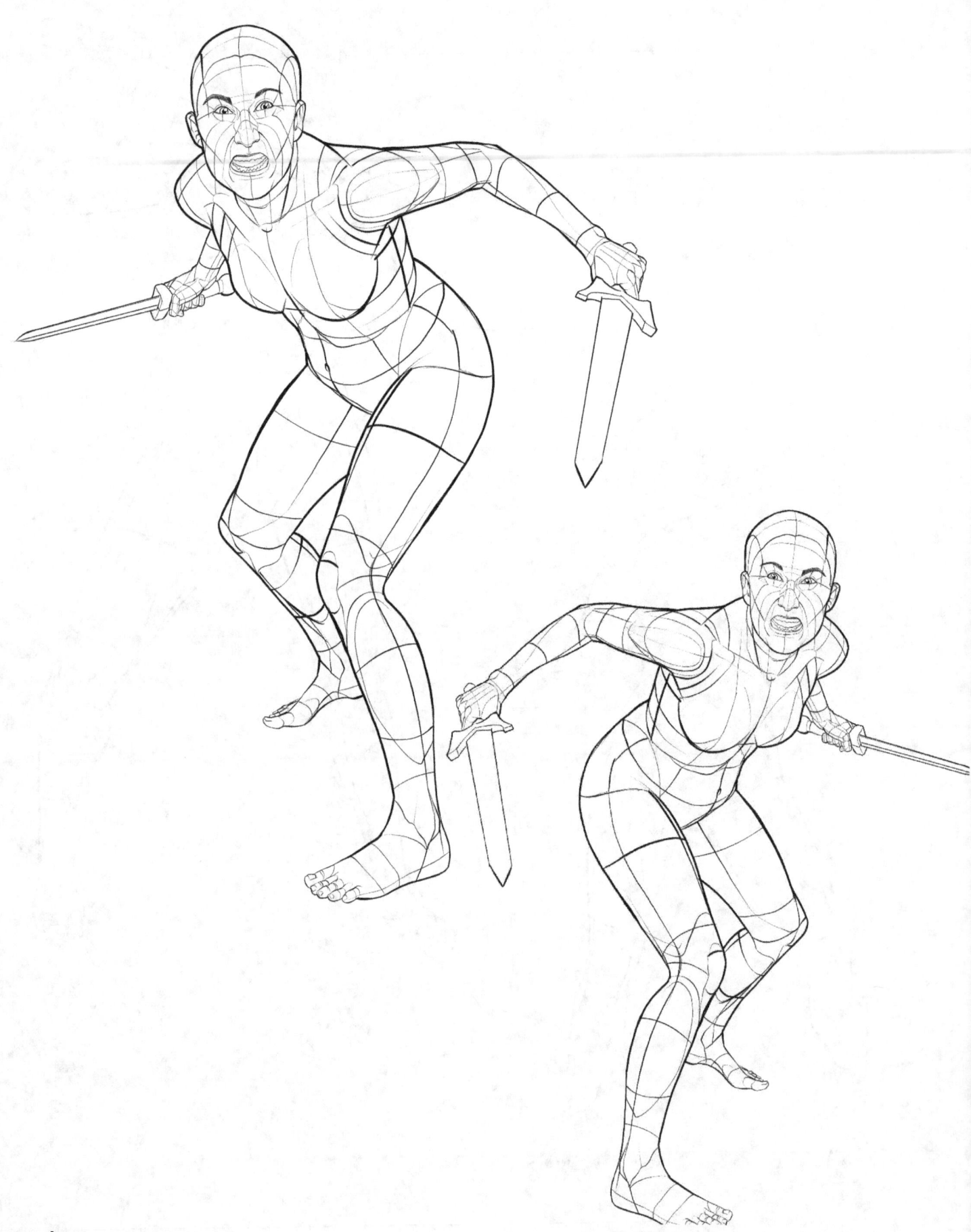

26 | Weilding Poses

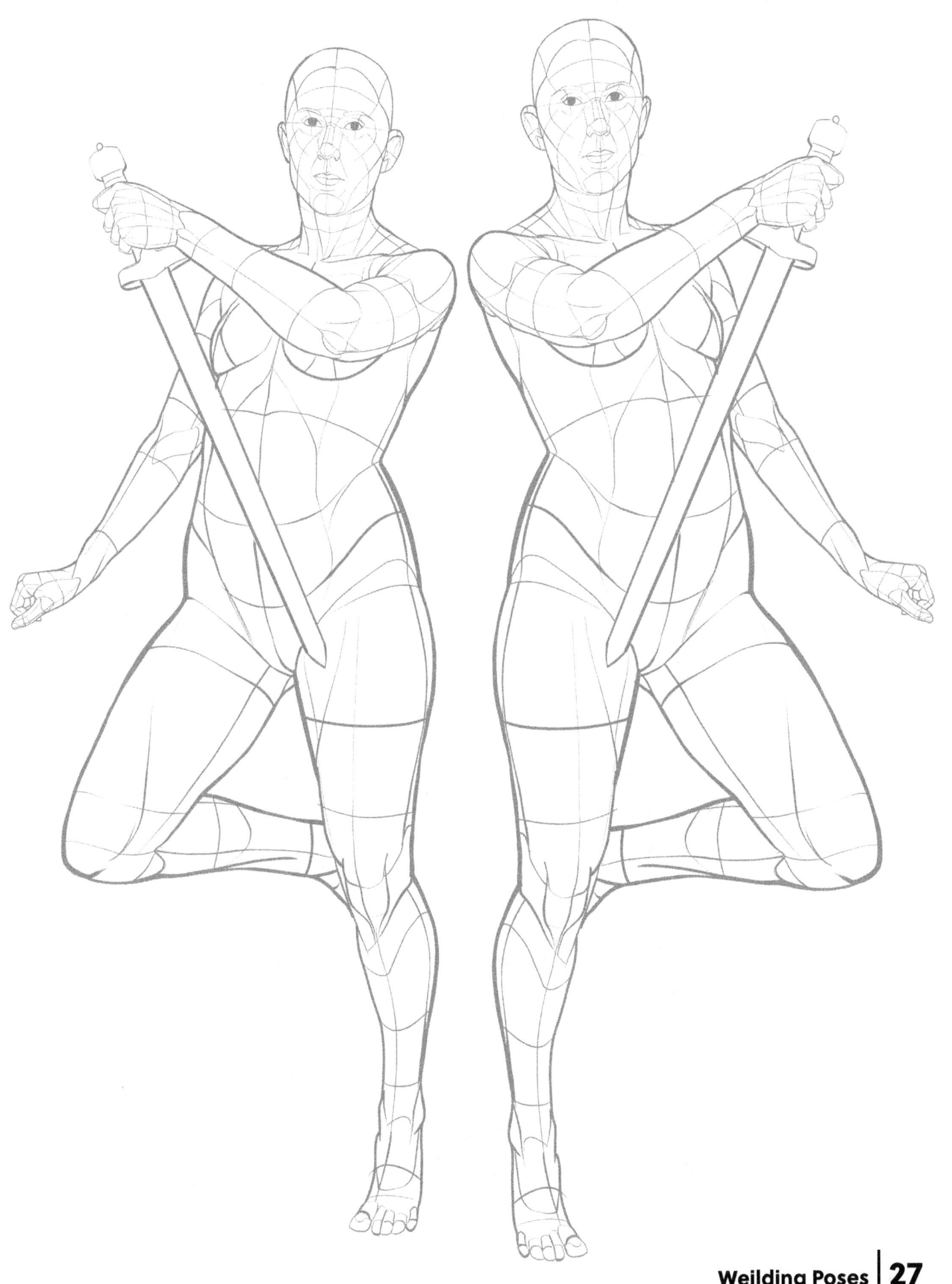

Weilding Poses | 27

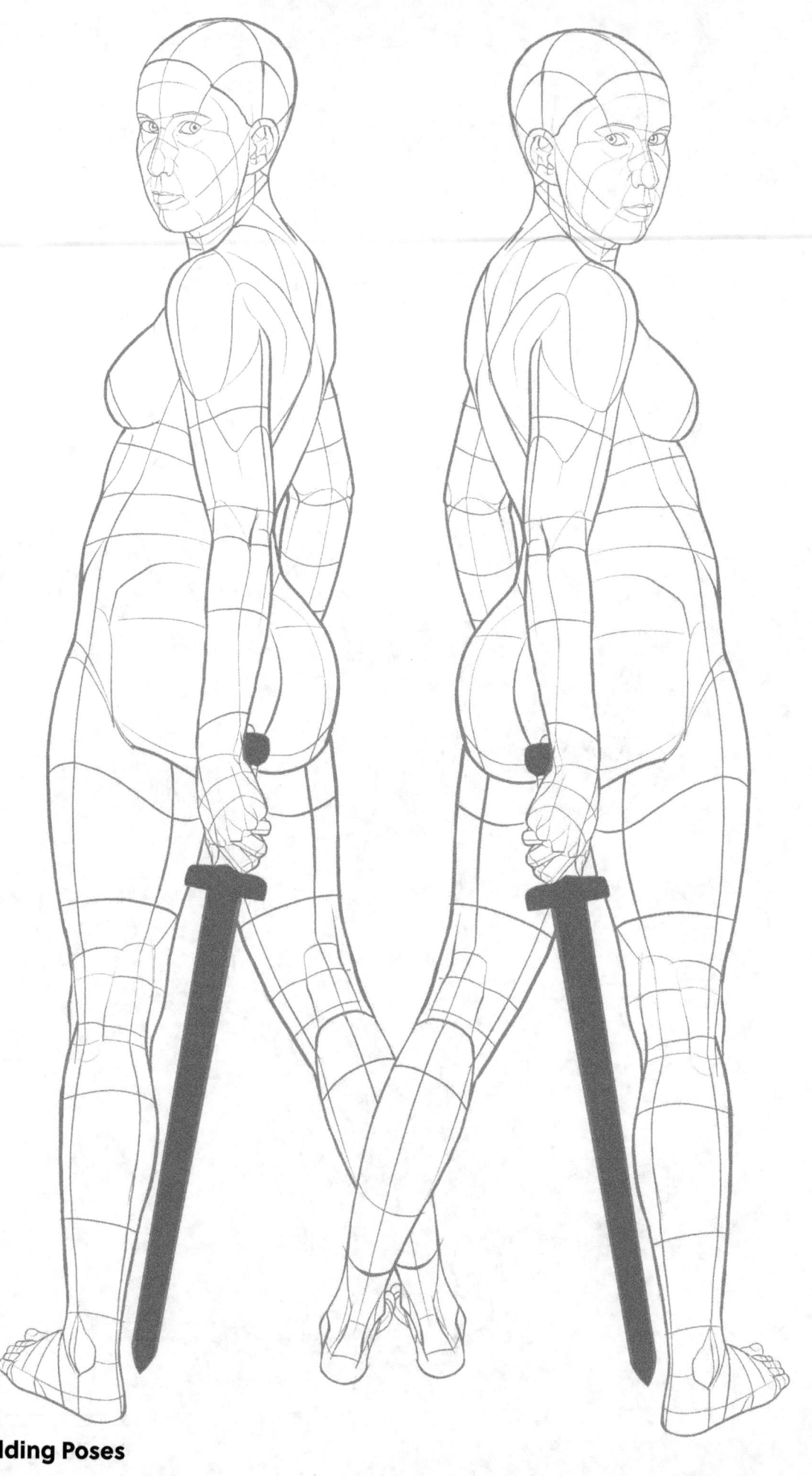

28 | Weilding Poses

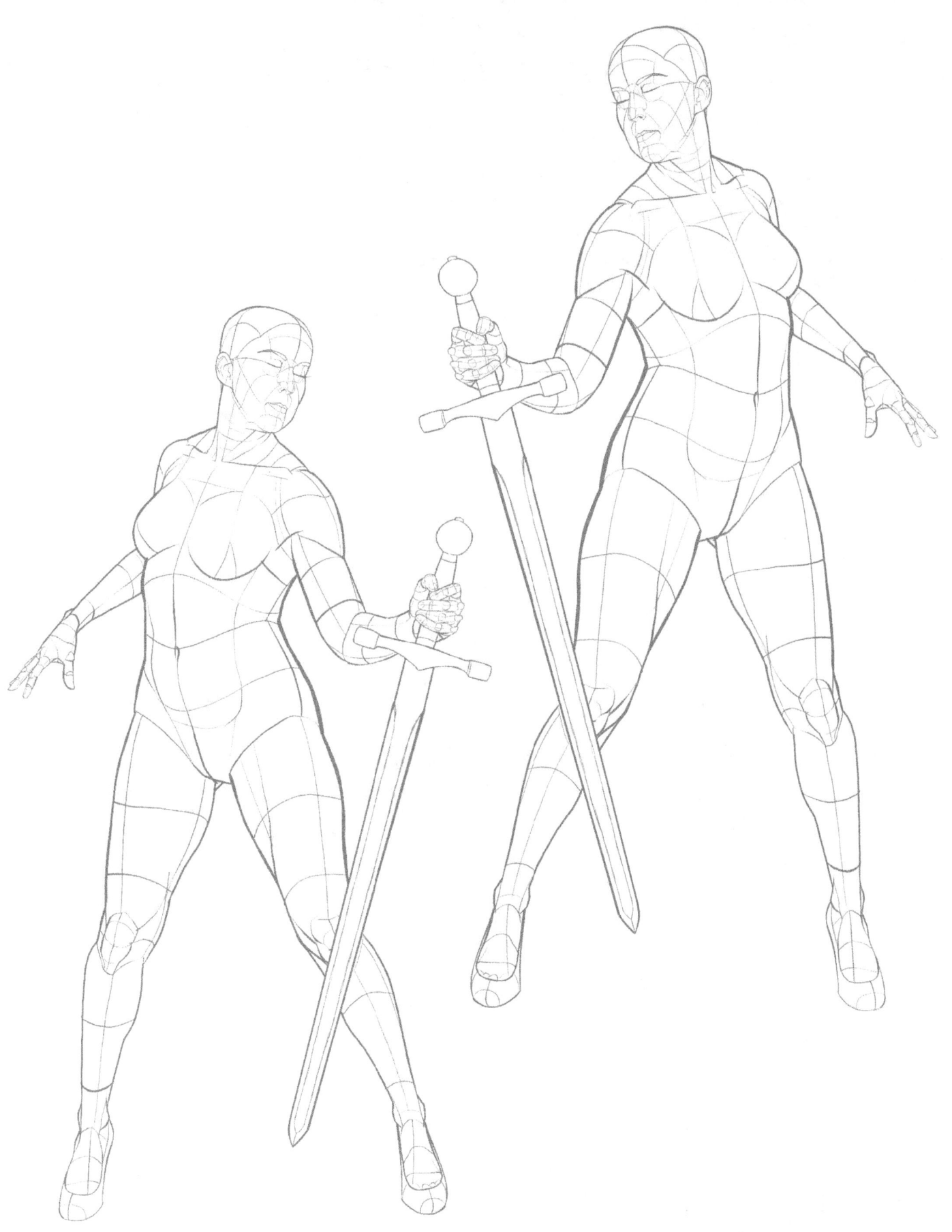

Weilding Poses | 29

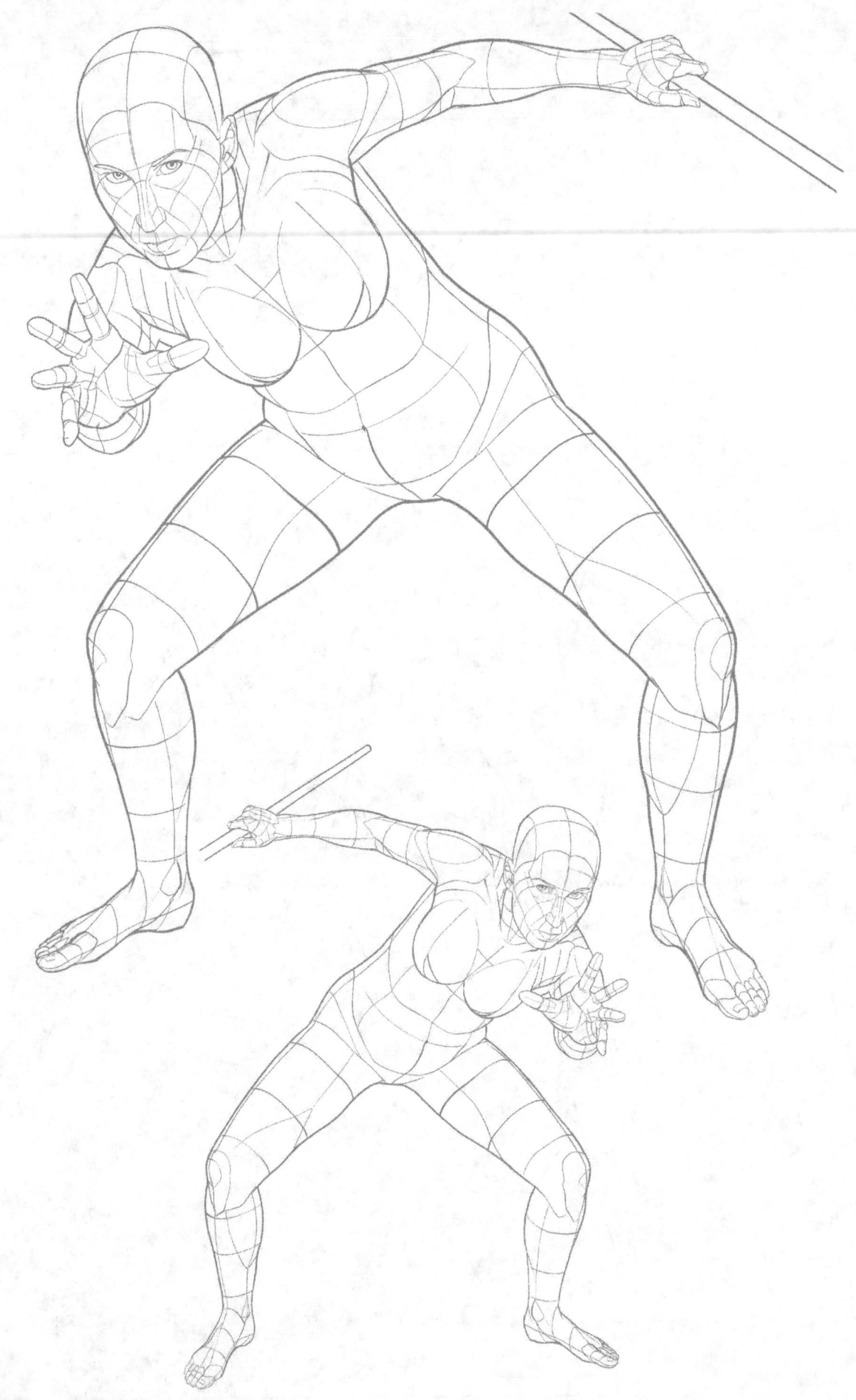

30 | Weilding Poses

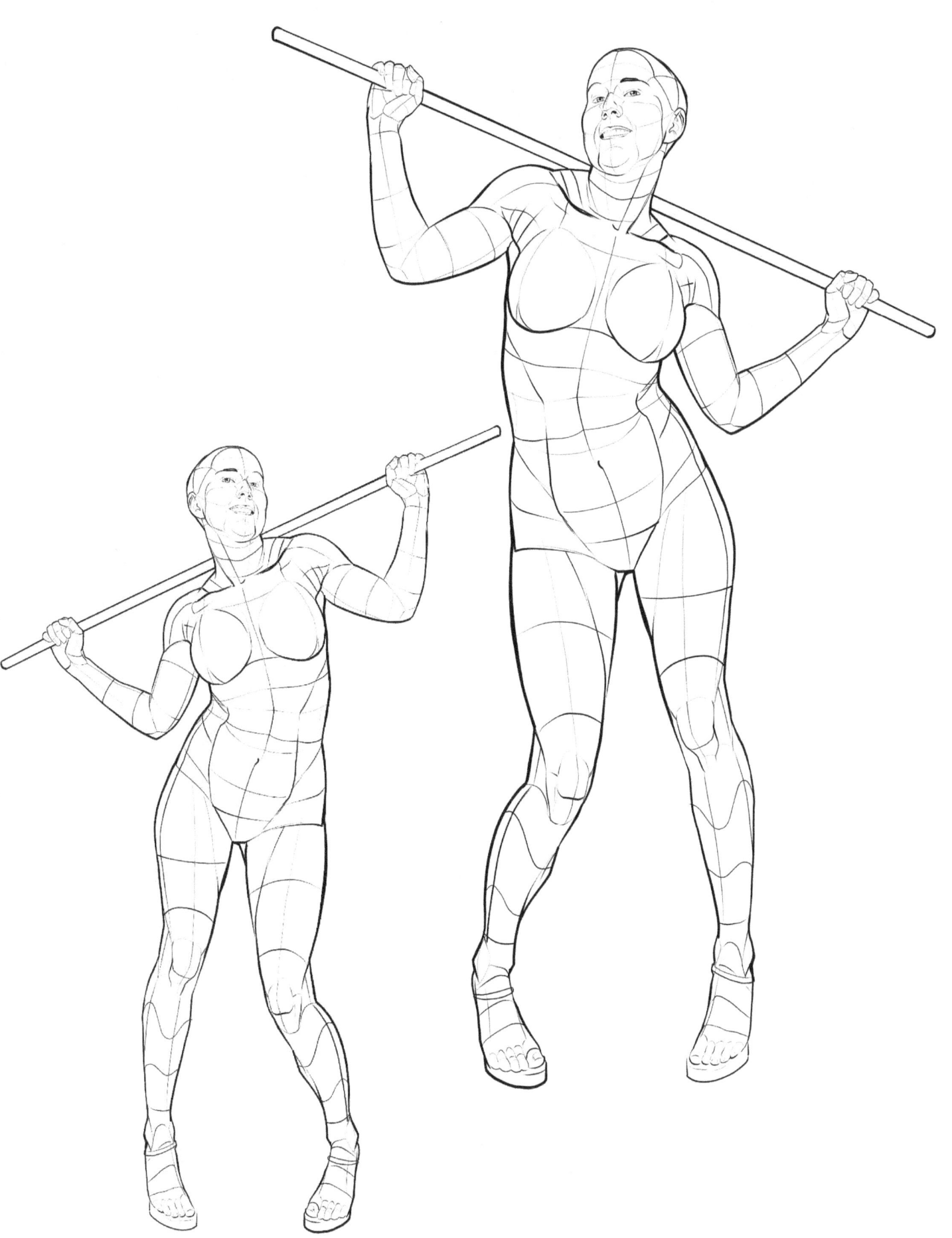

Weilding Poses | 31

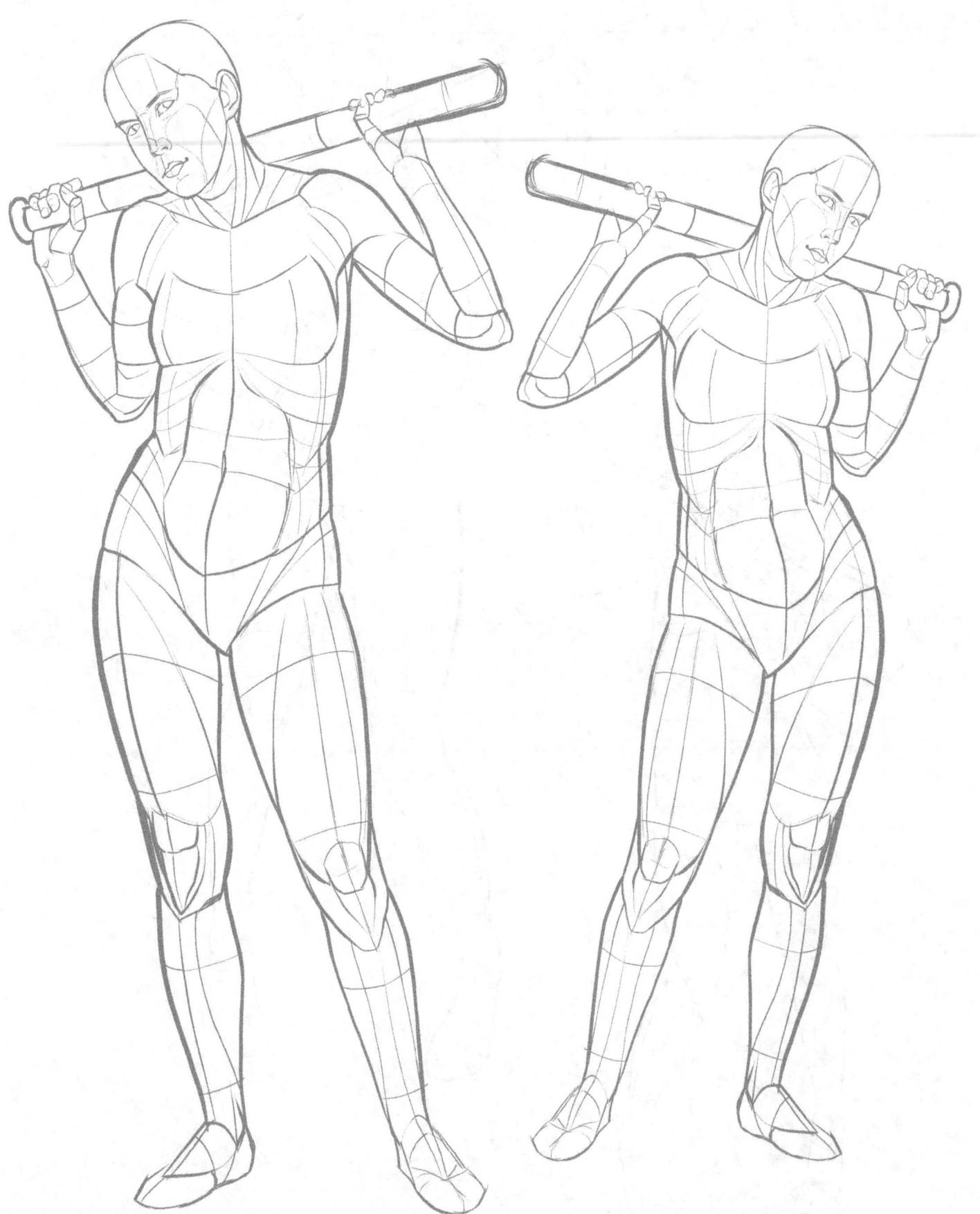

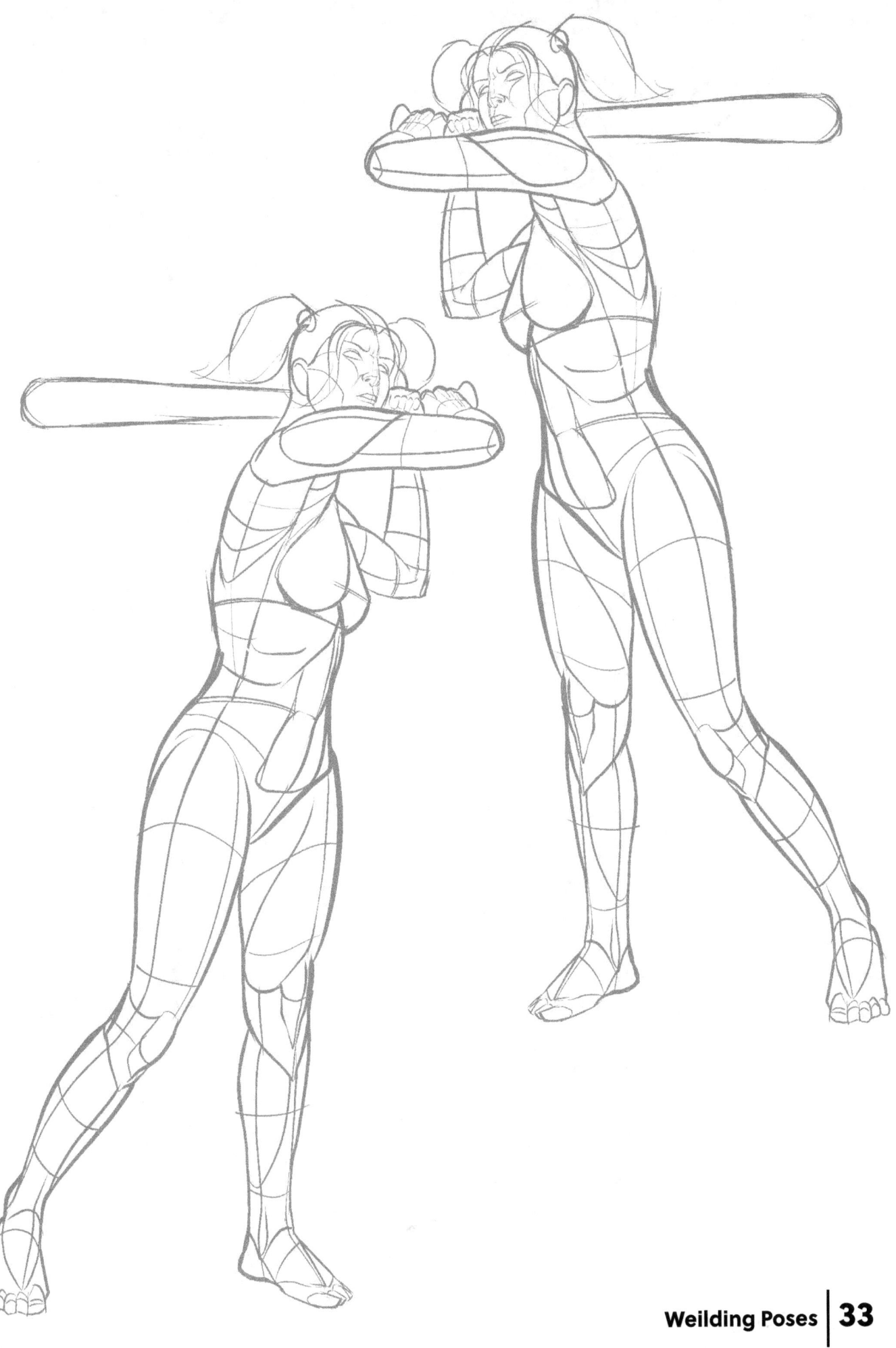

Weilding Poses | 33

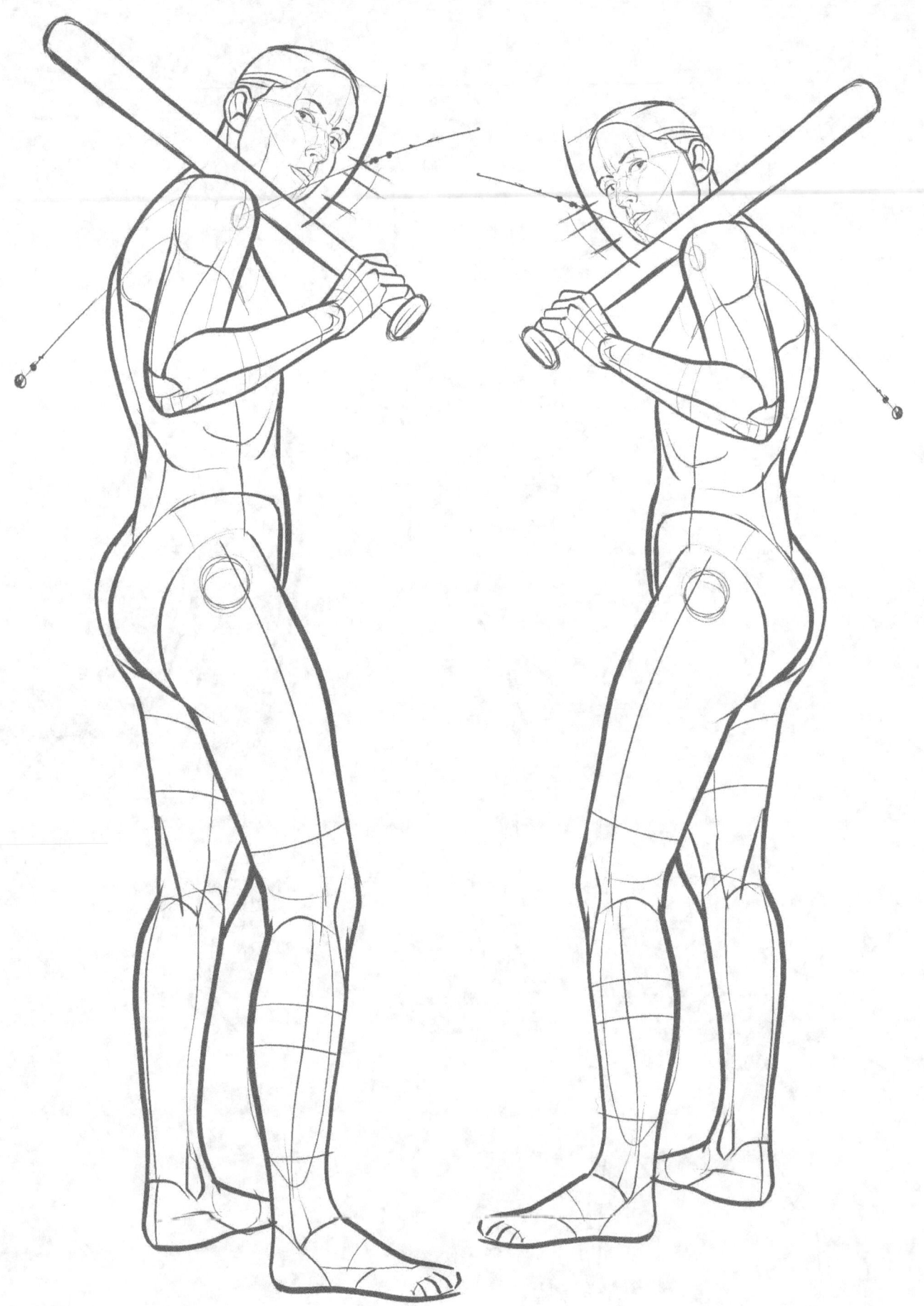

34 | Weilding Poses

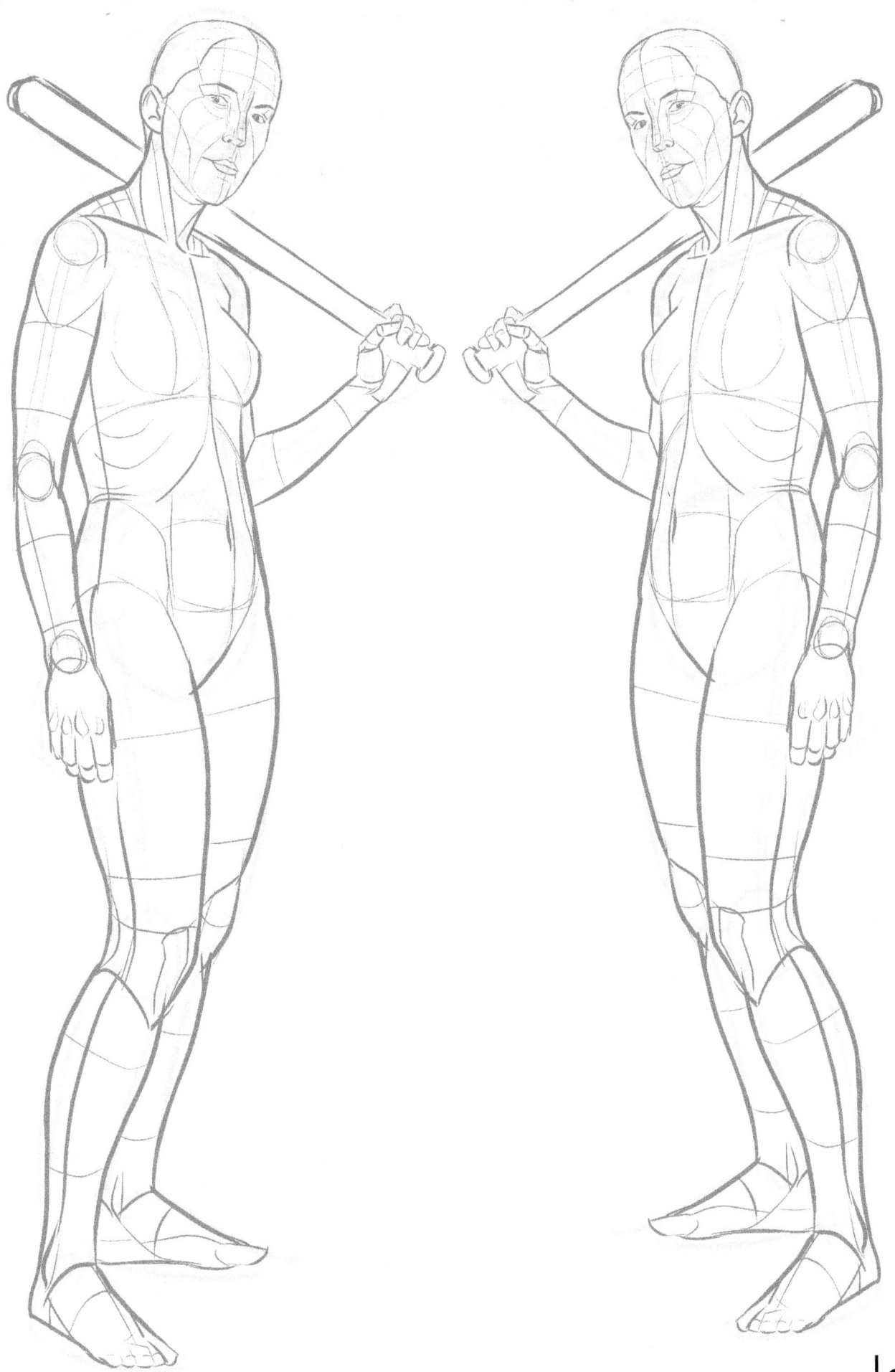

Weilding Poses | 35

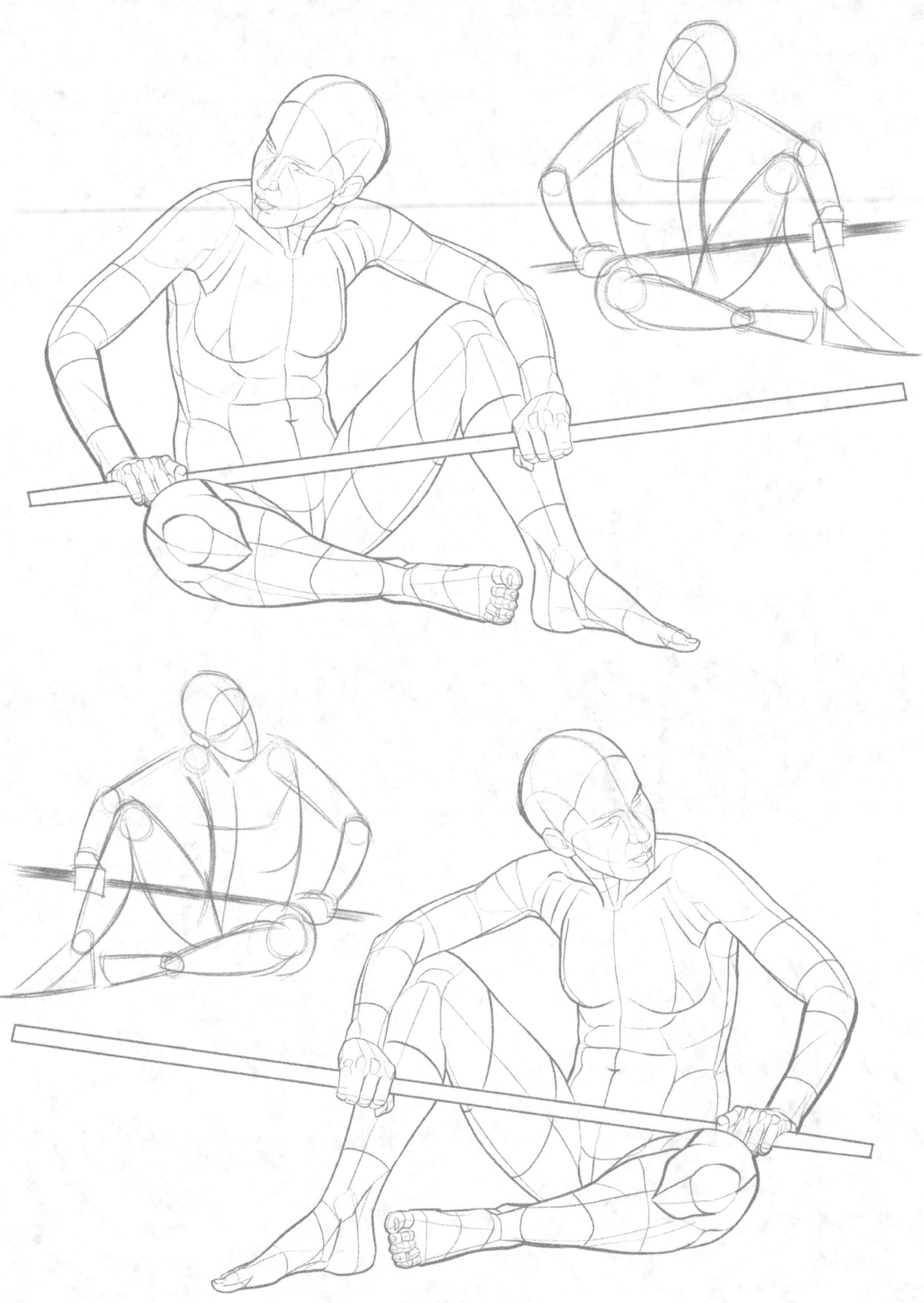

36 | Weilding Poses

Standing Poses

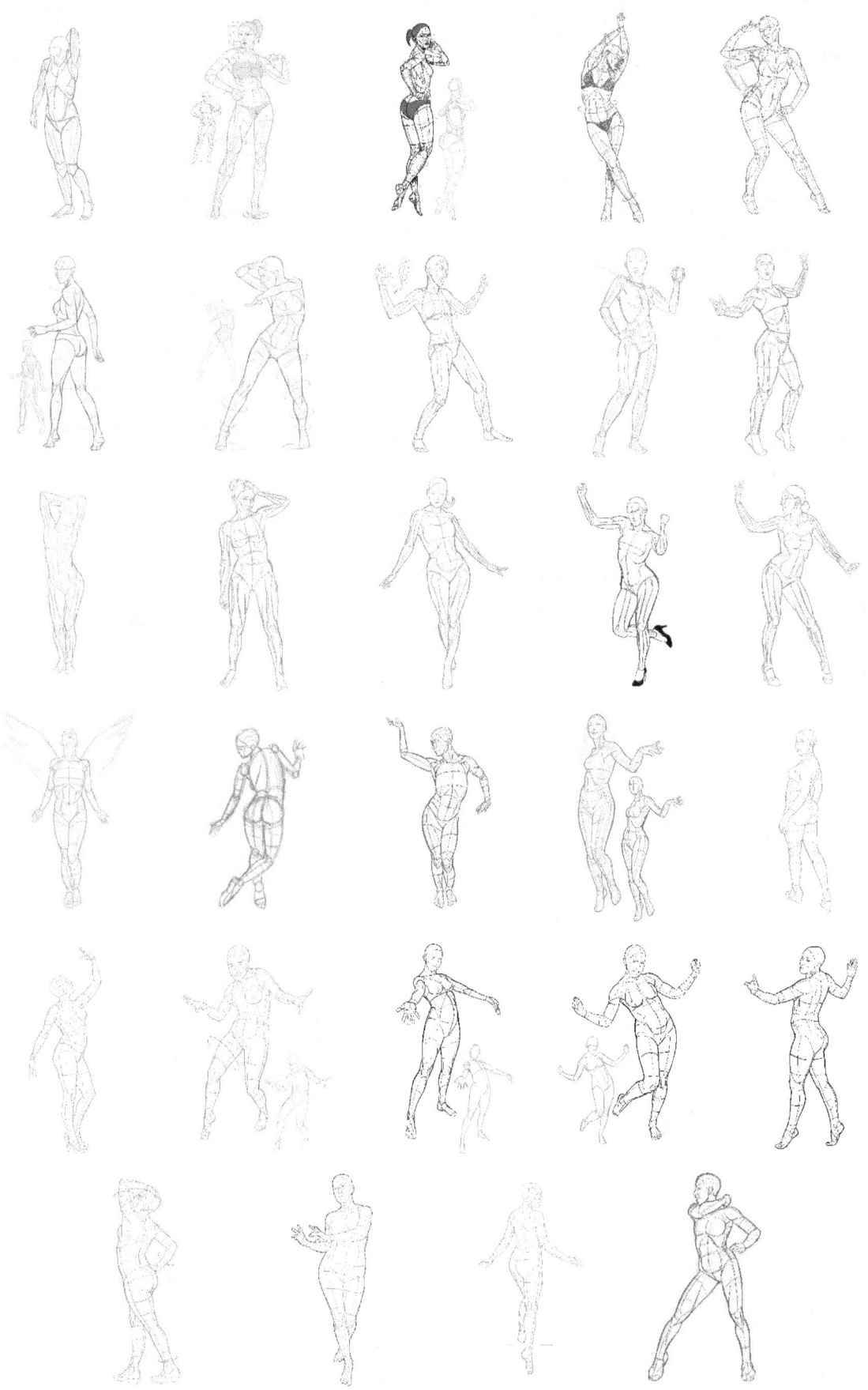

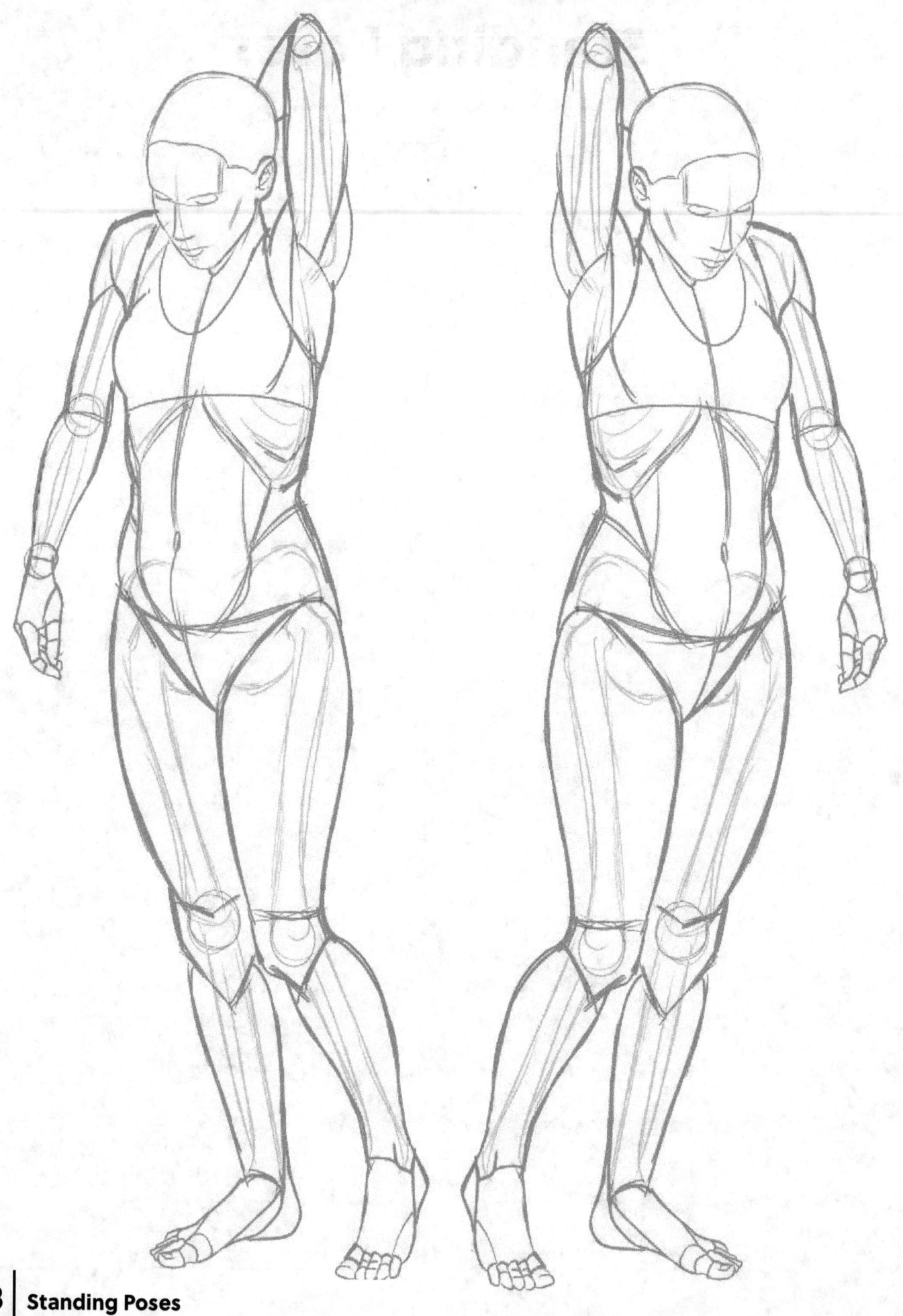

Standing Poses

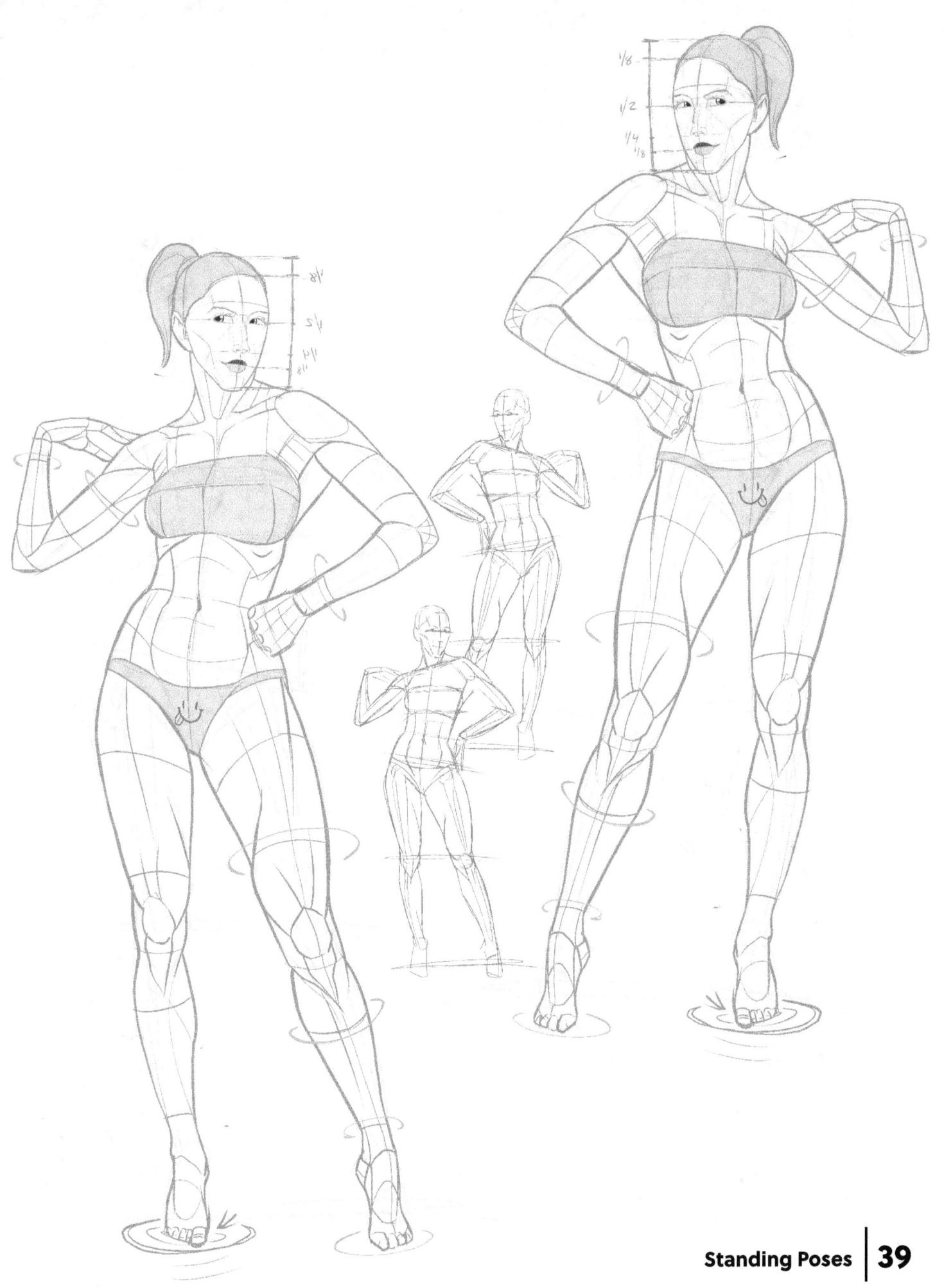

Standing Poses | 39

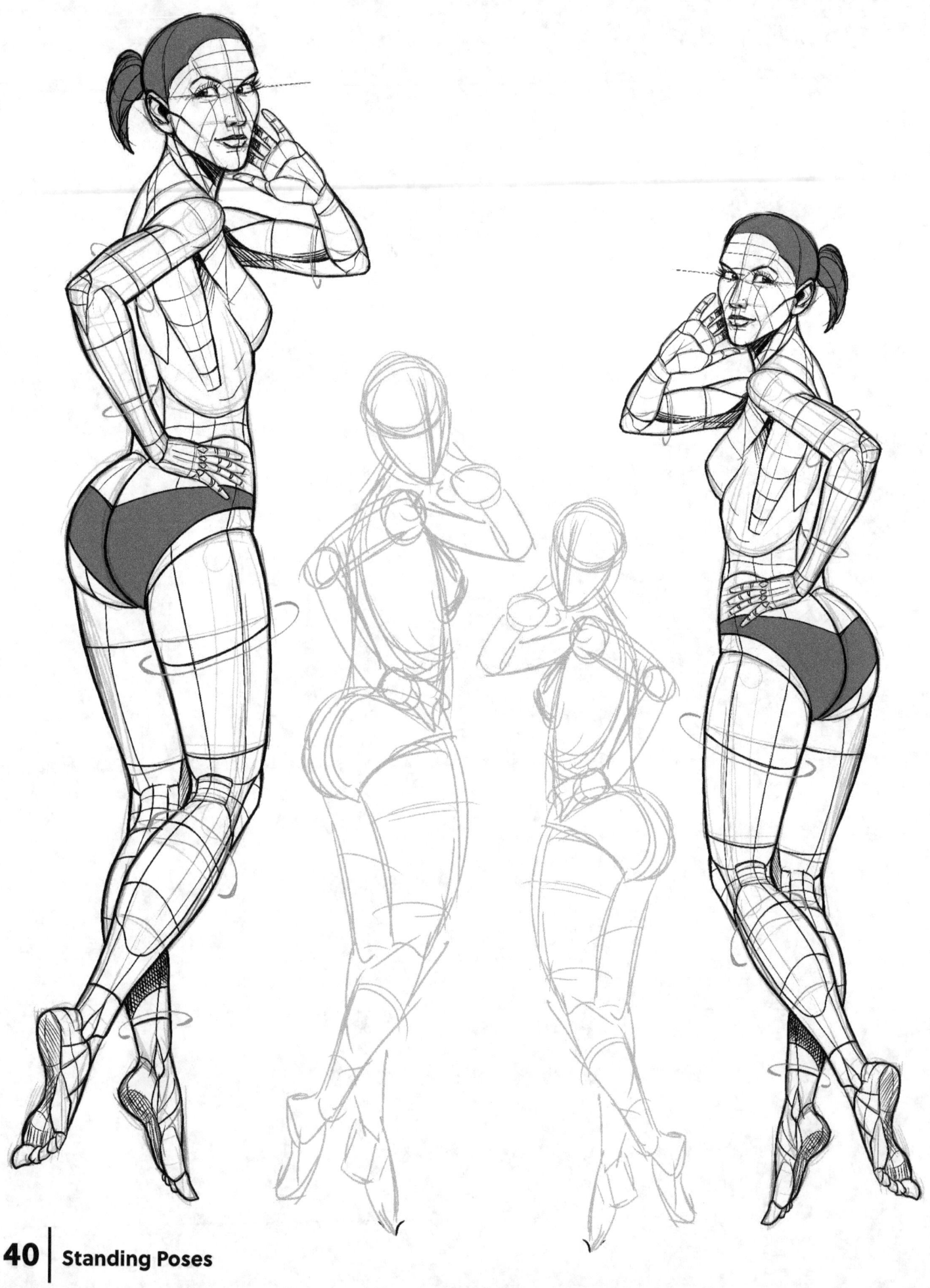

40 | Standing Poses

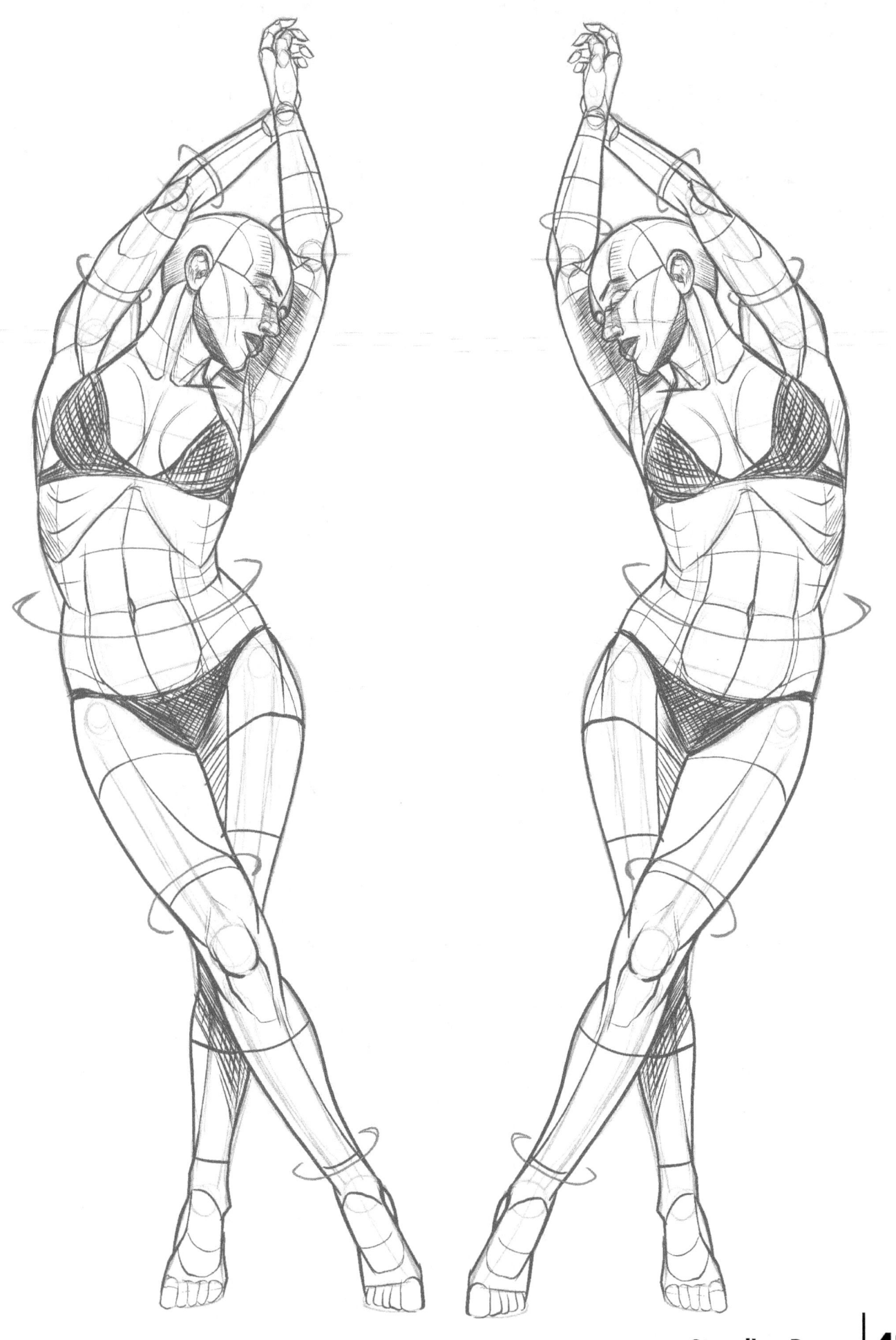

Standing Poses | 41

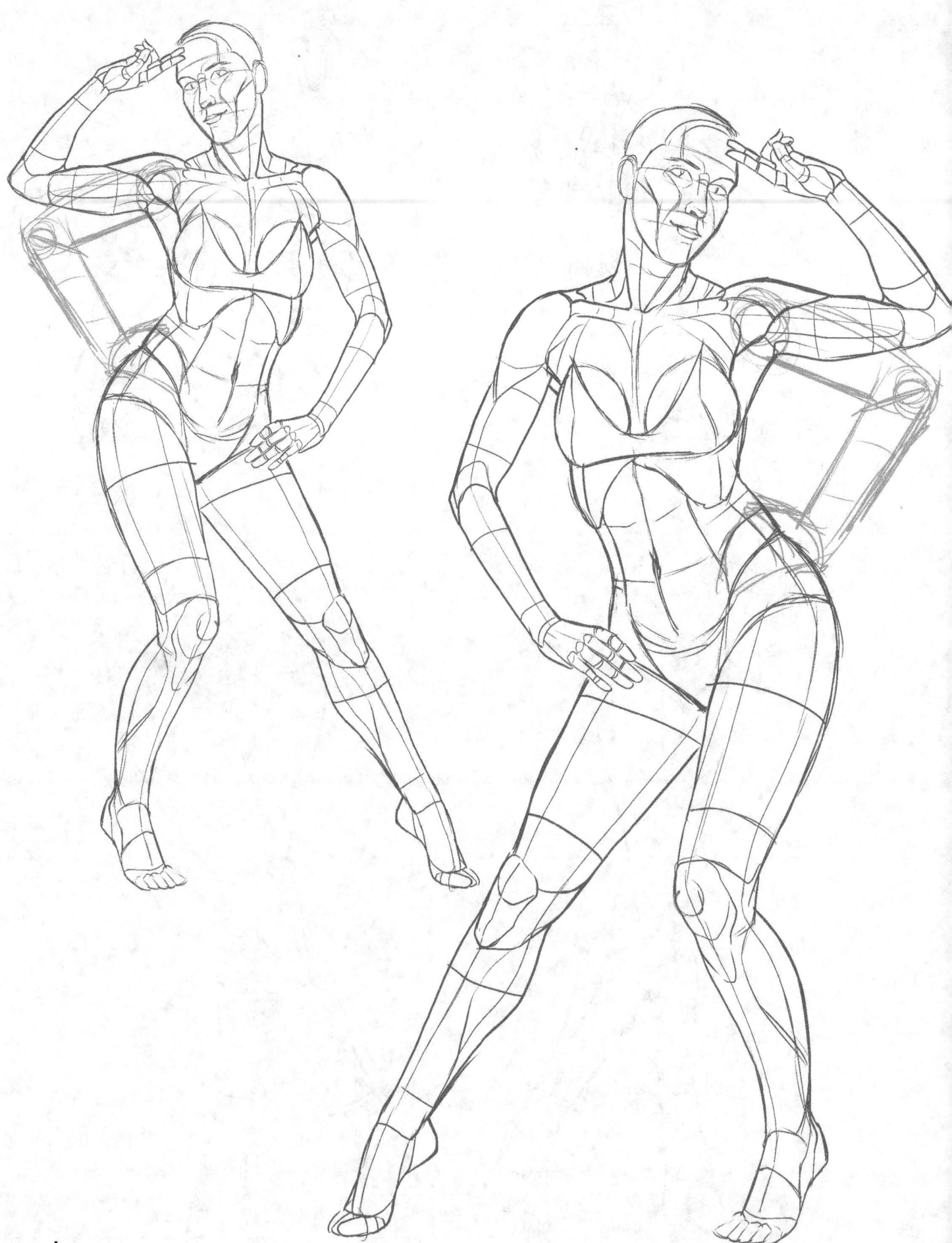

Standing Poses

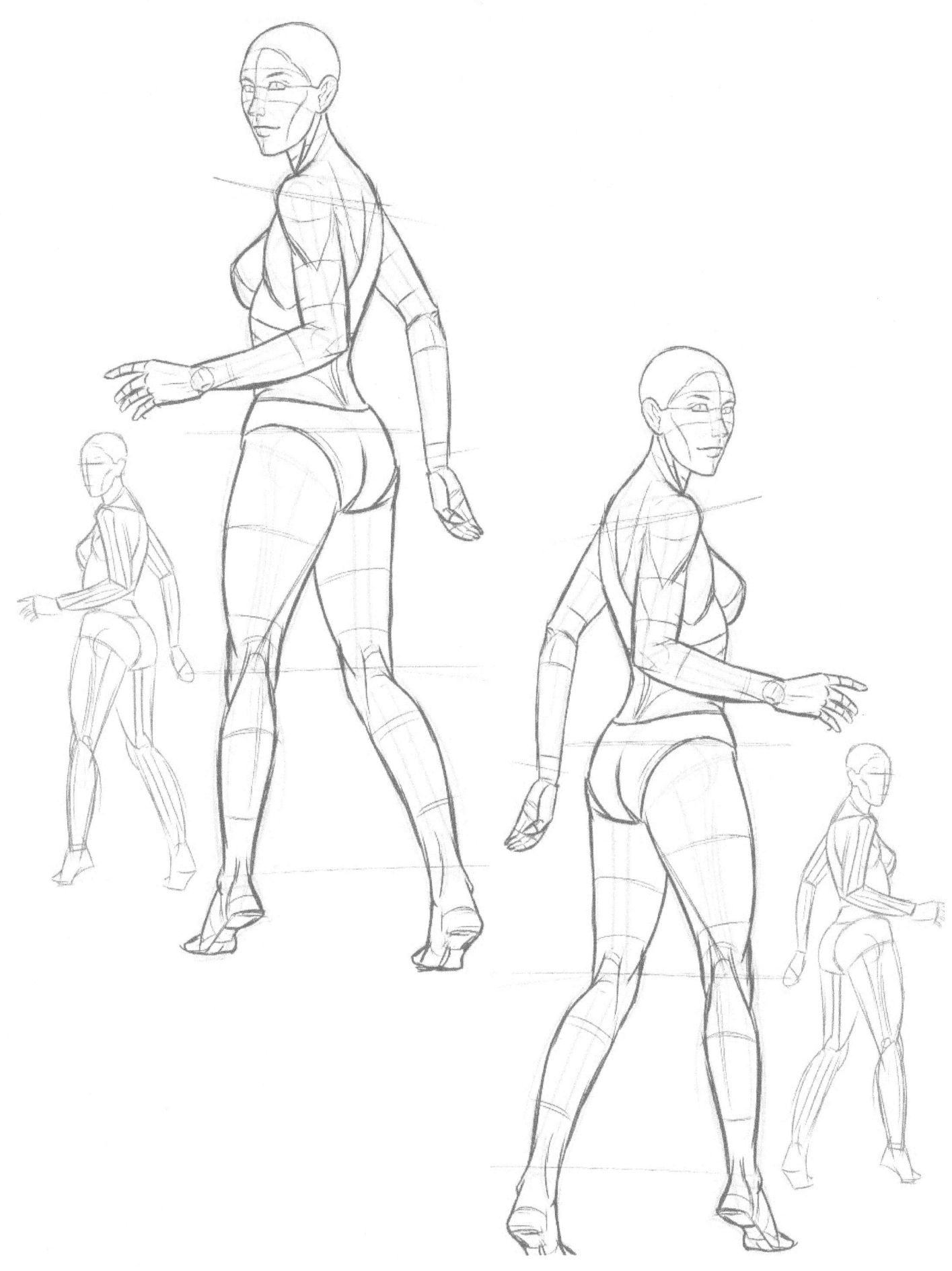

Standing Poses | 43

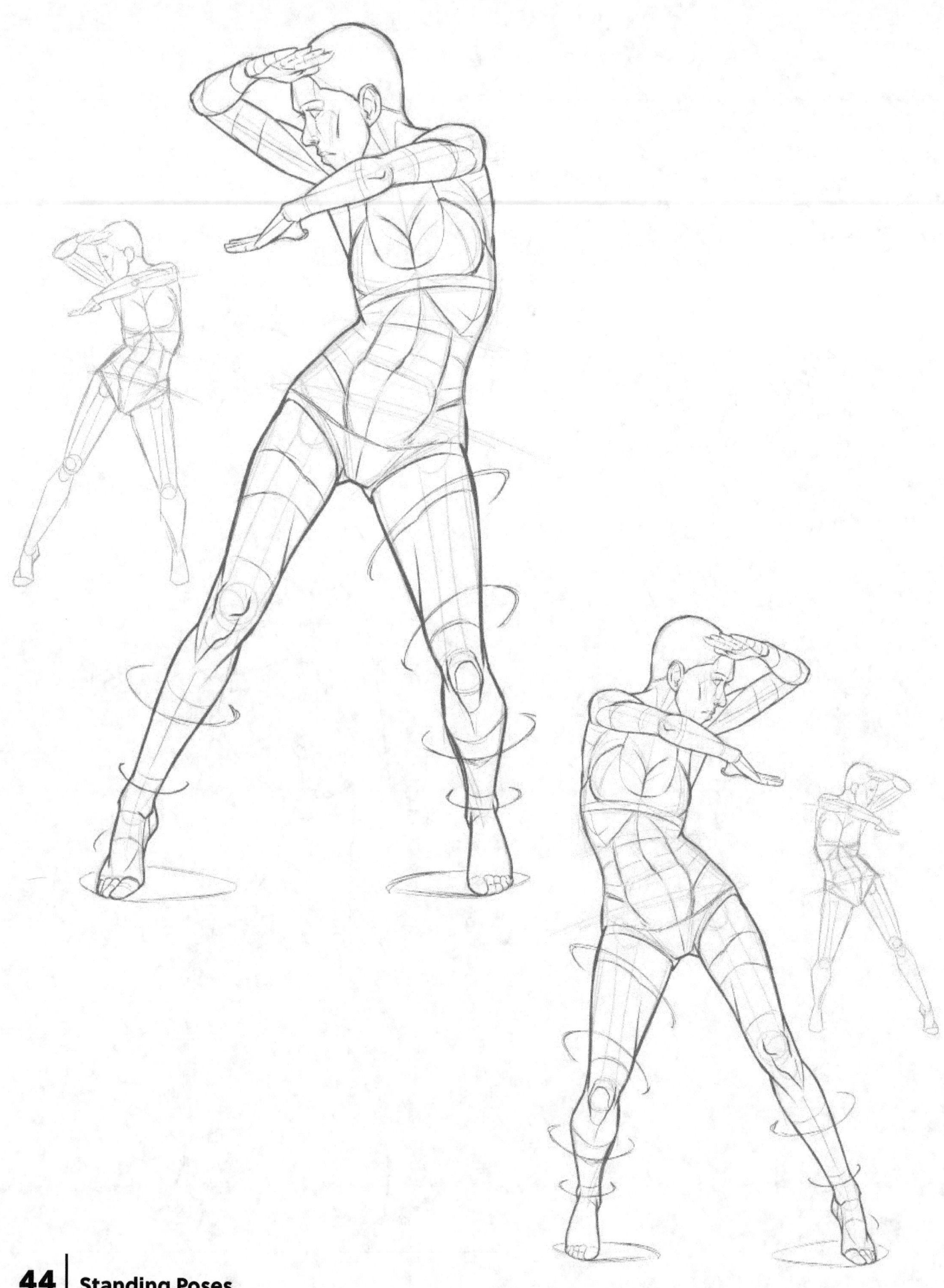

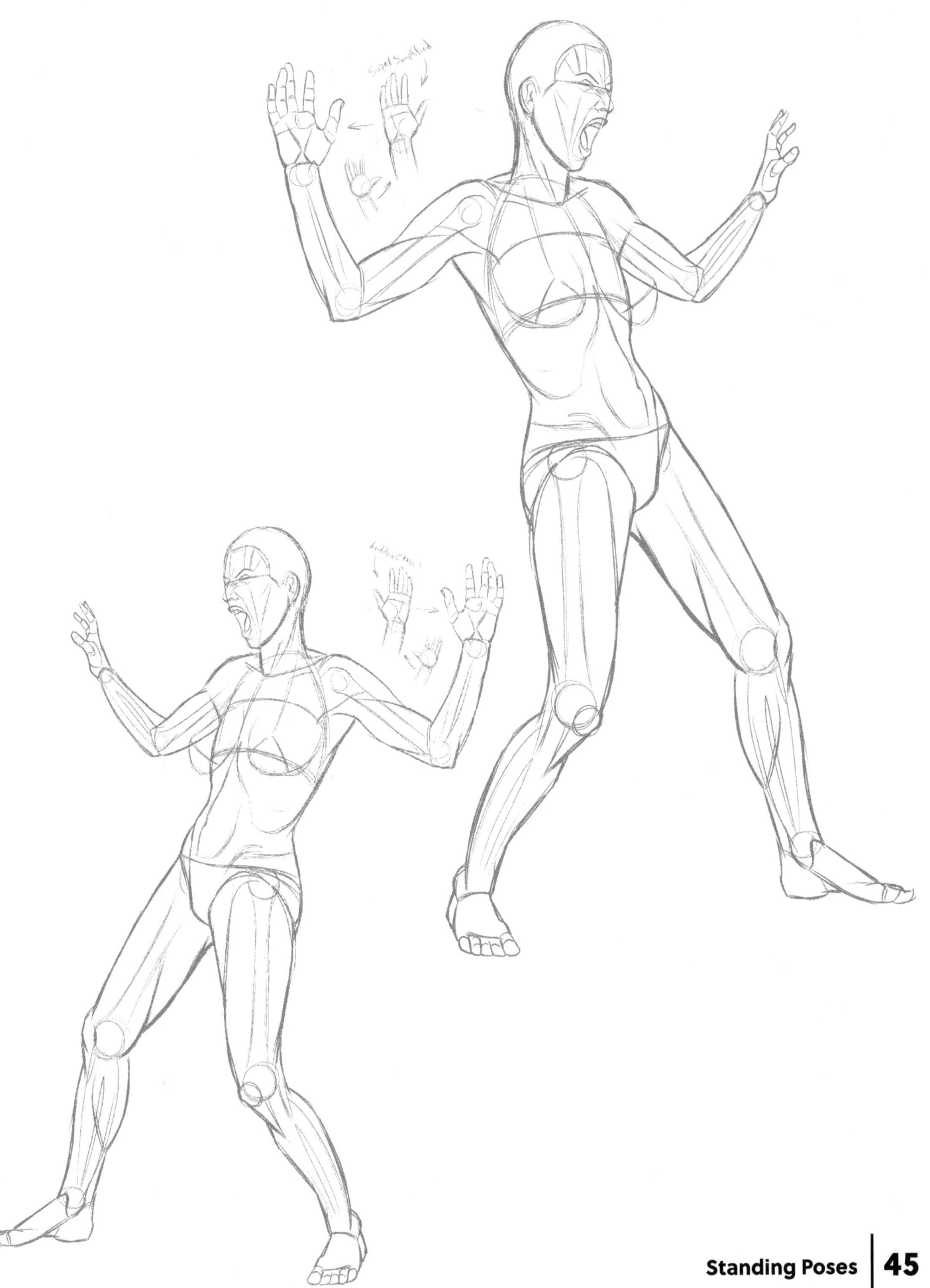

Standing Poses | 45

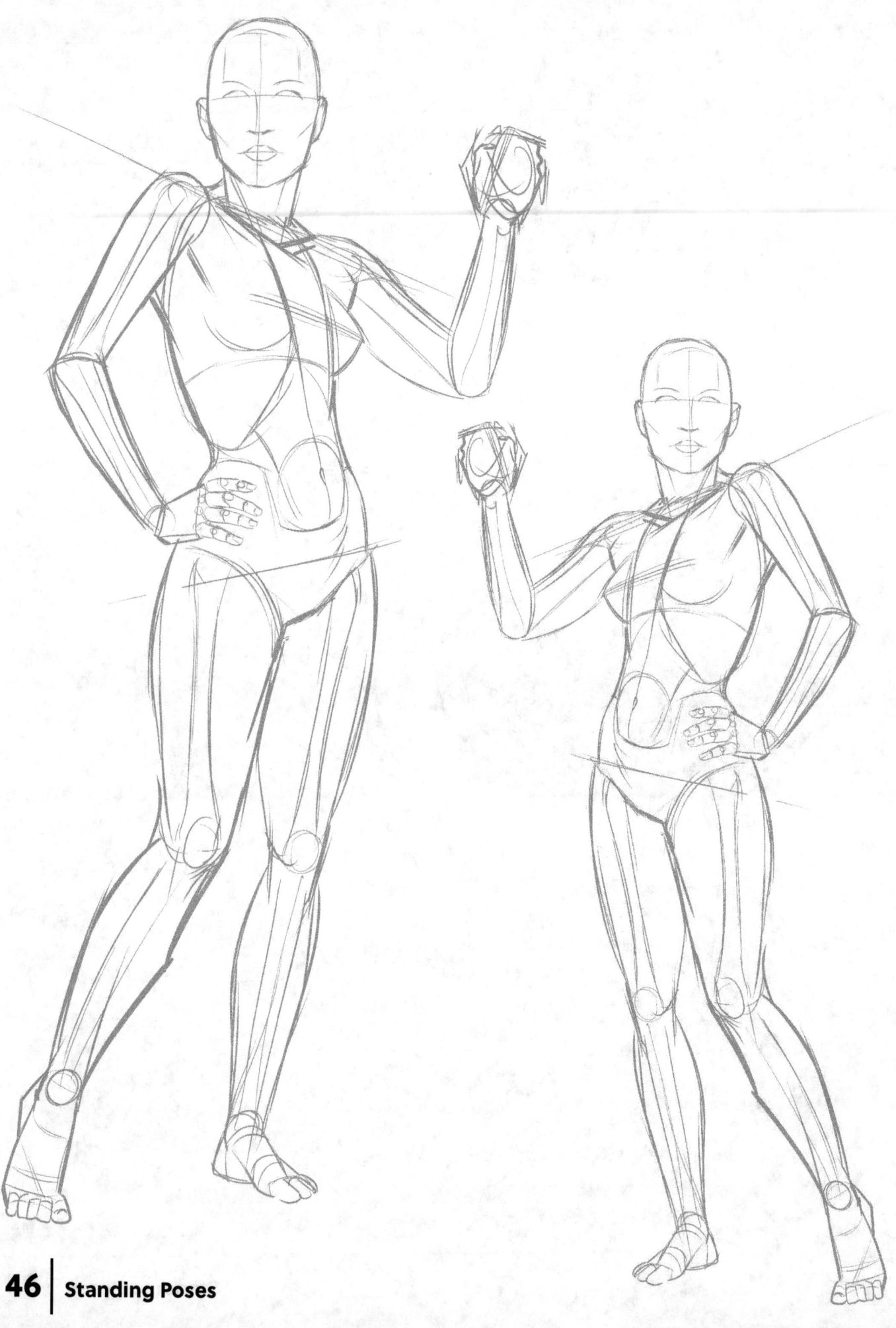

46 | **Standing Poses**

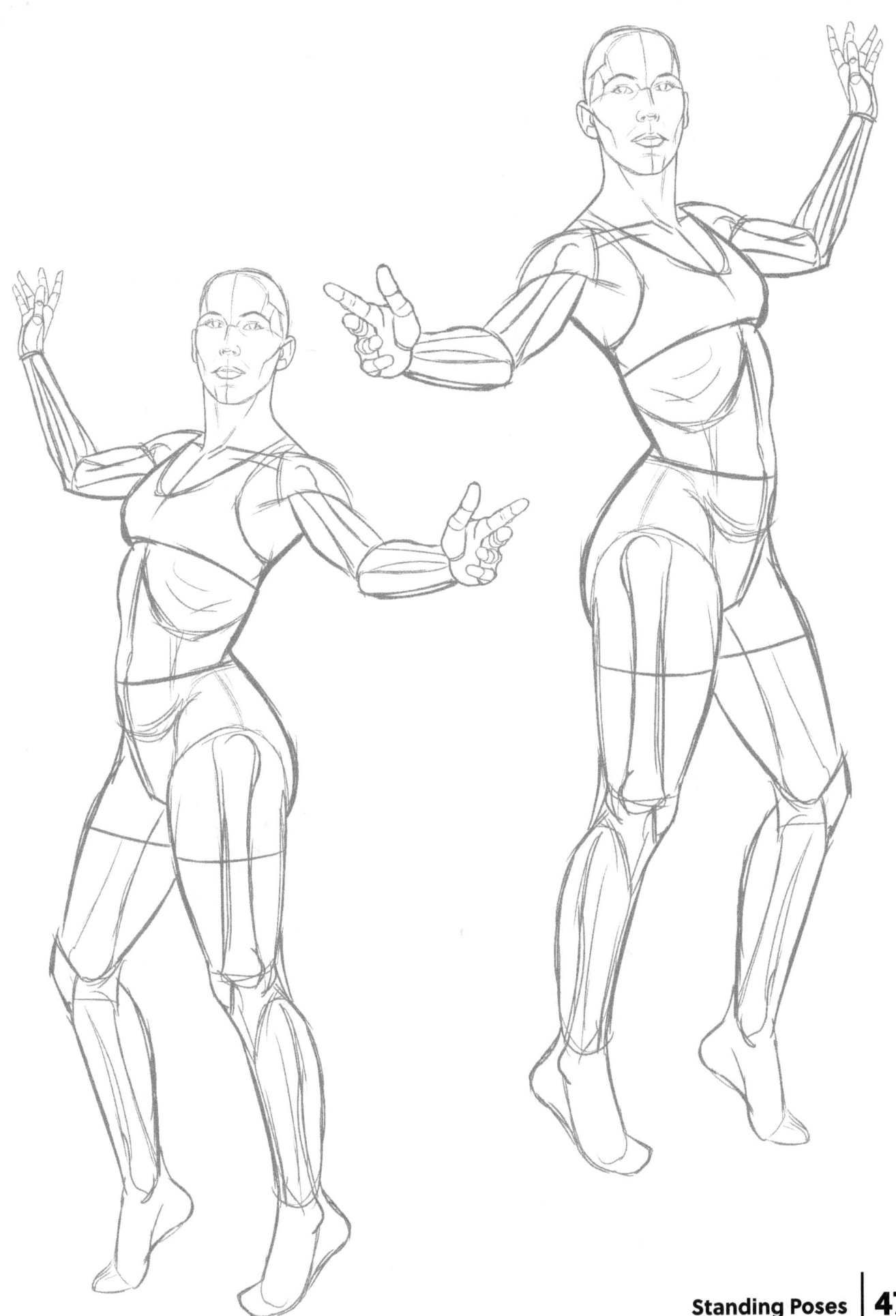

Standing Poses | 47

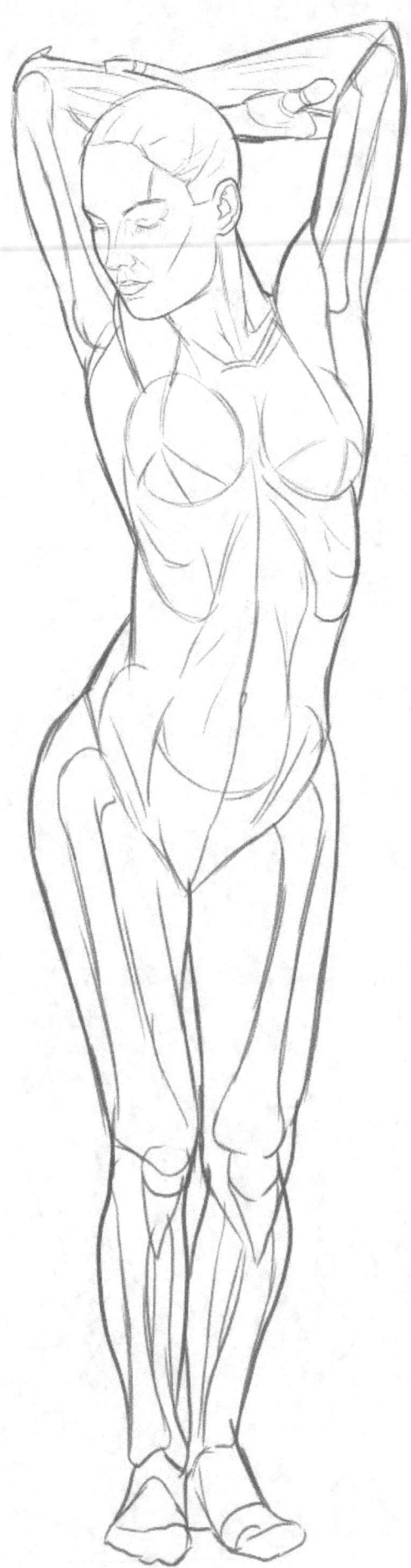
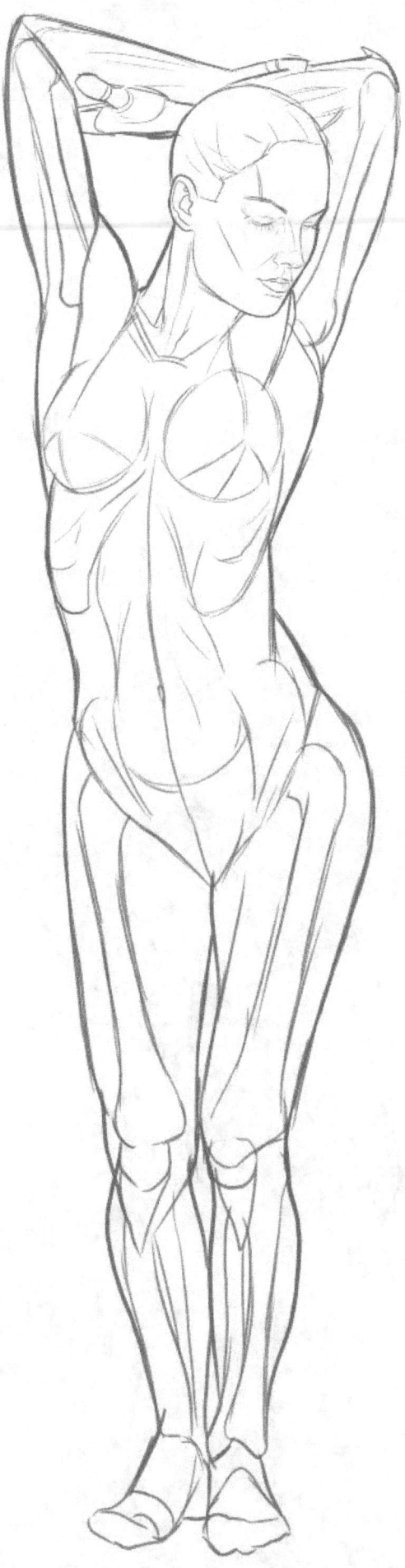

48 | Standing Poses

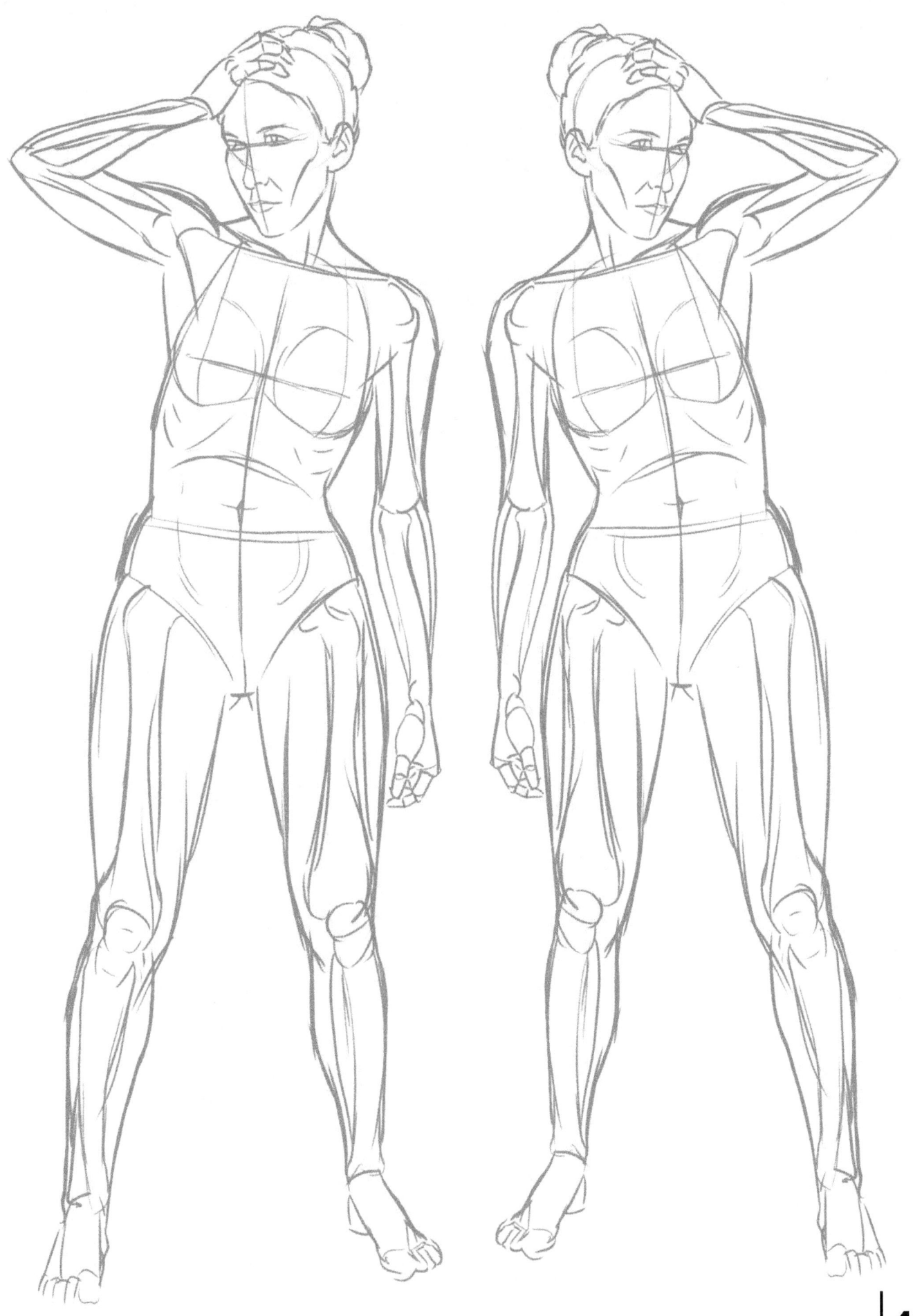

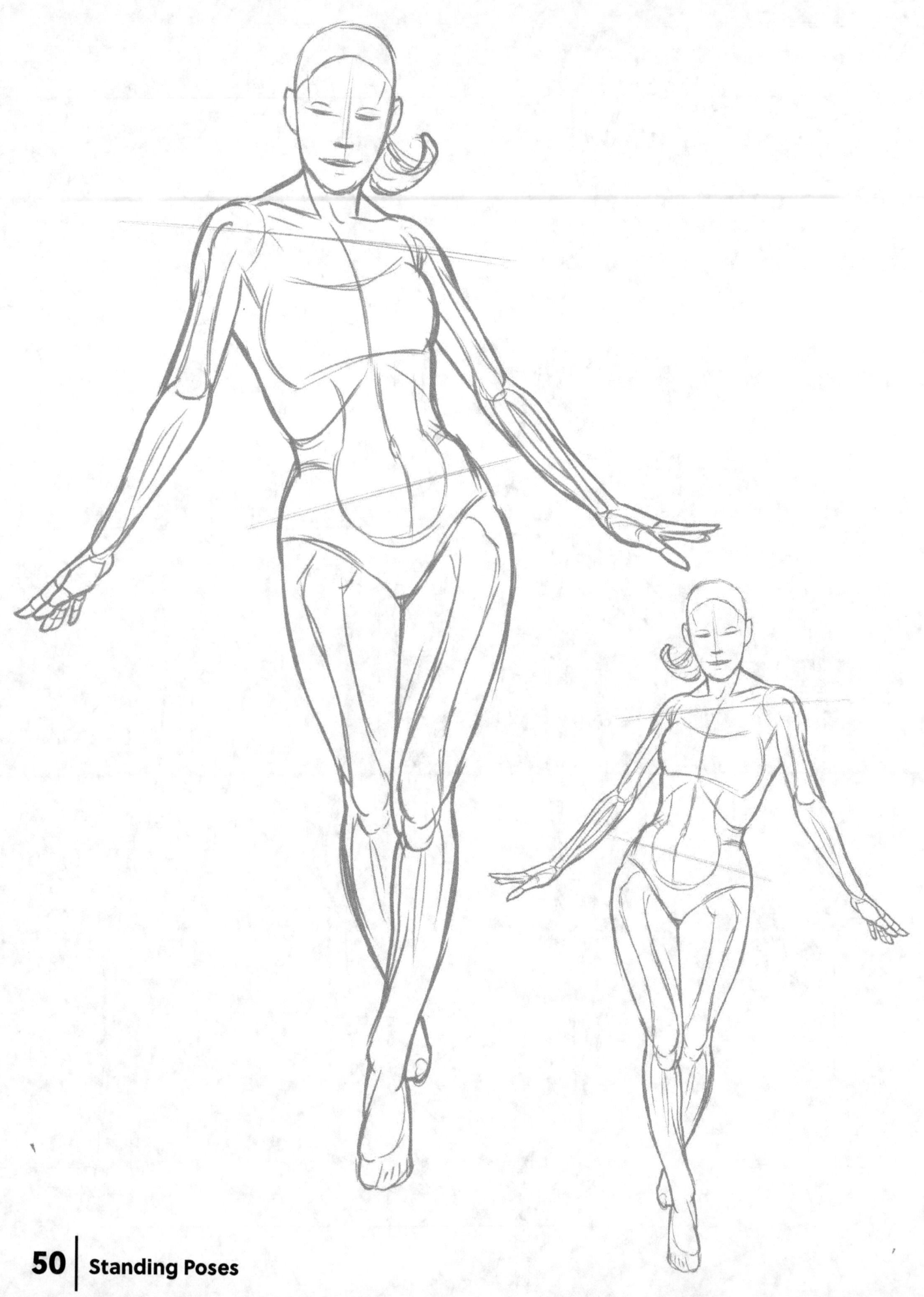

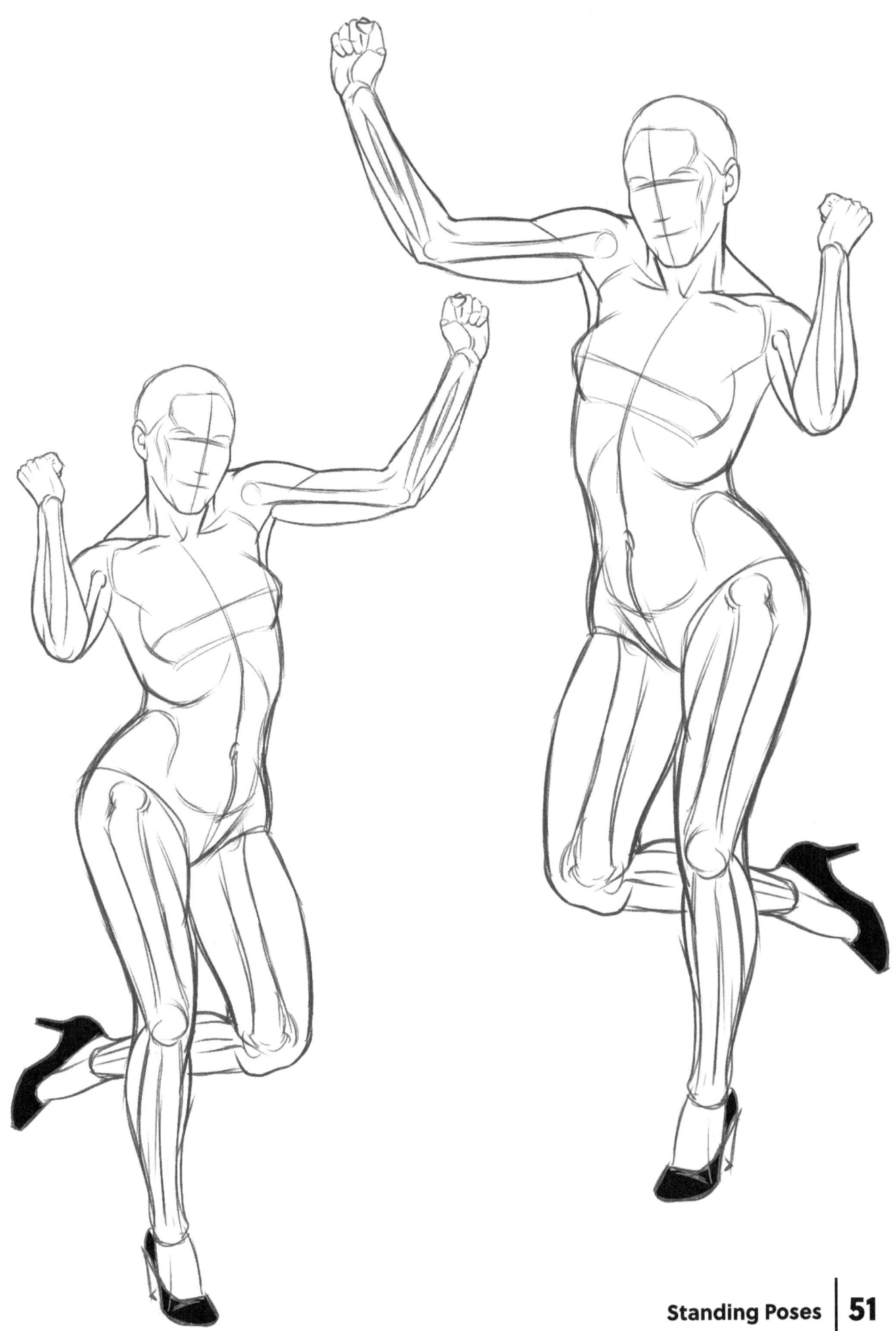

Standing Poses | 51

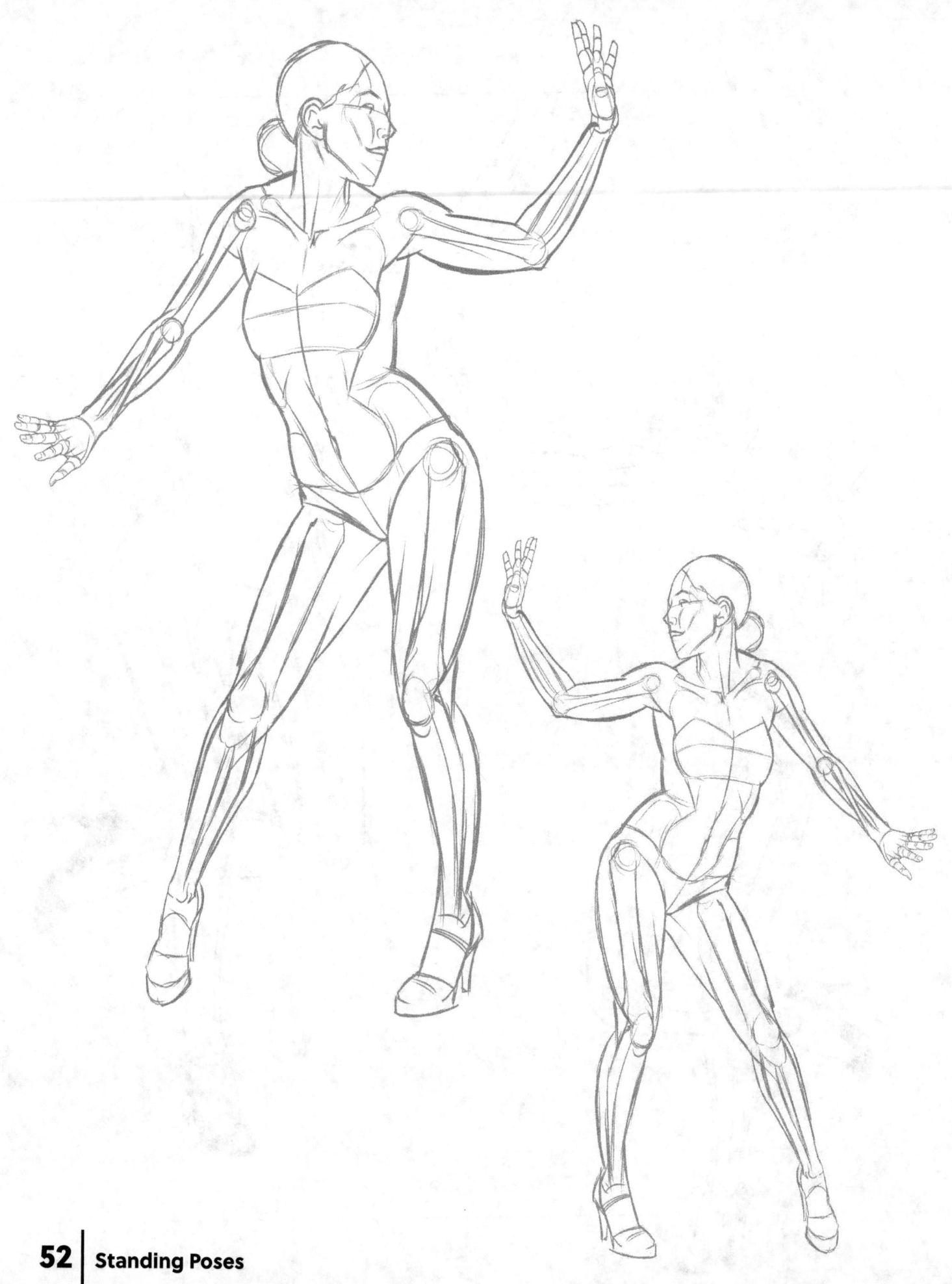

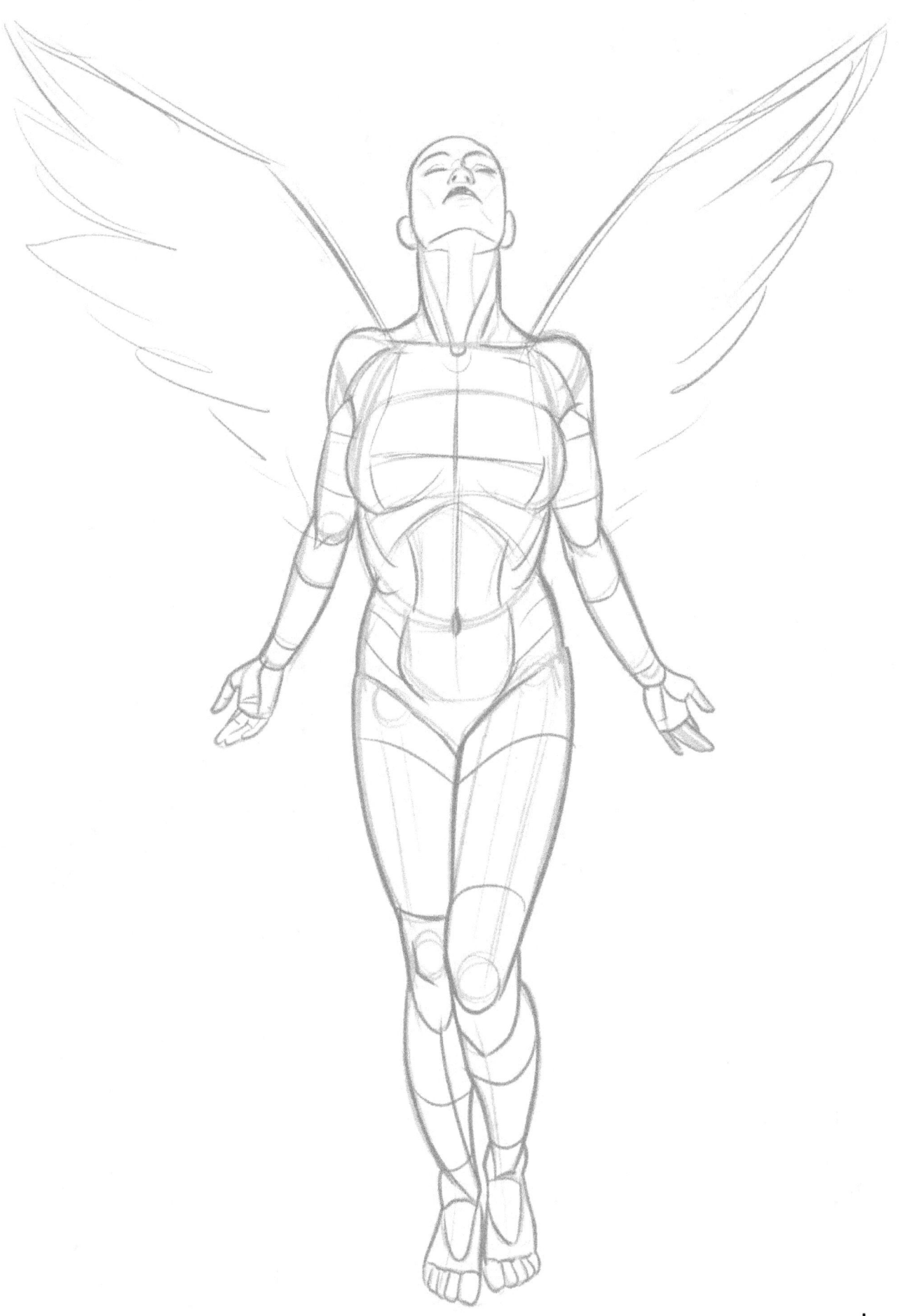

Standing Poses | 53

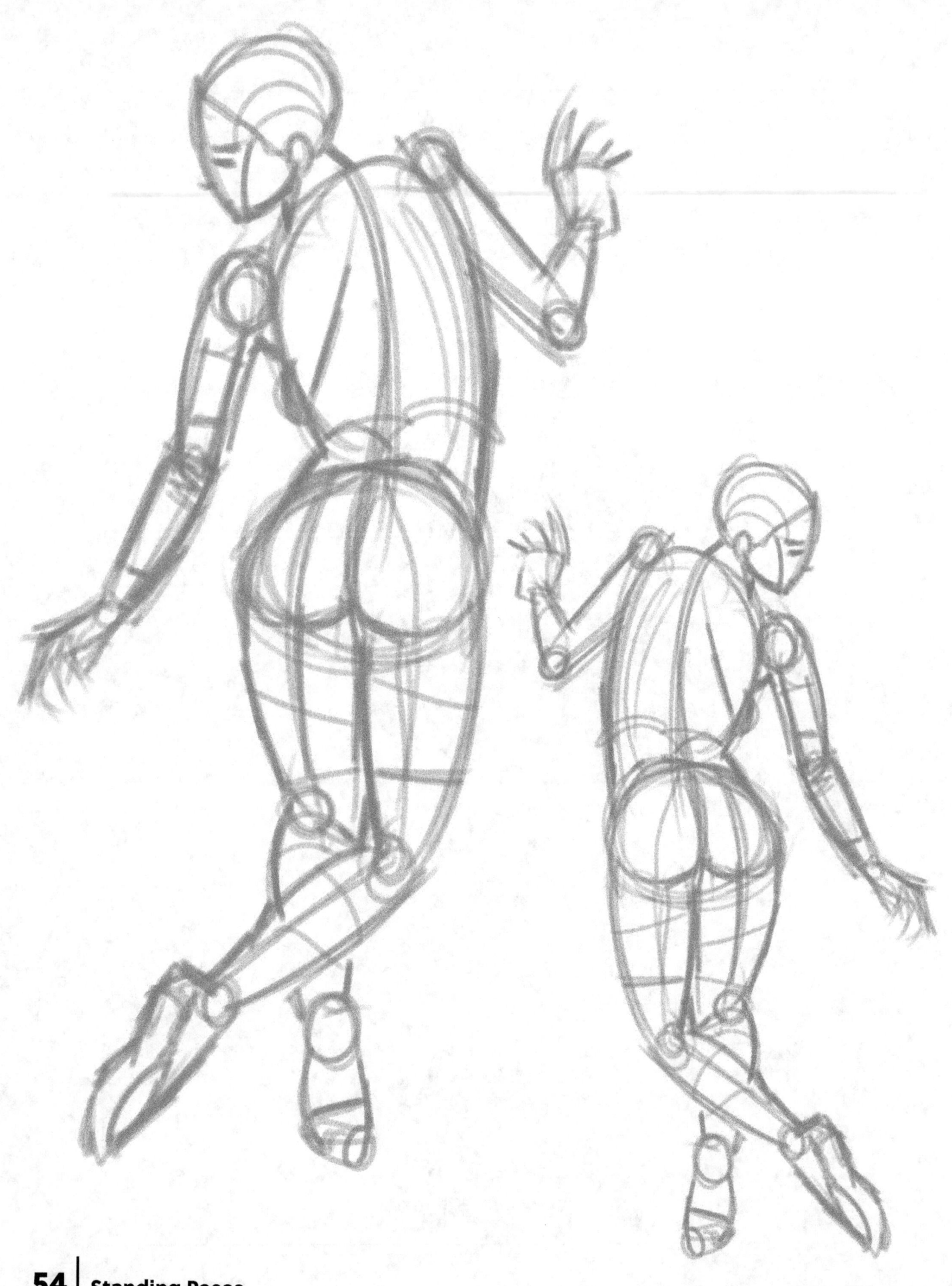

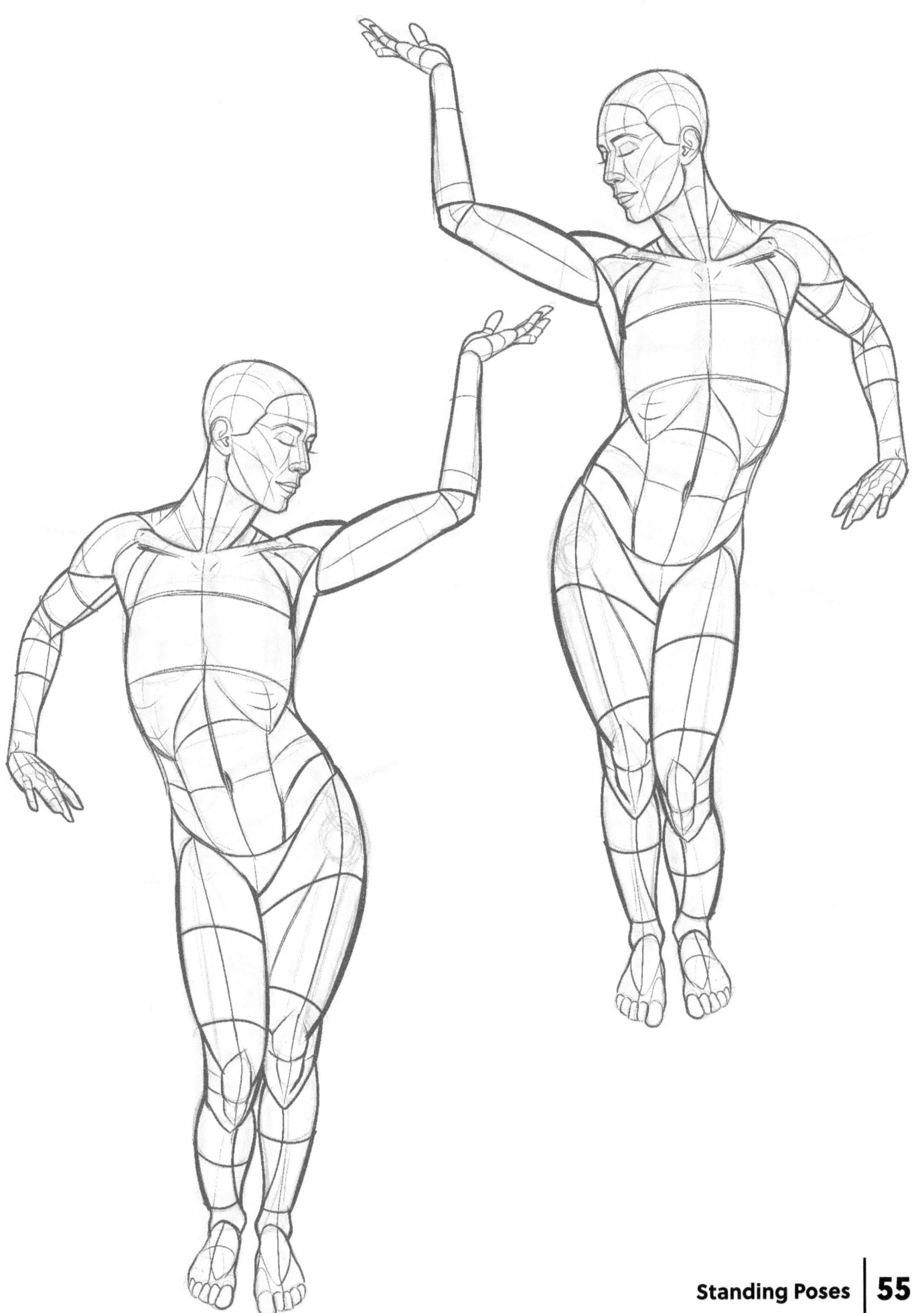

Standing Poses | 55

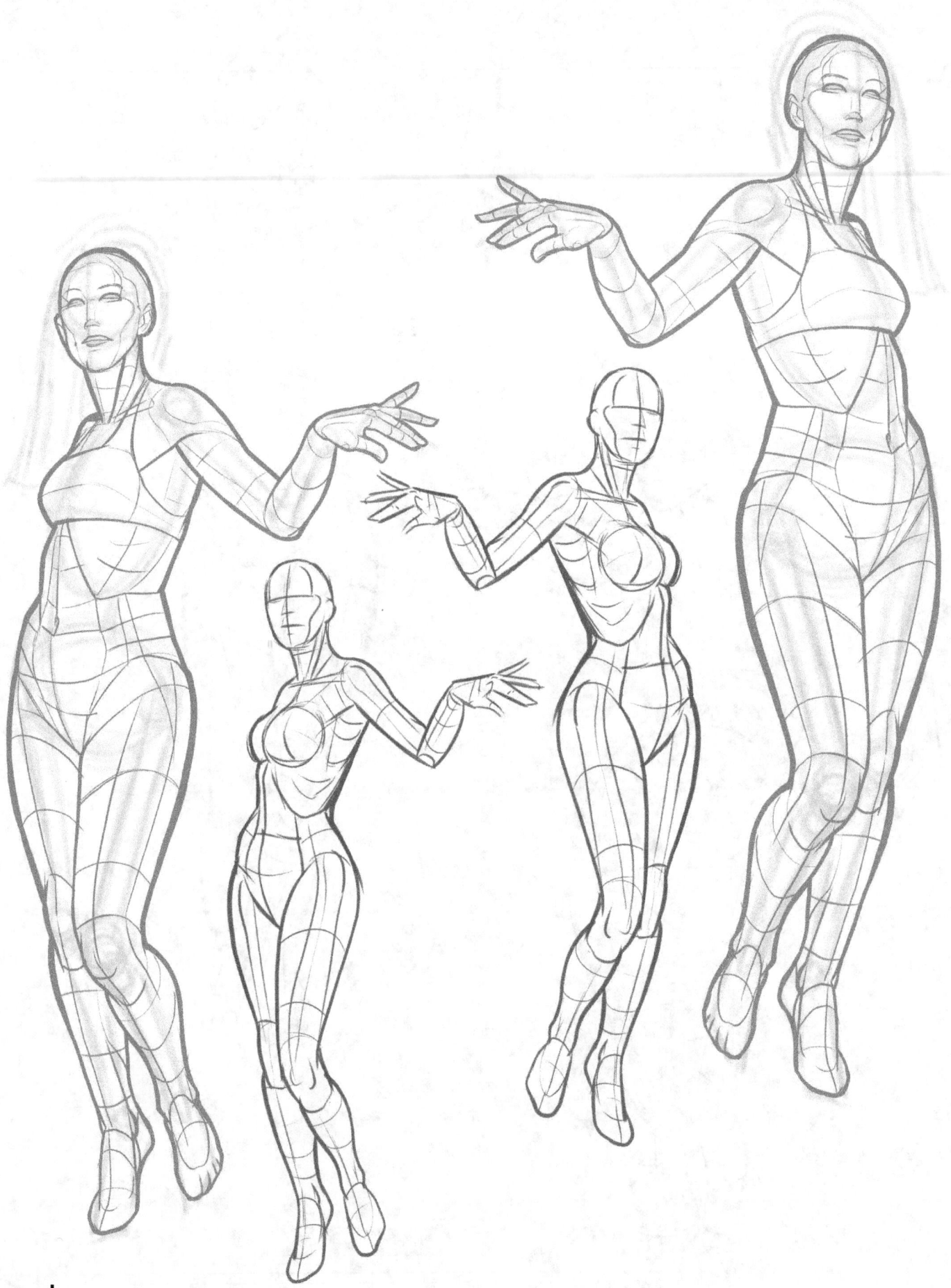

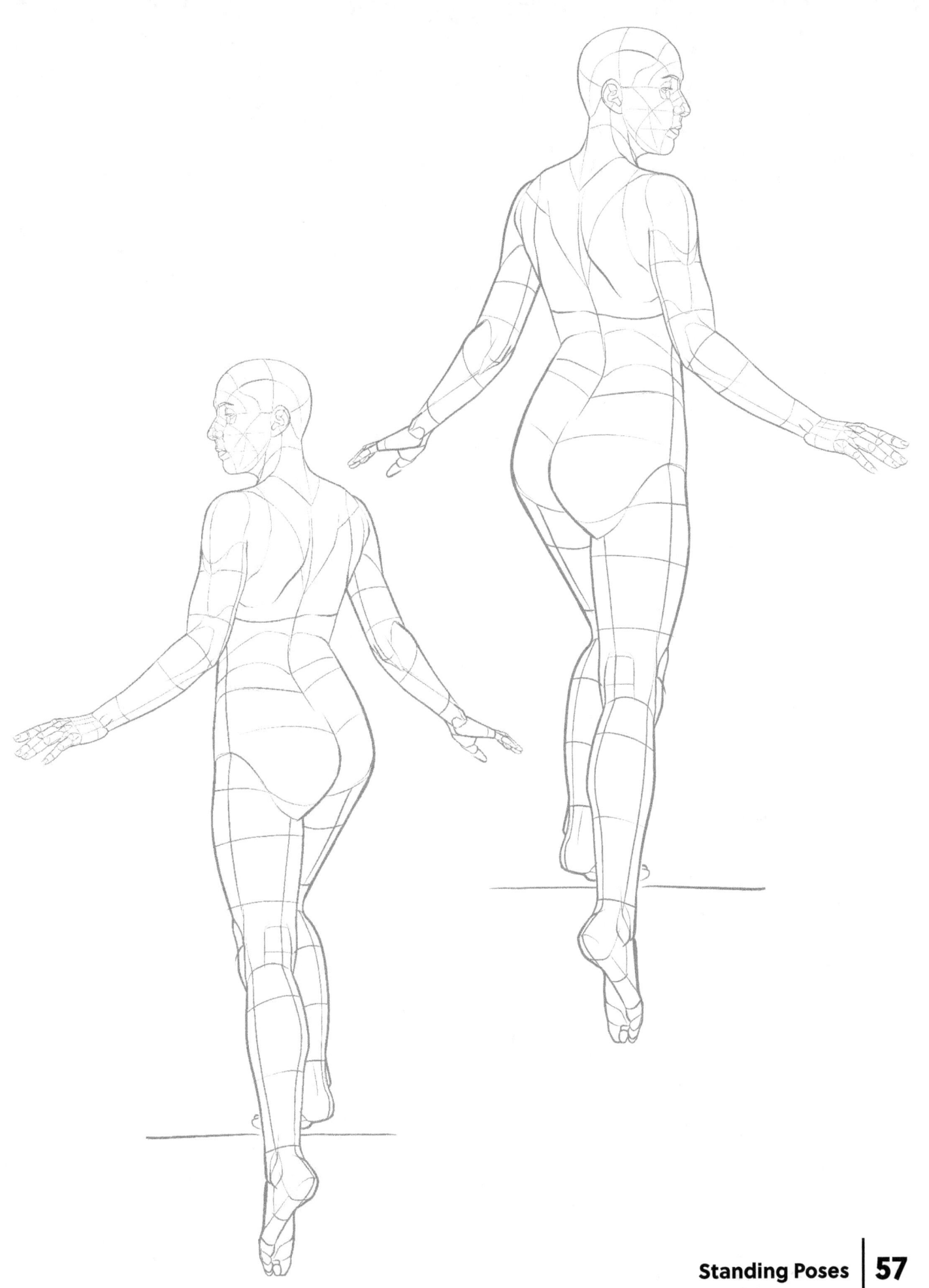

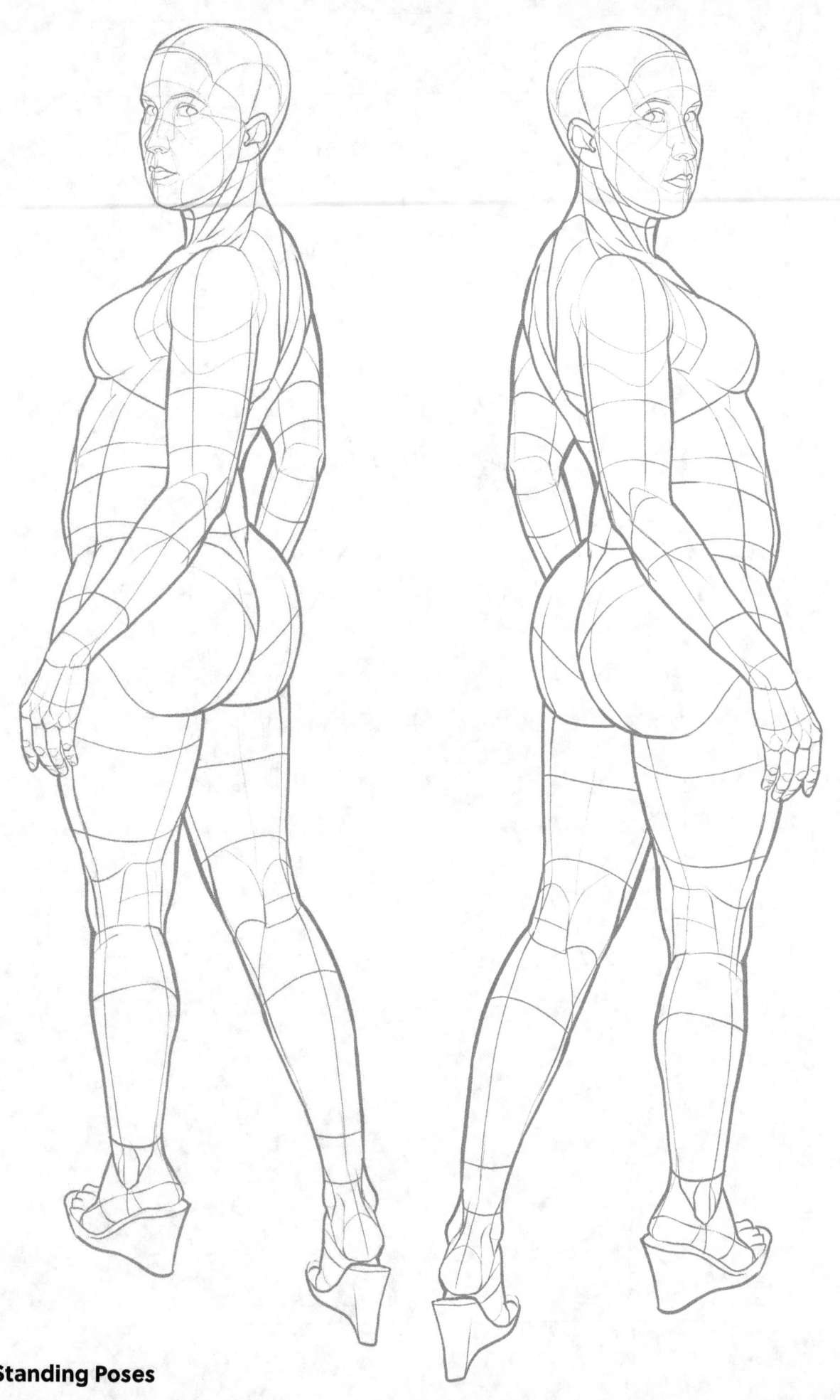

Standing Poses

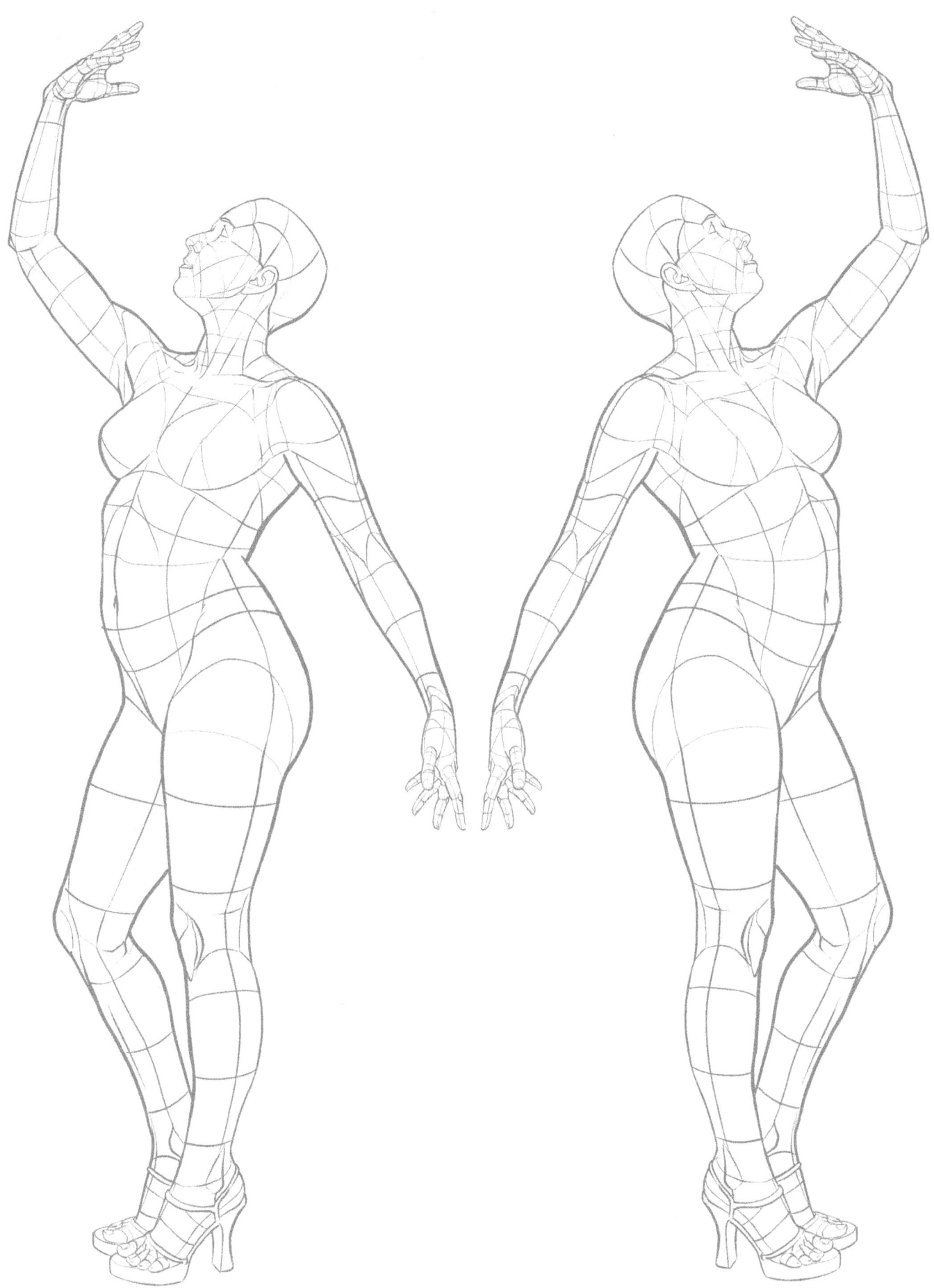

Standing Poses | 59

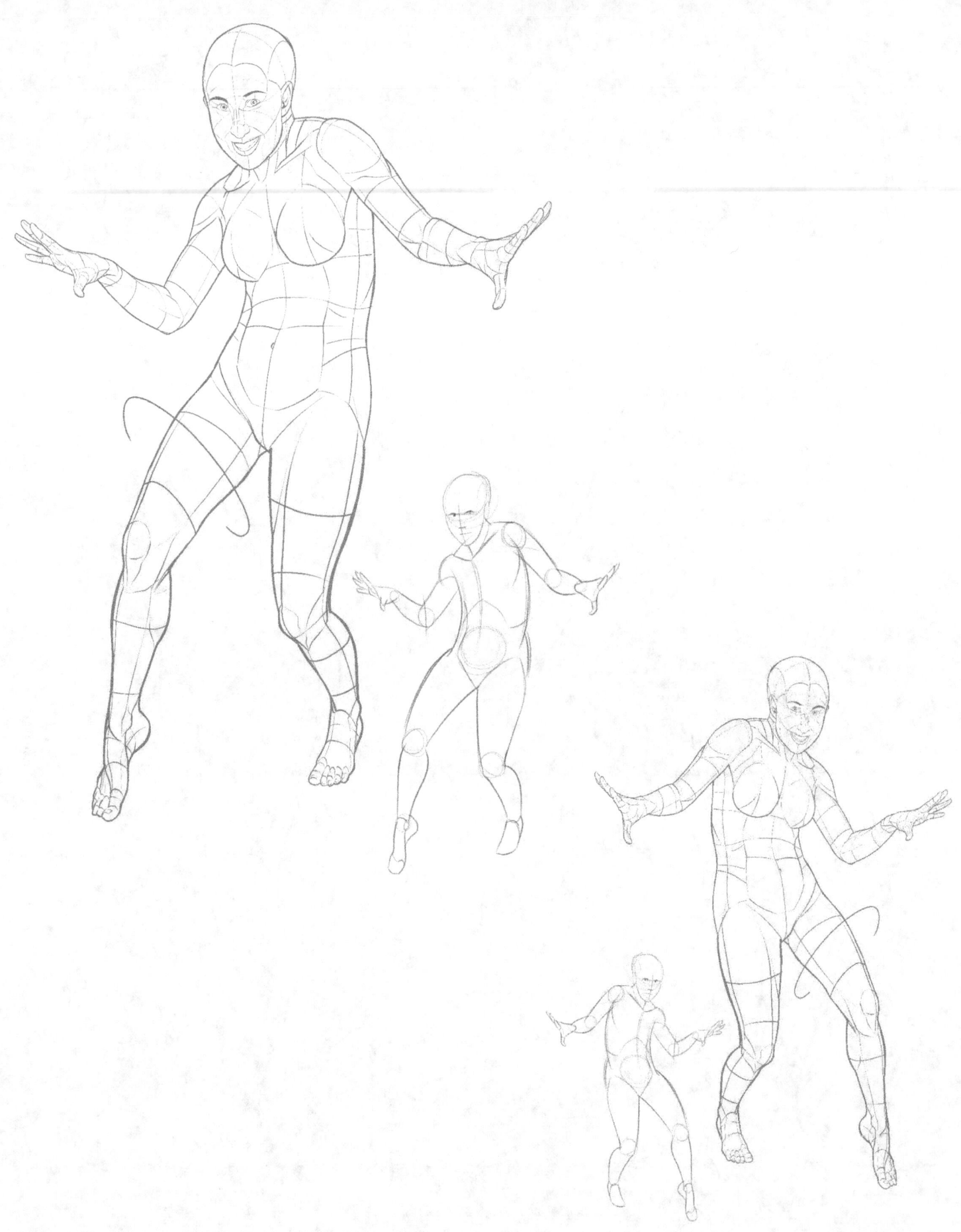

60 | Standing Poses

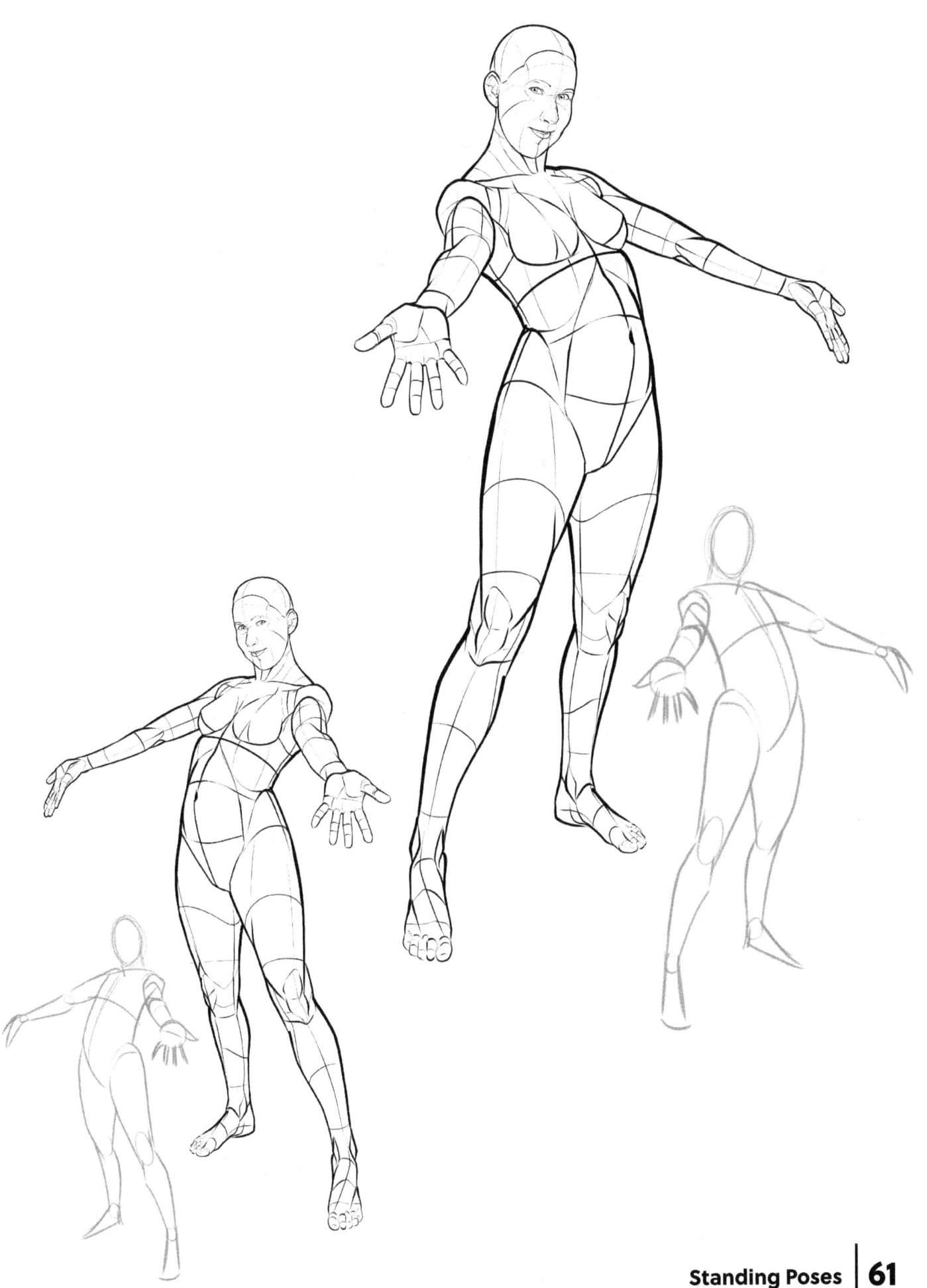

Standing Poses | 61

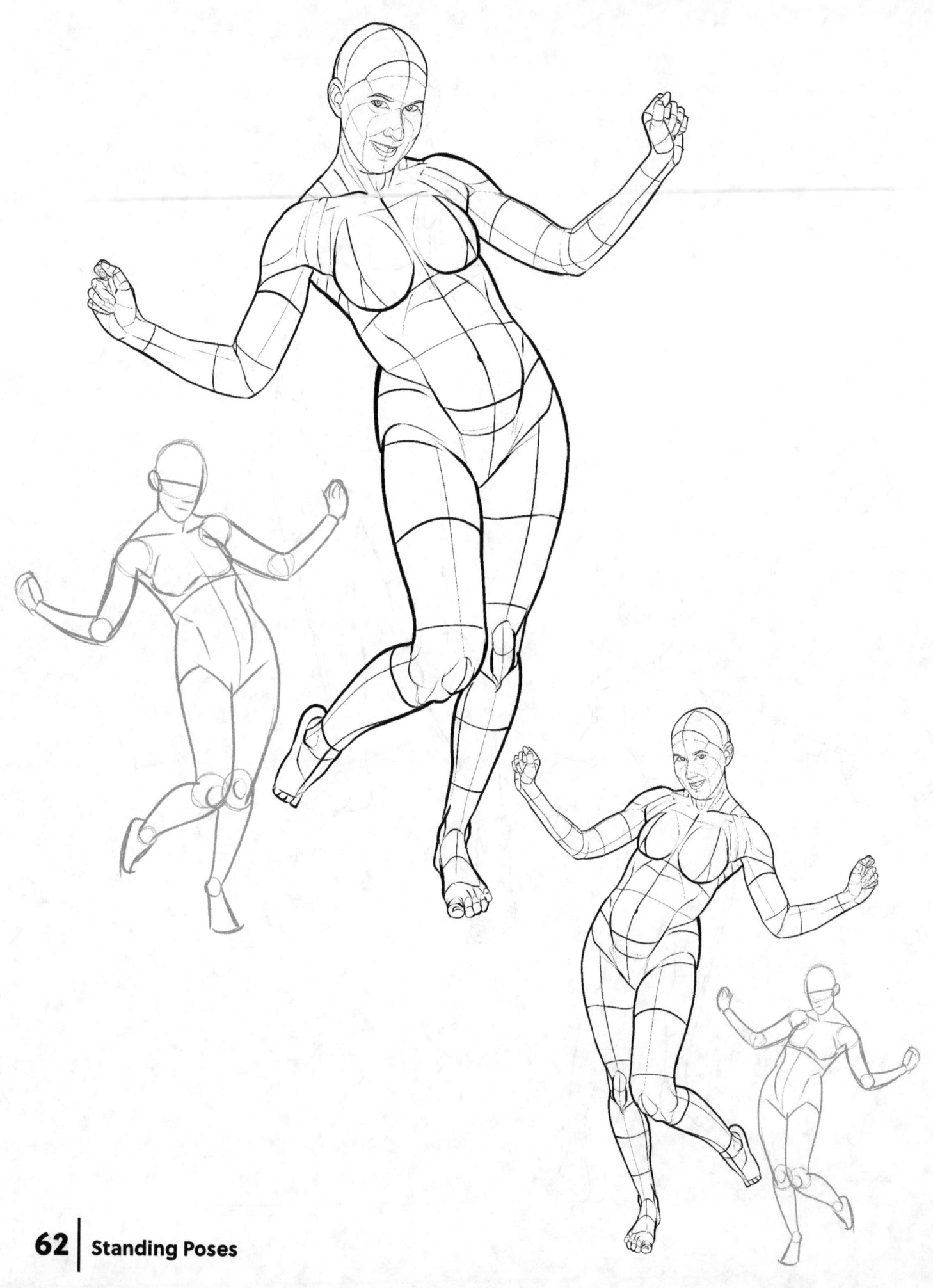

62 | Standing Poses

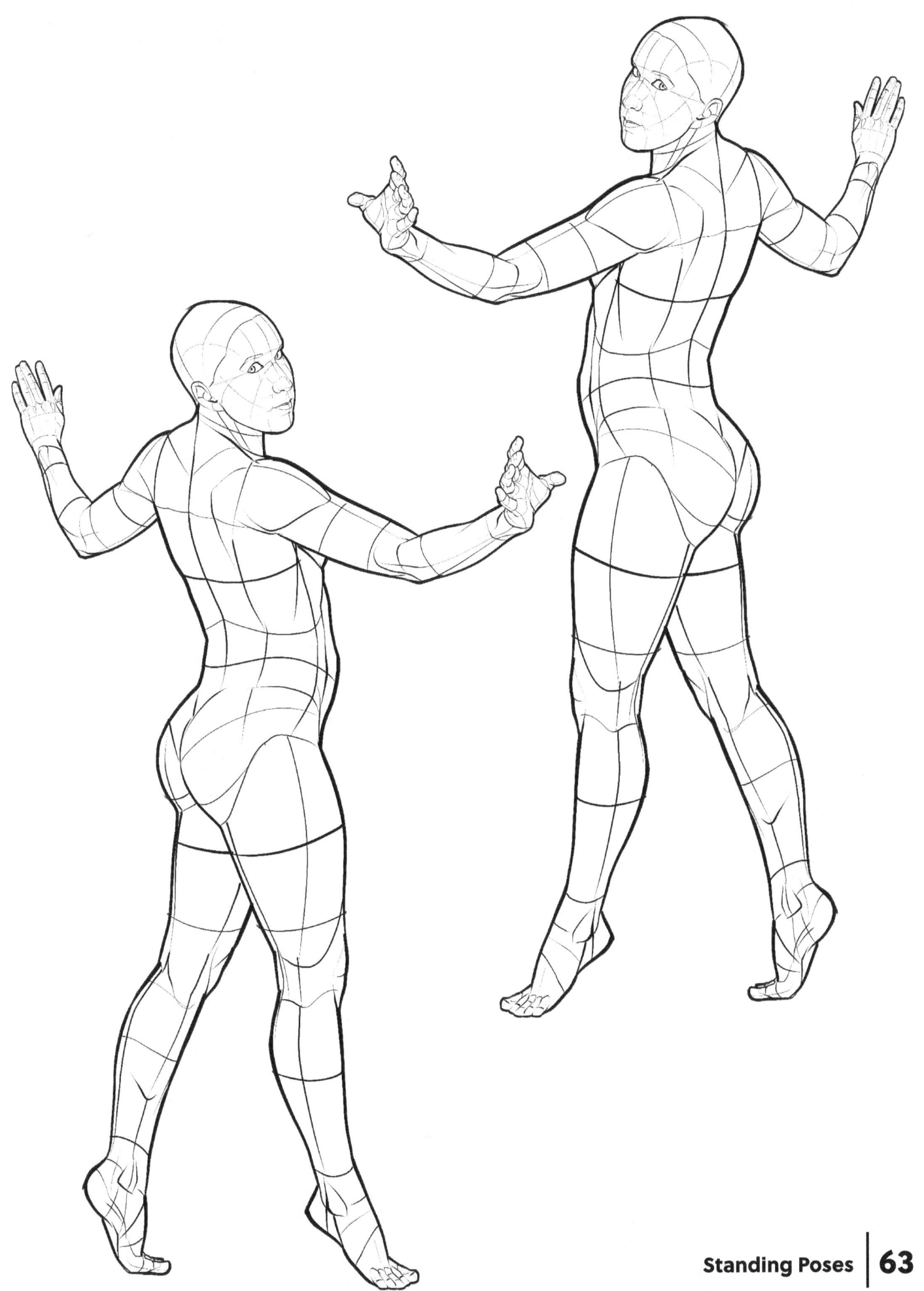

Standing Poses | **63**

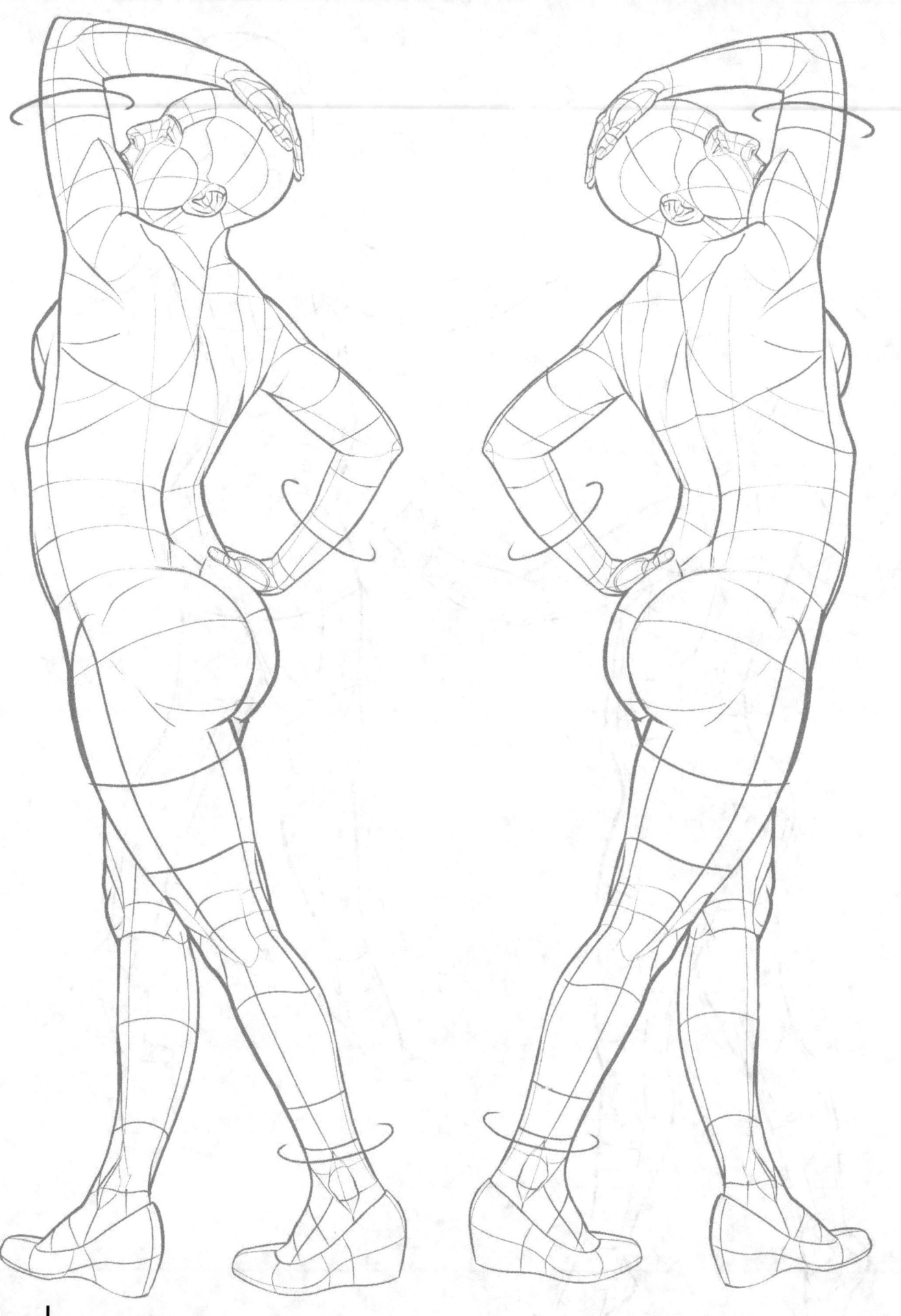

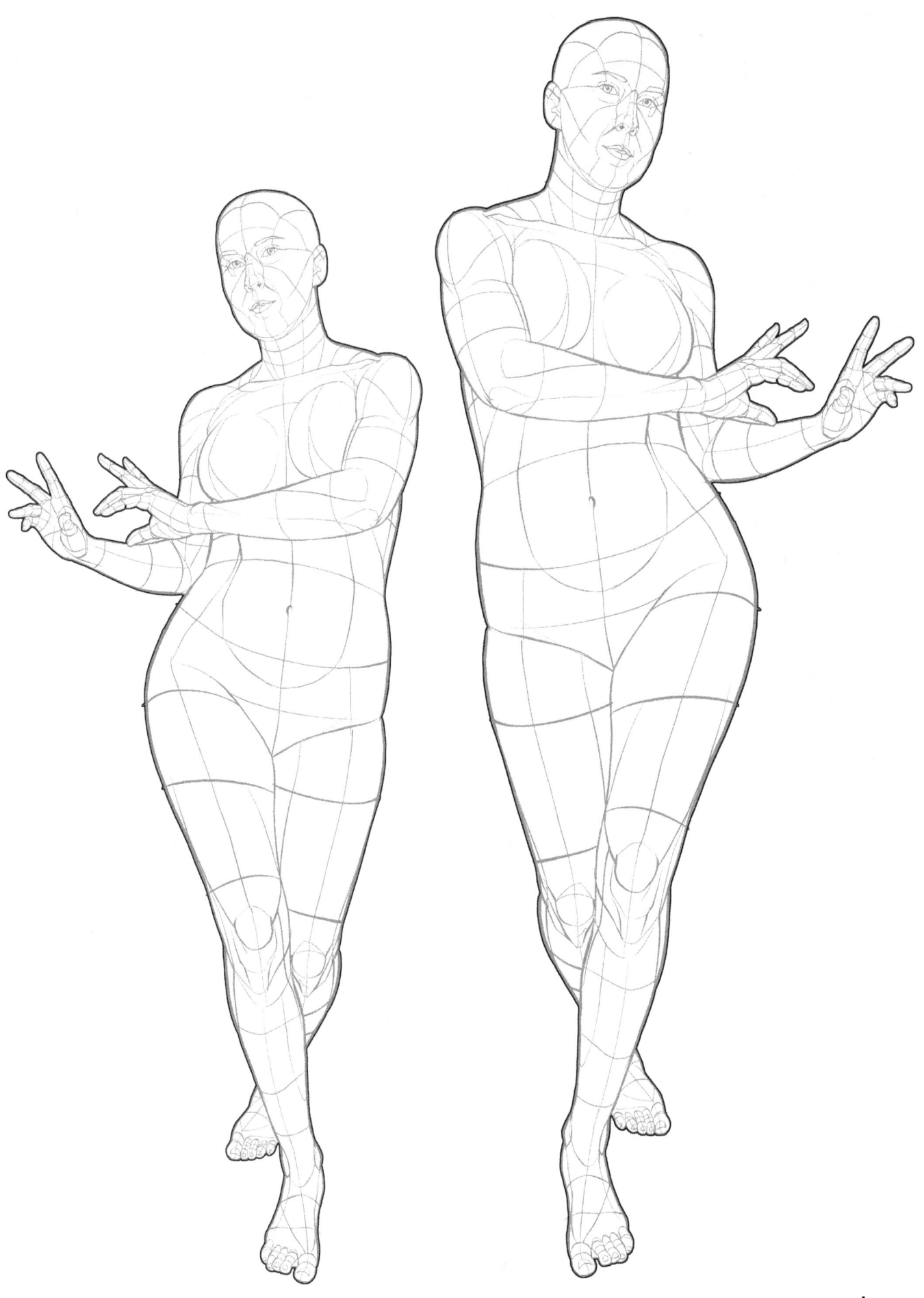

Standing Poses | 65

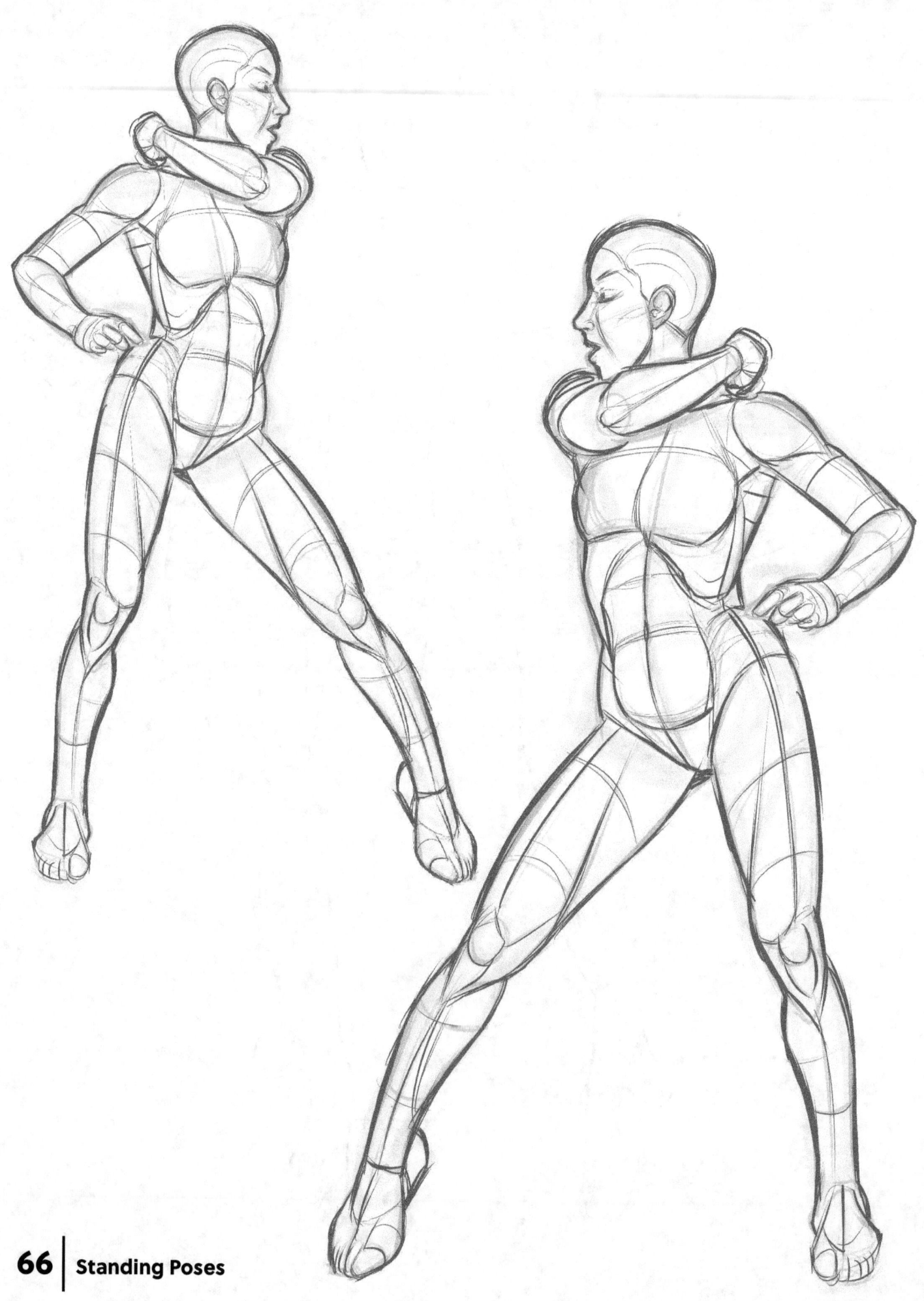

66 | Standing Poses

Sitting Poses

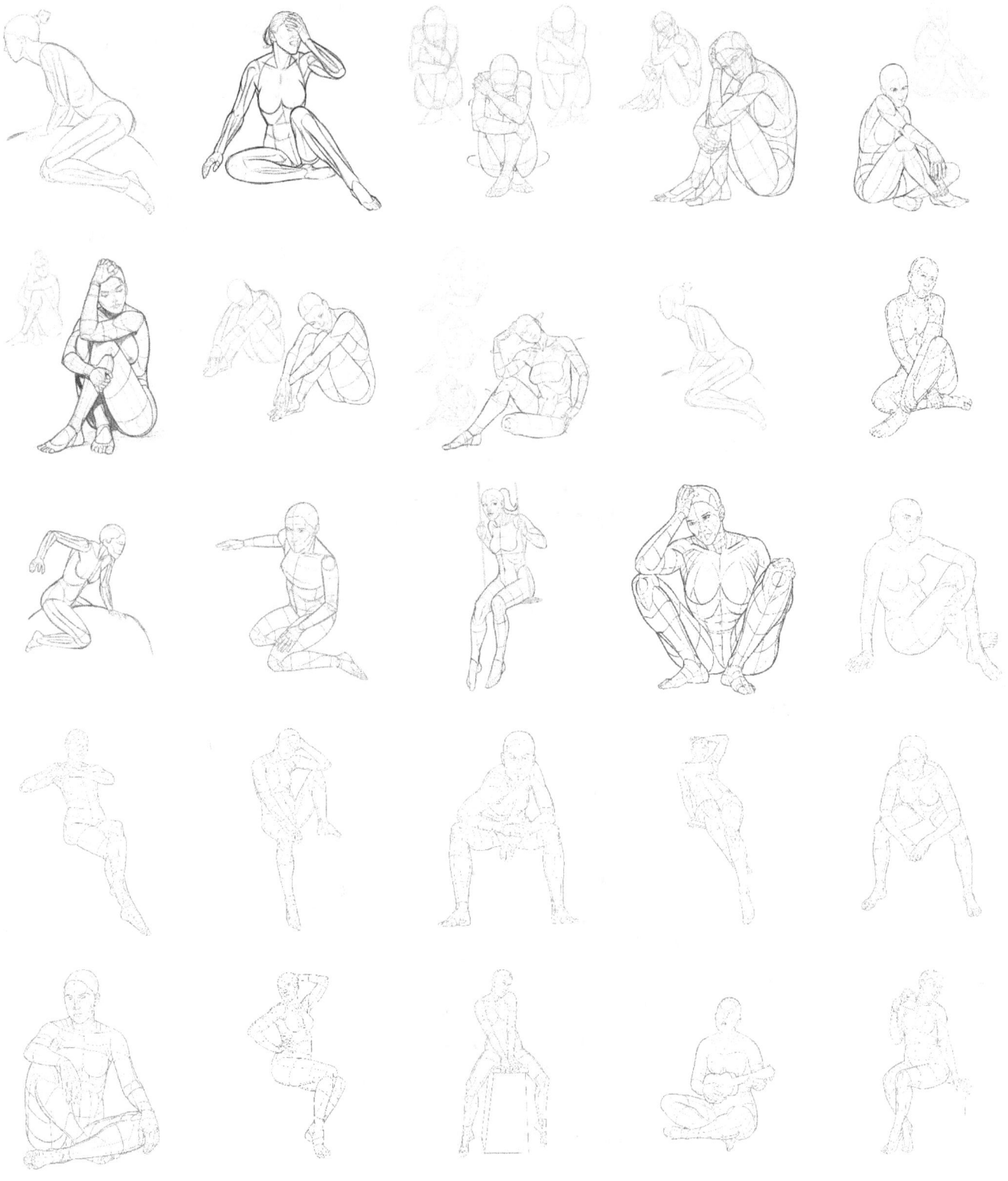

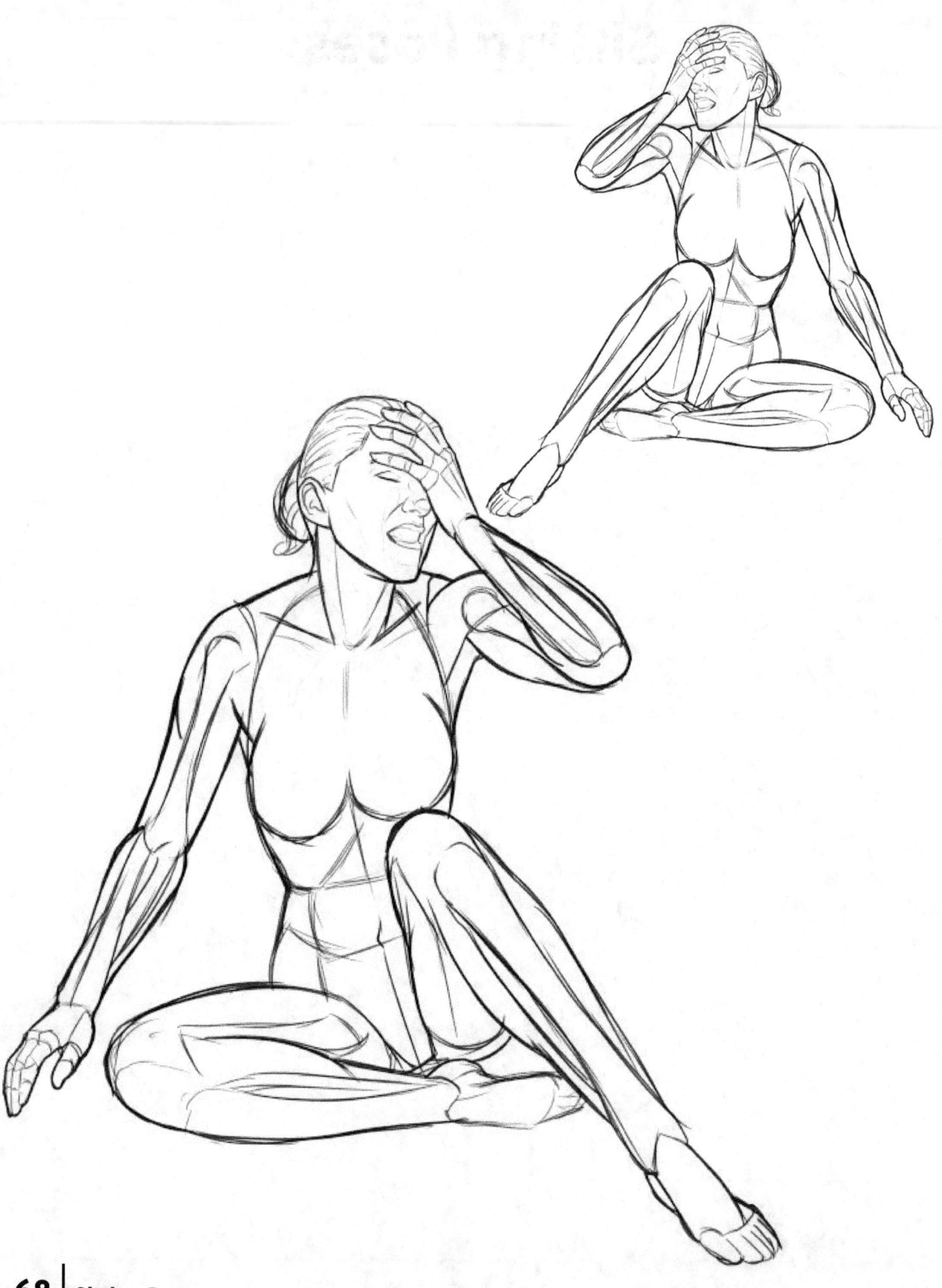

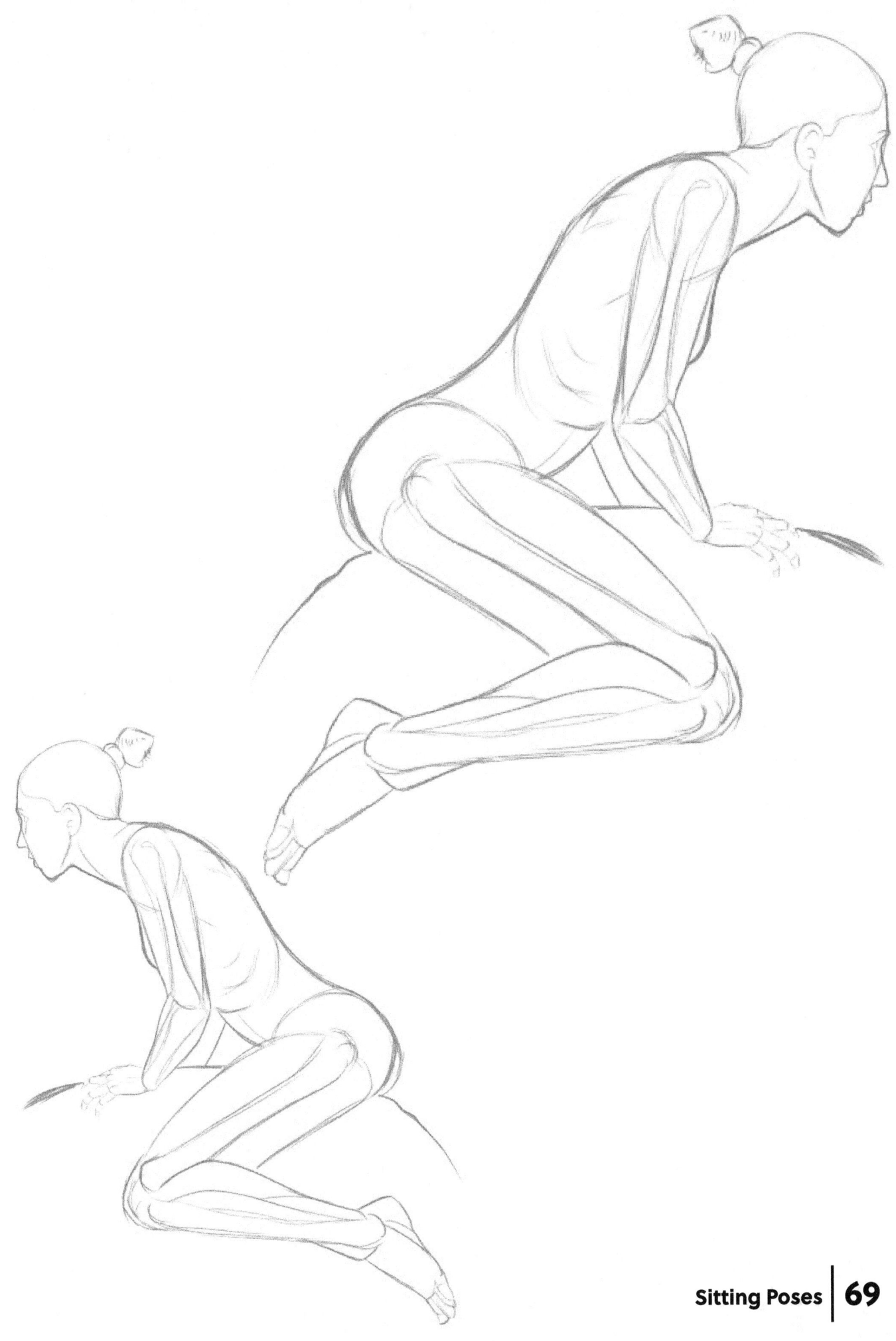

Sitting Poses | **69**

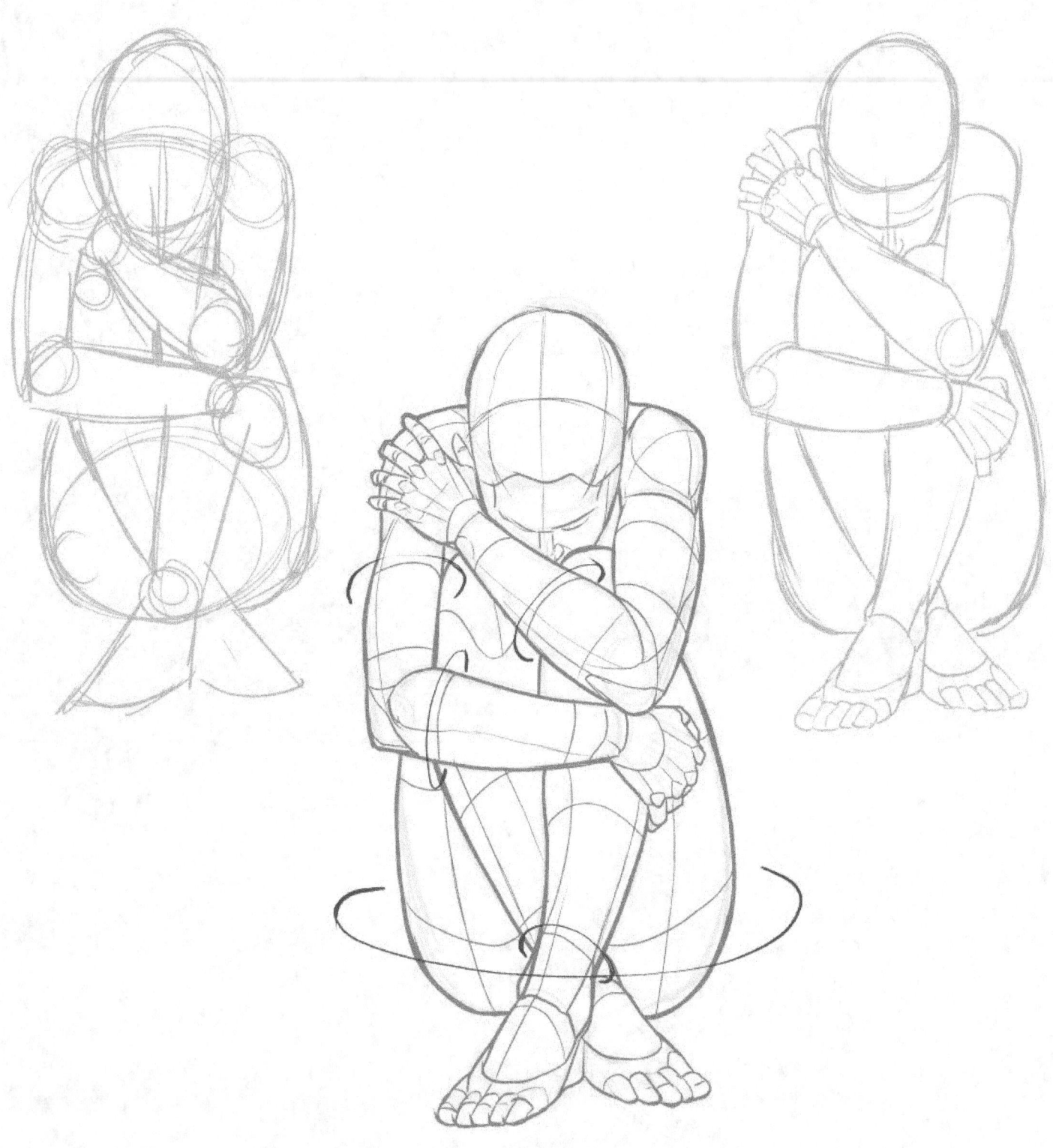

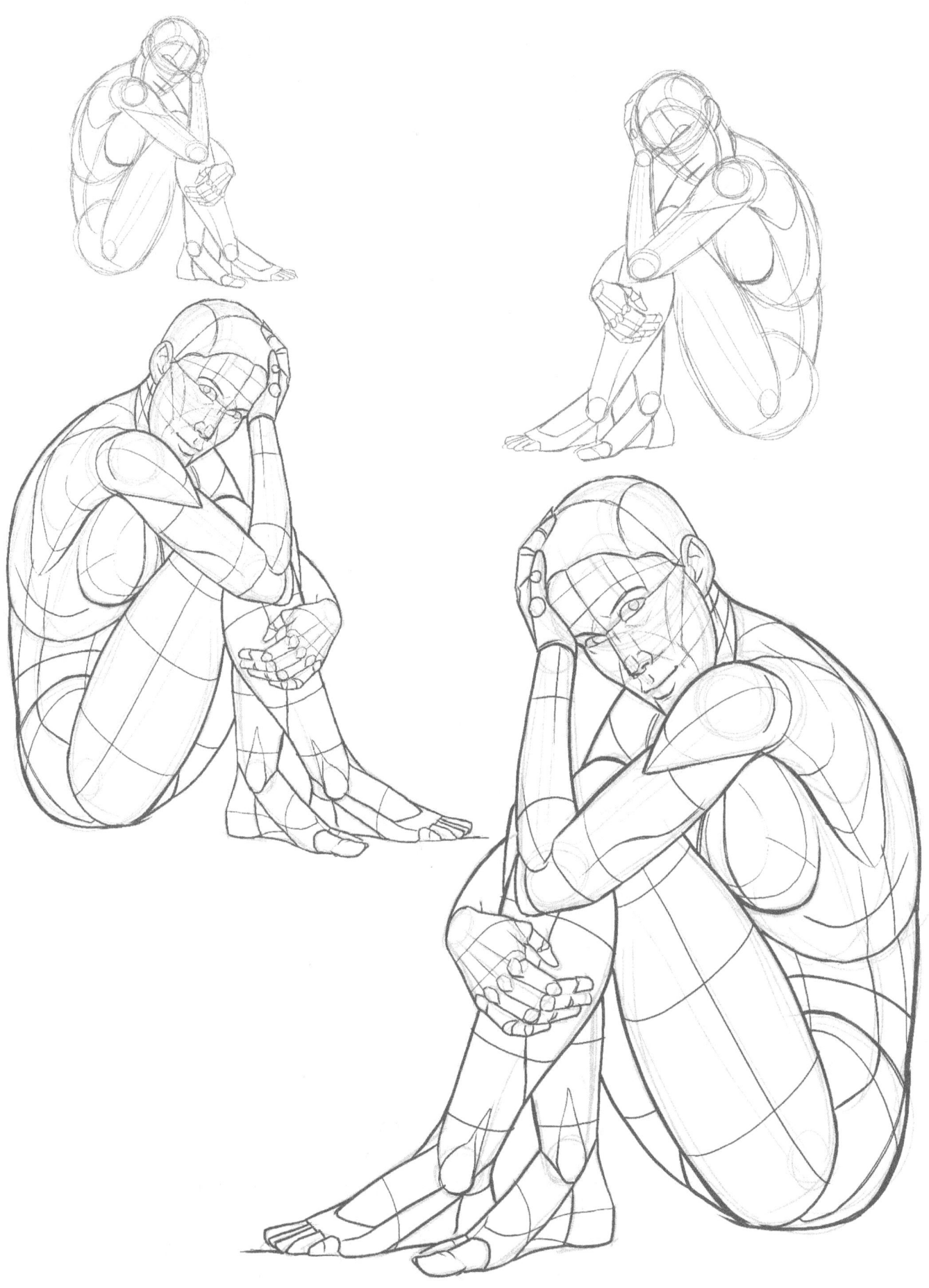

Sitting Poses

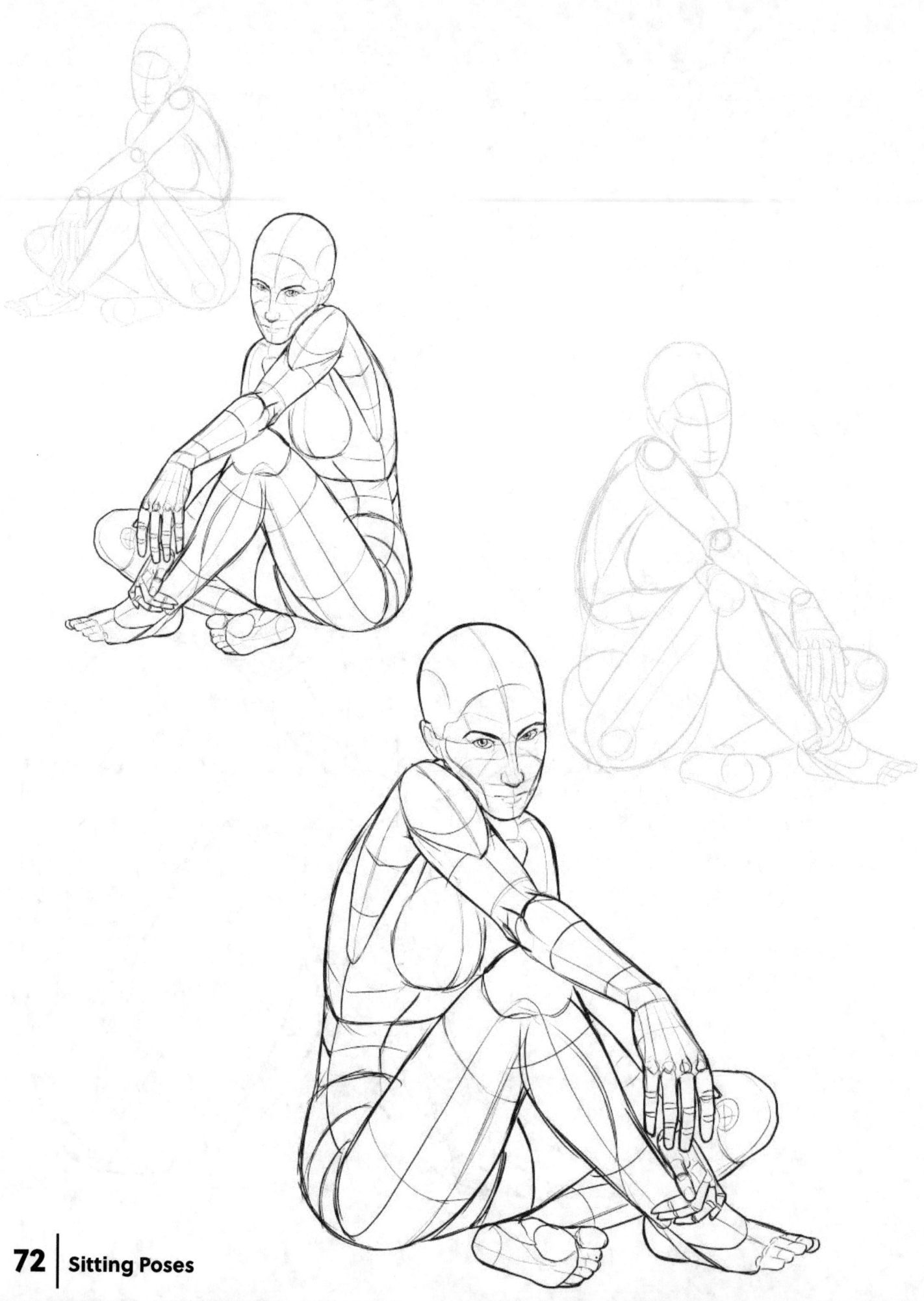

72 | Sitting Poses

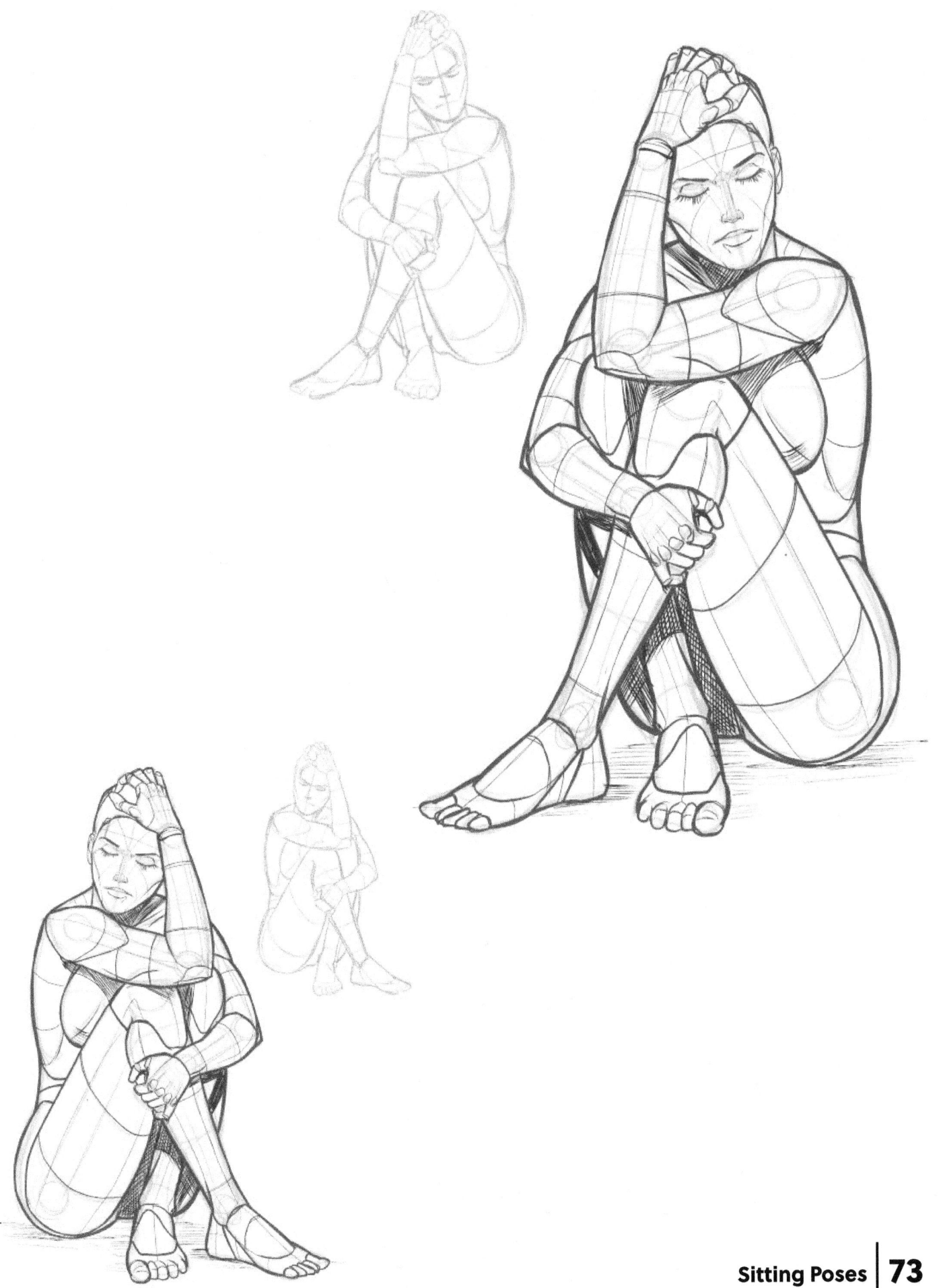

Sitting Poses | 73

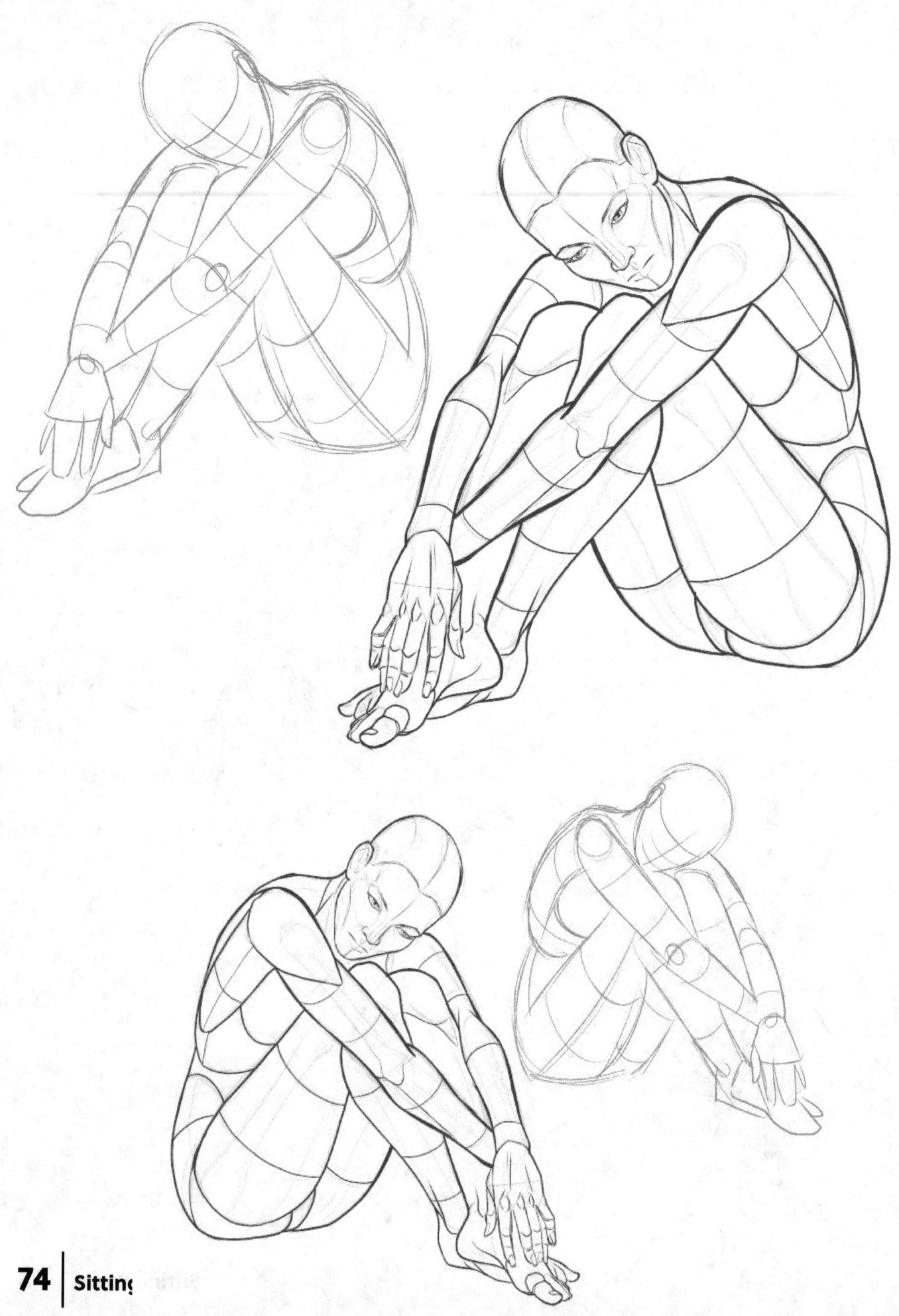

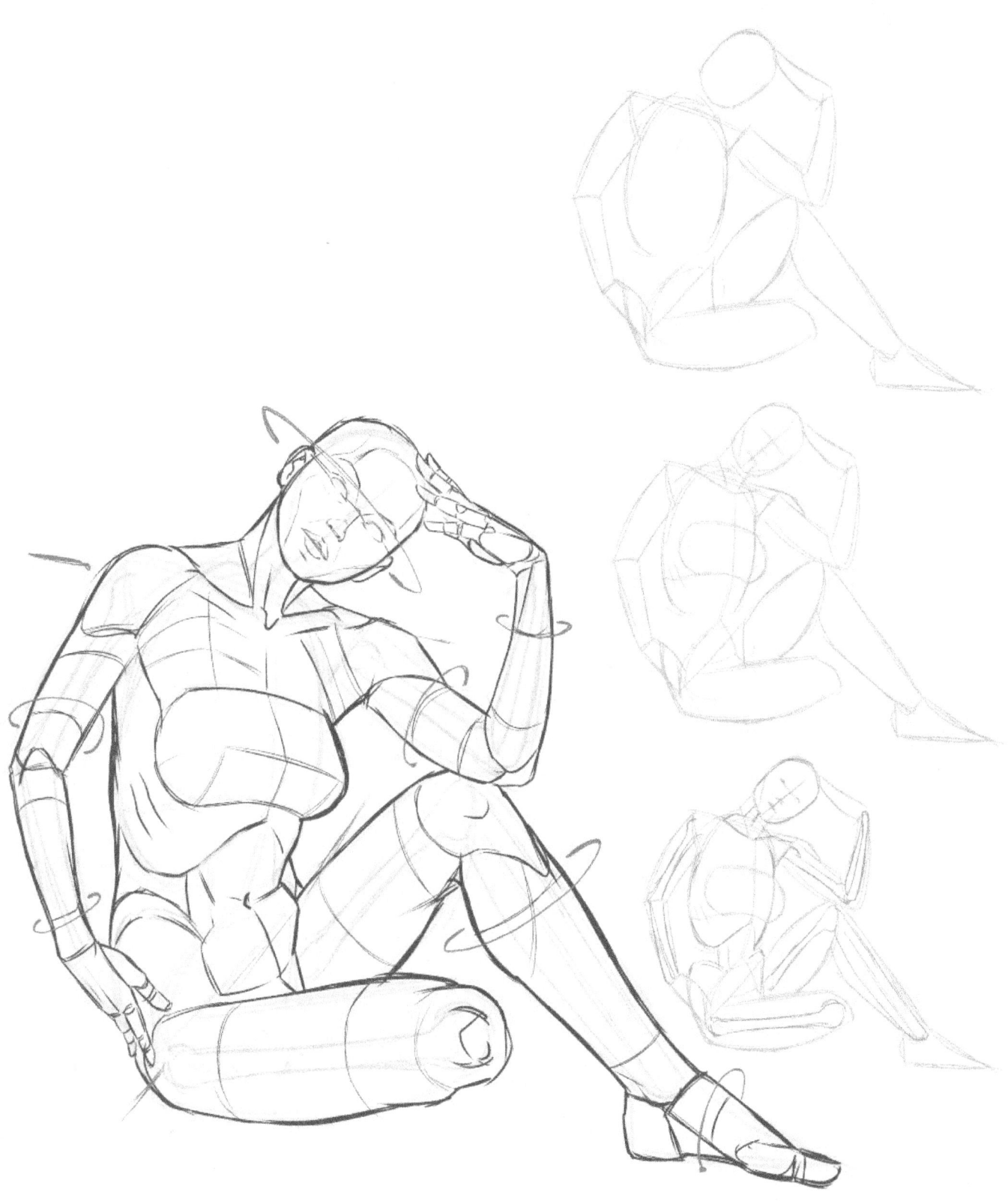

Sitting Poses | **75**

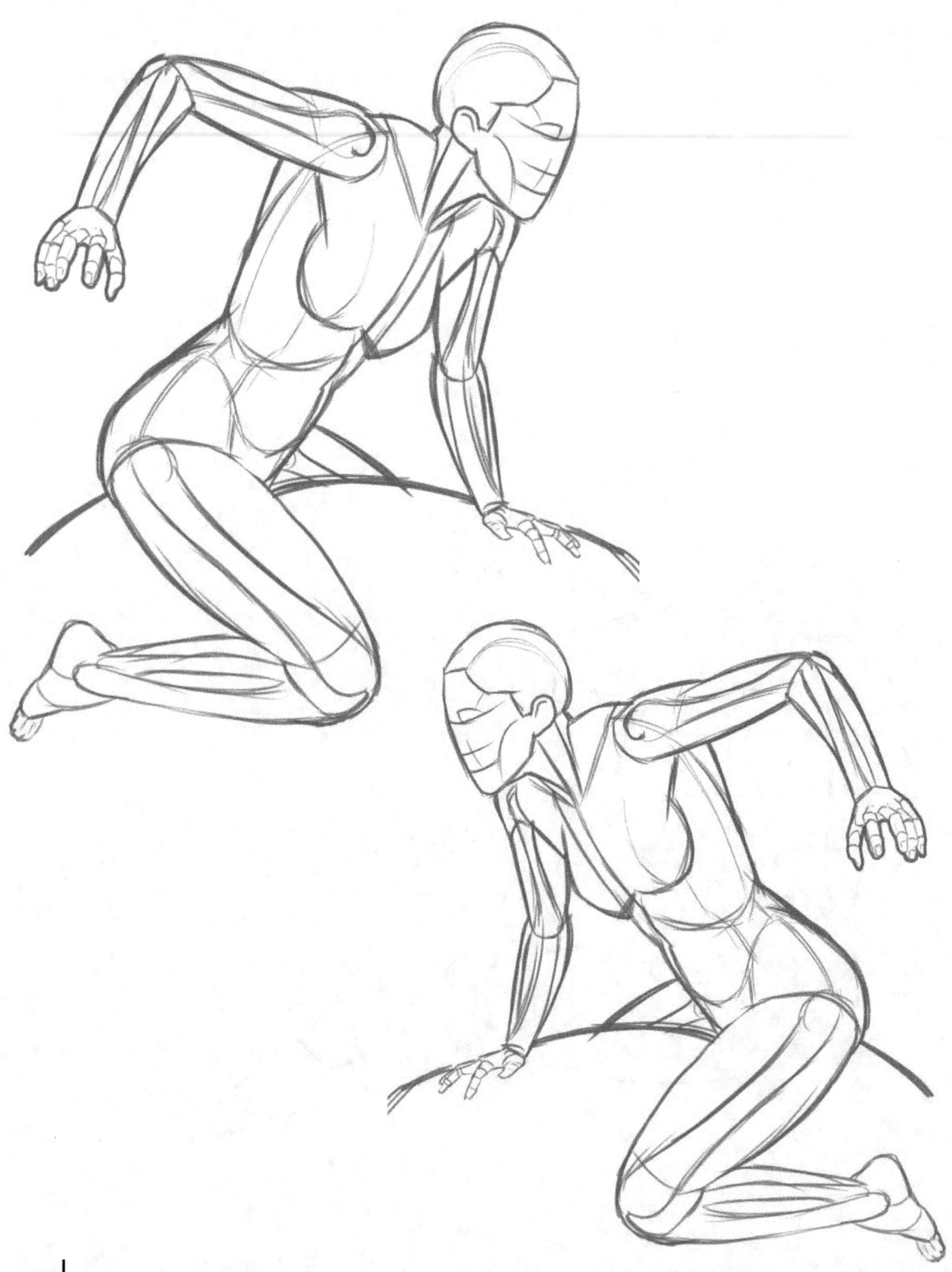

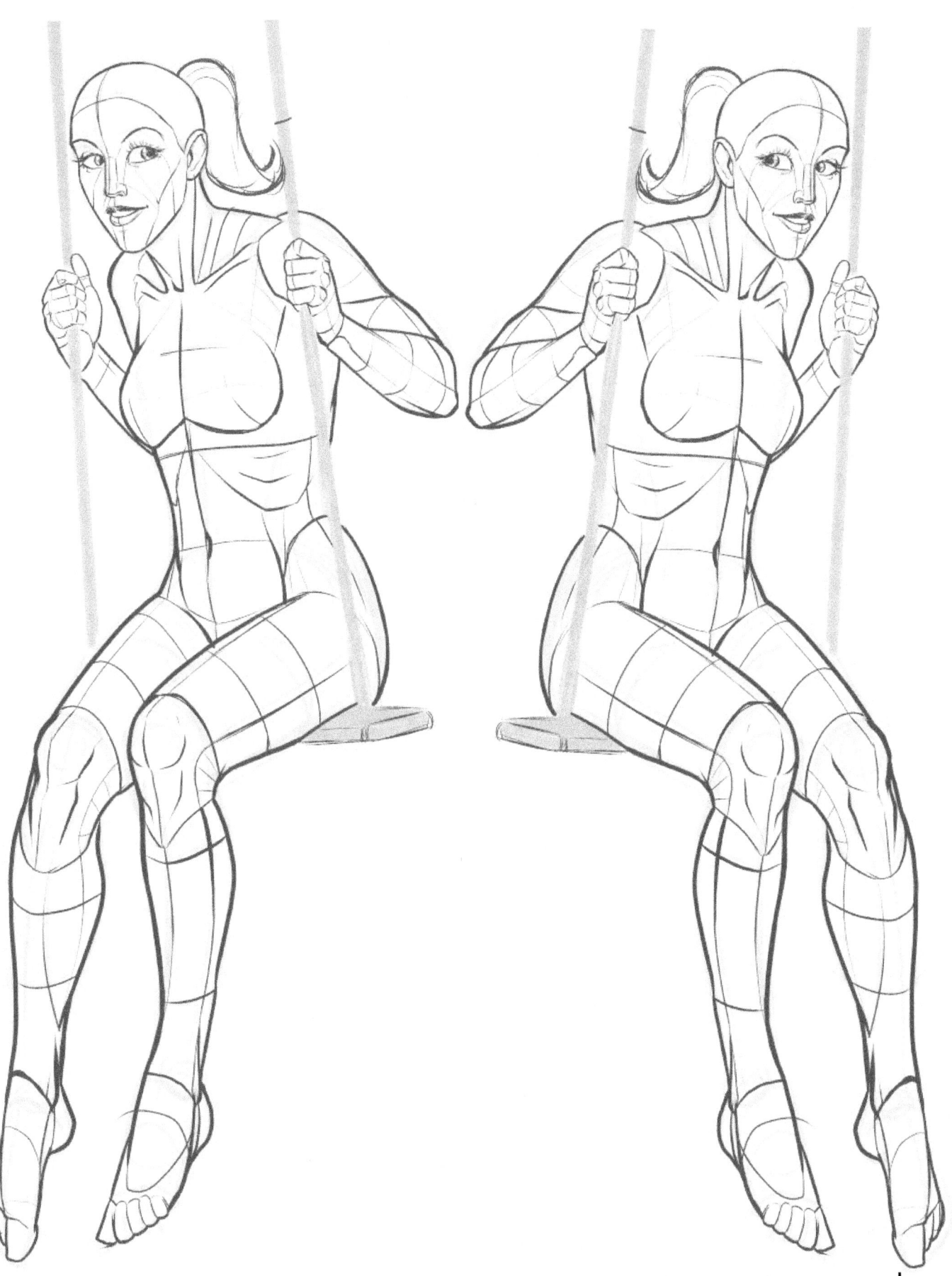

Sitting Poses | 77

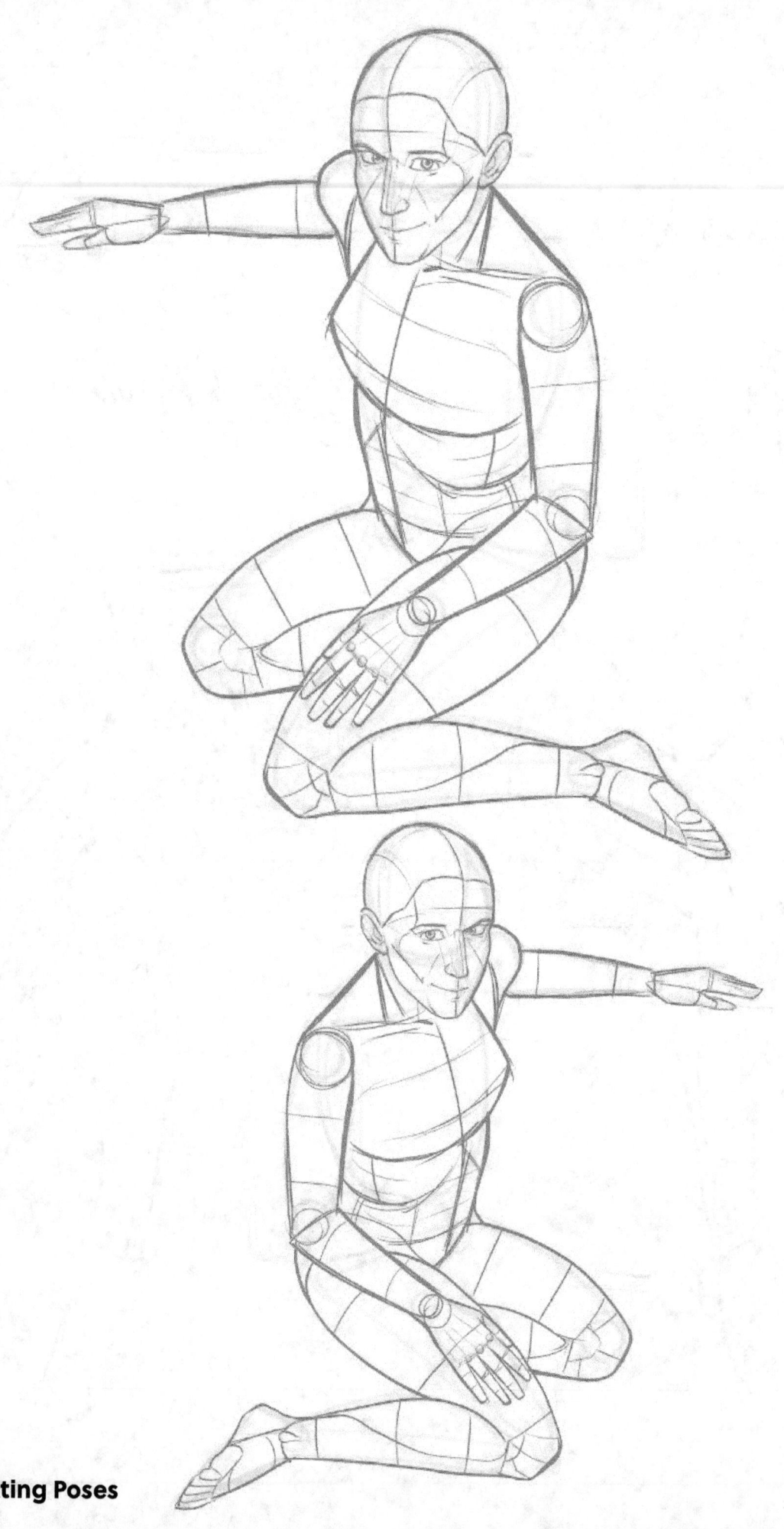

Sitting Poses

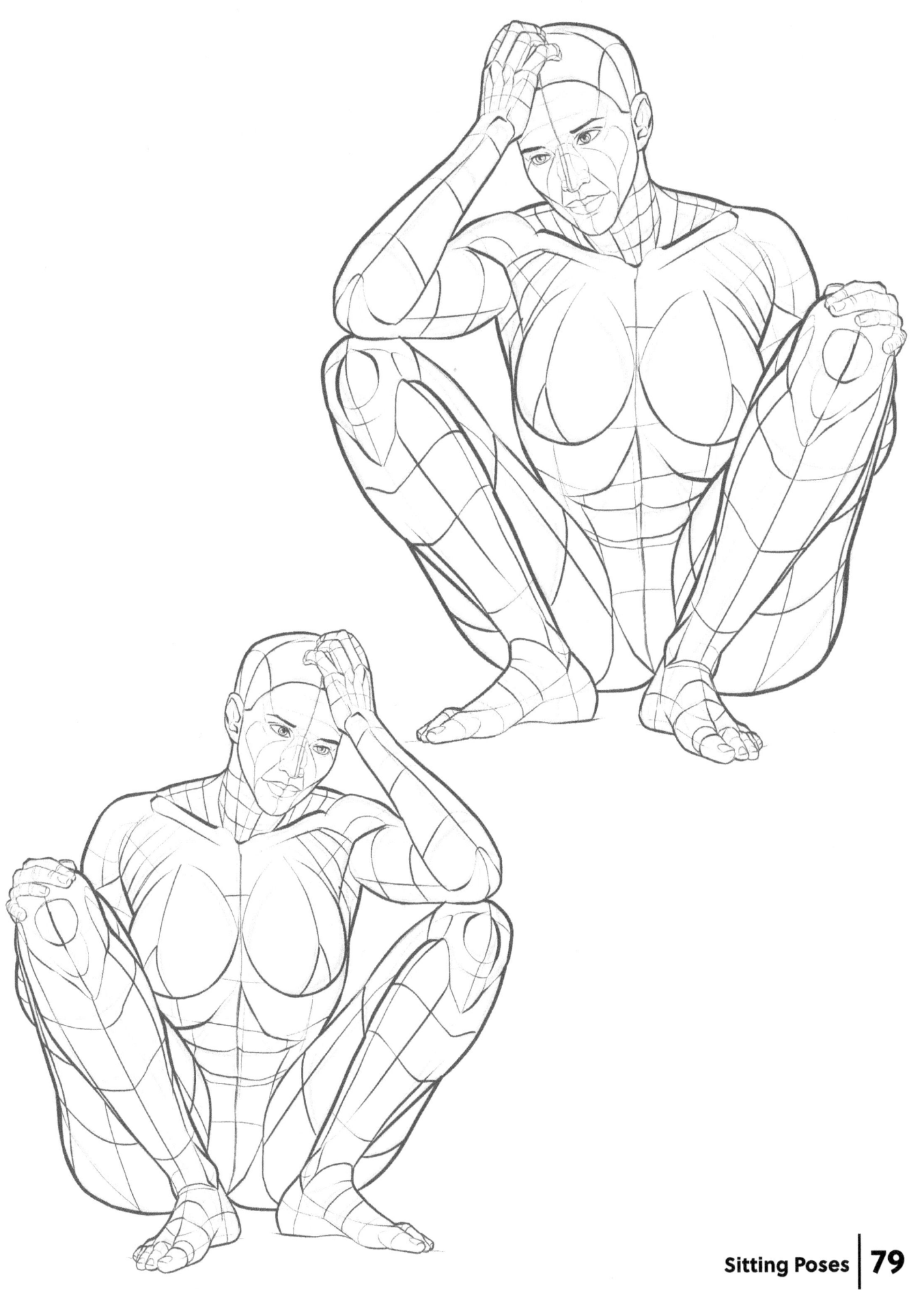

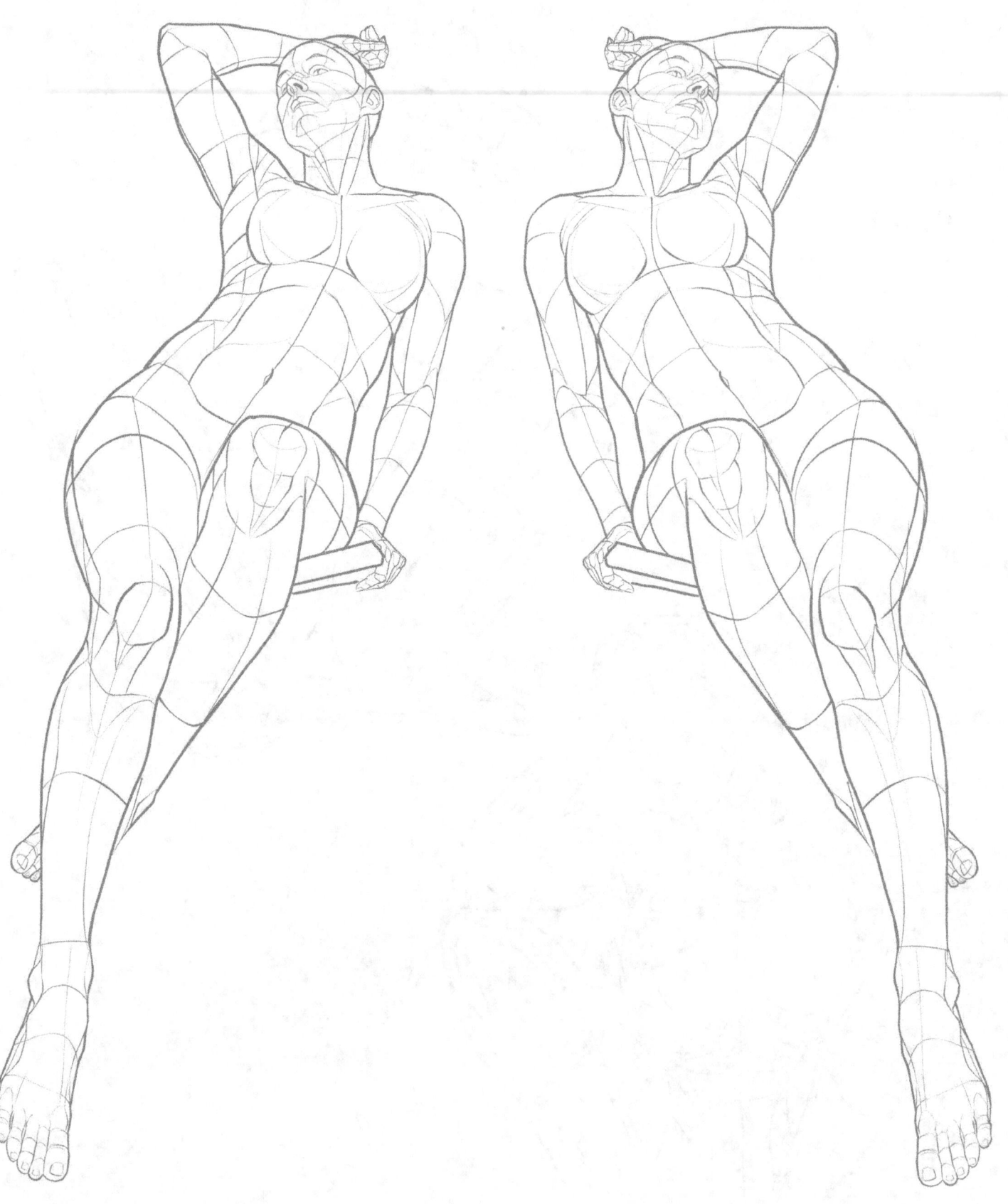

Sitting Poses

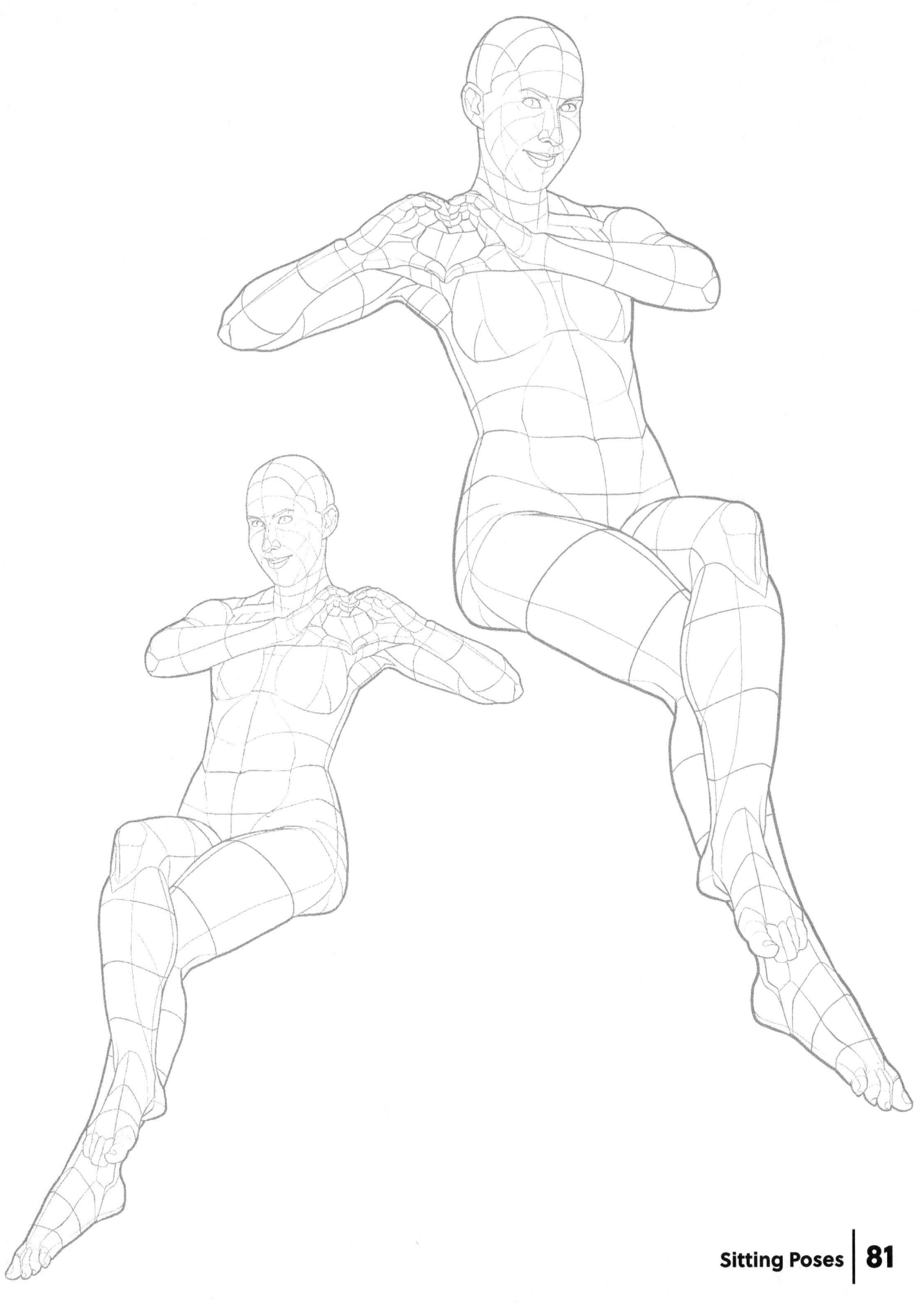

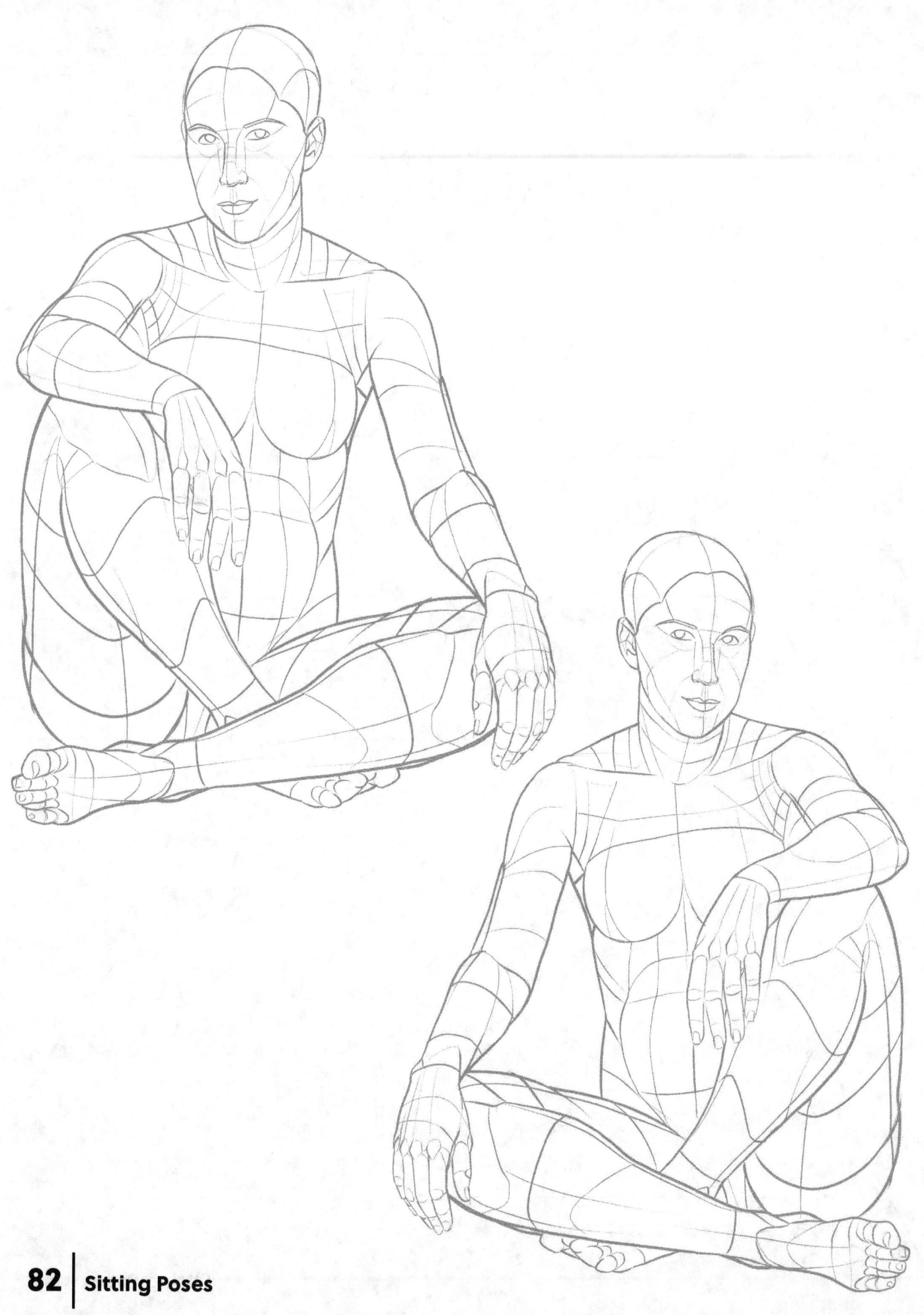

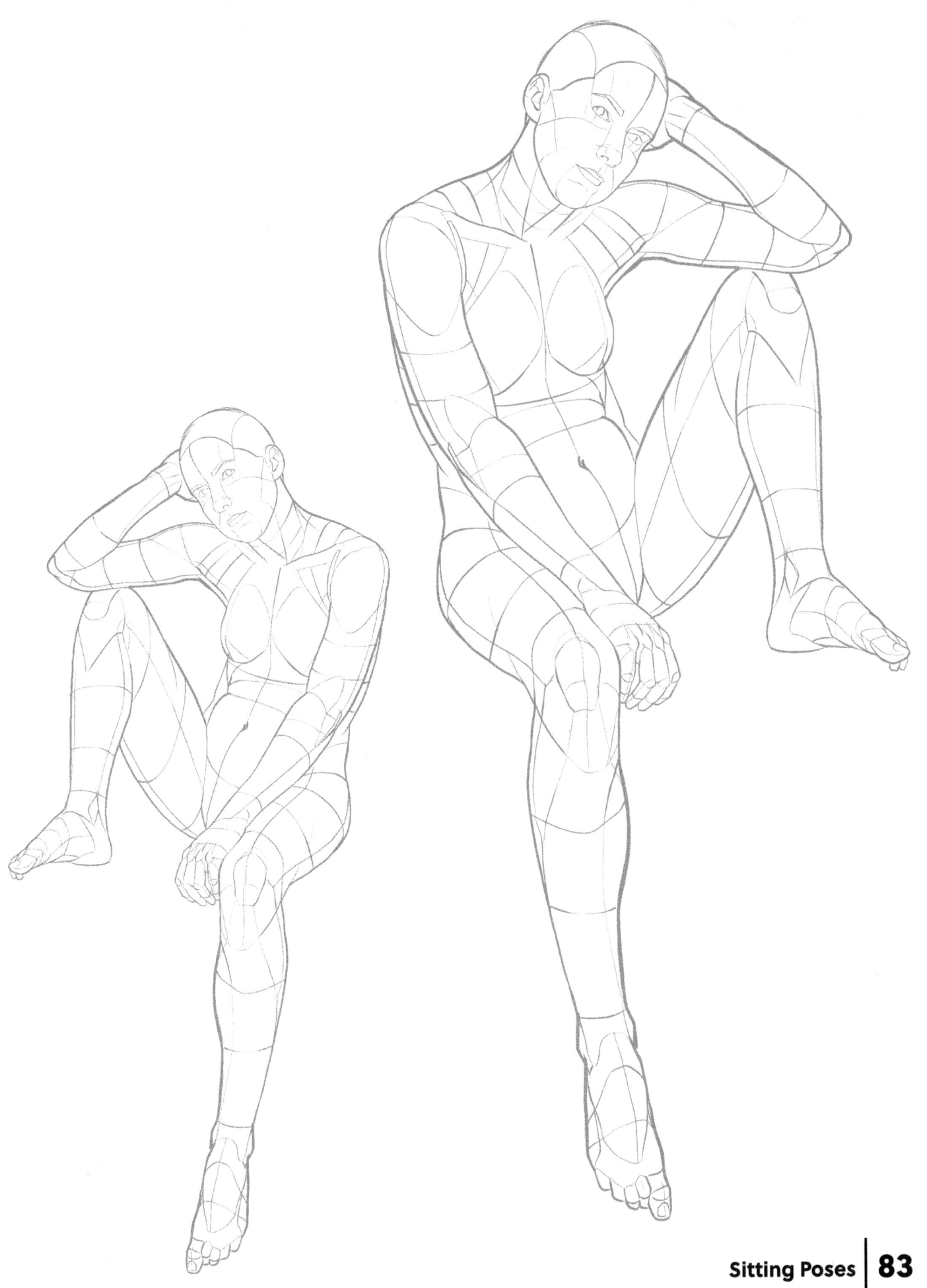

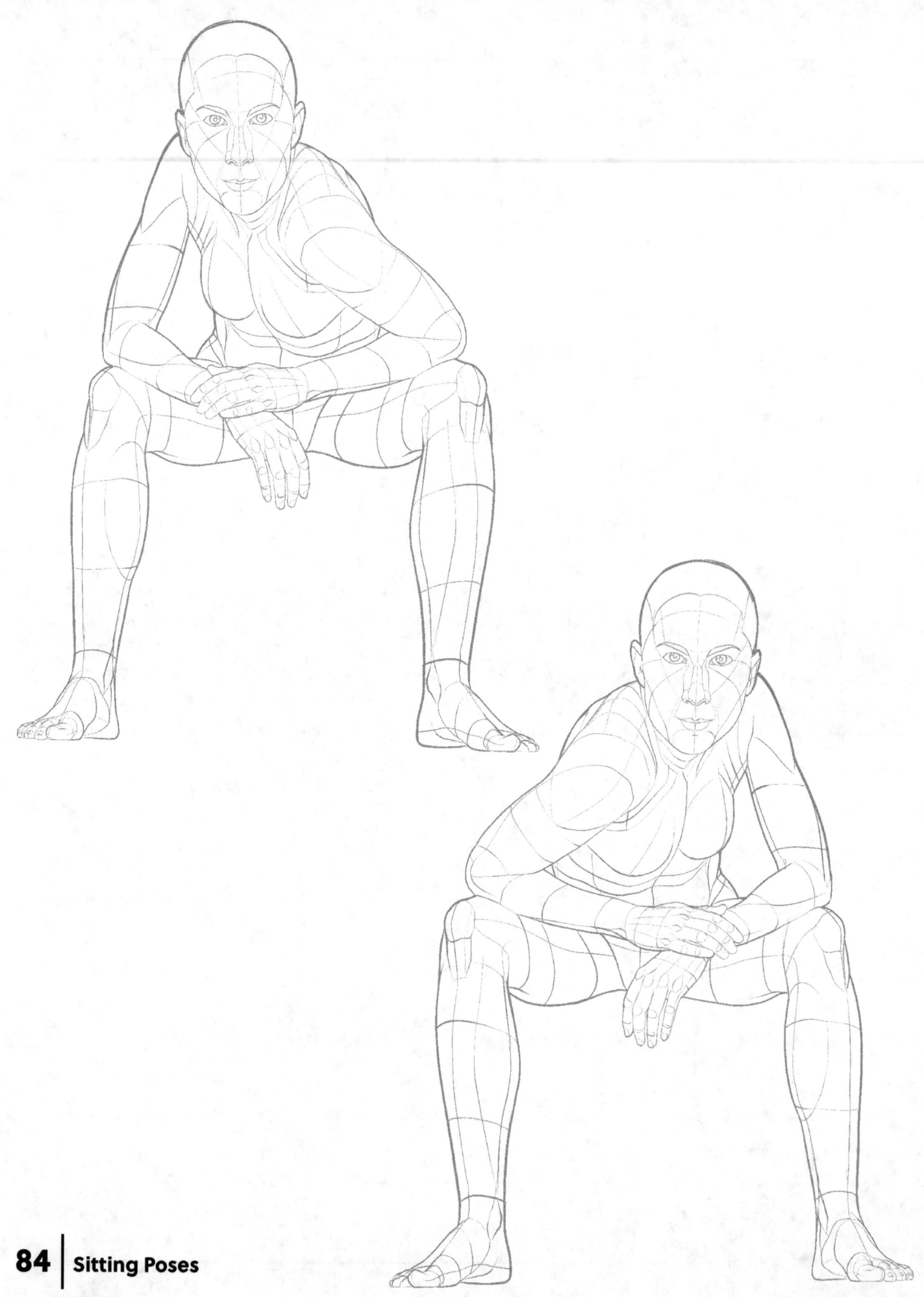

84 | Sitting Poses

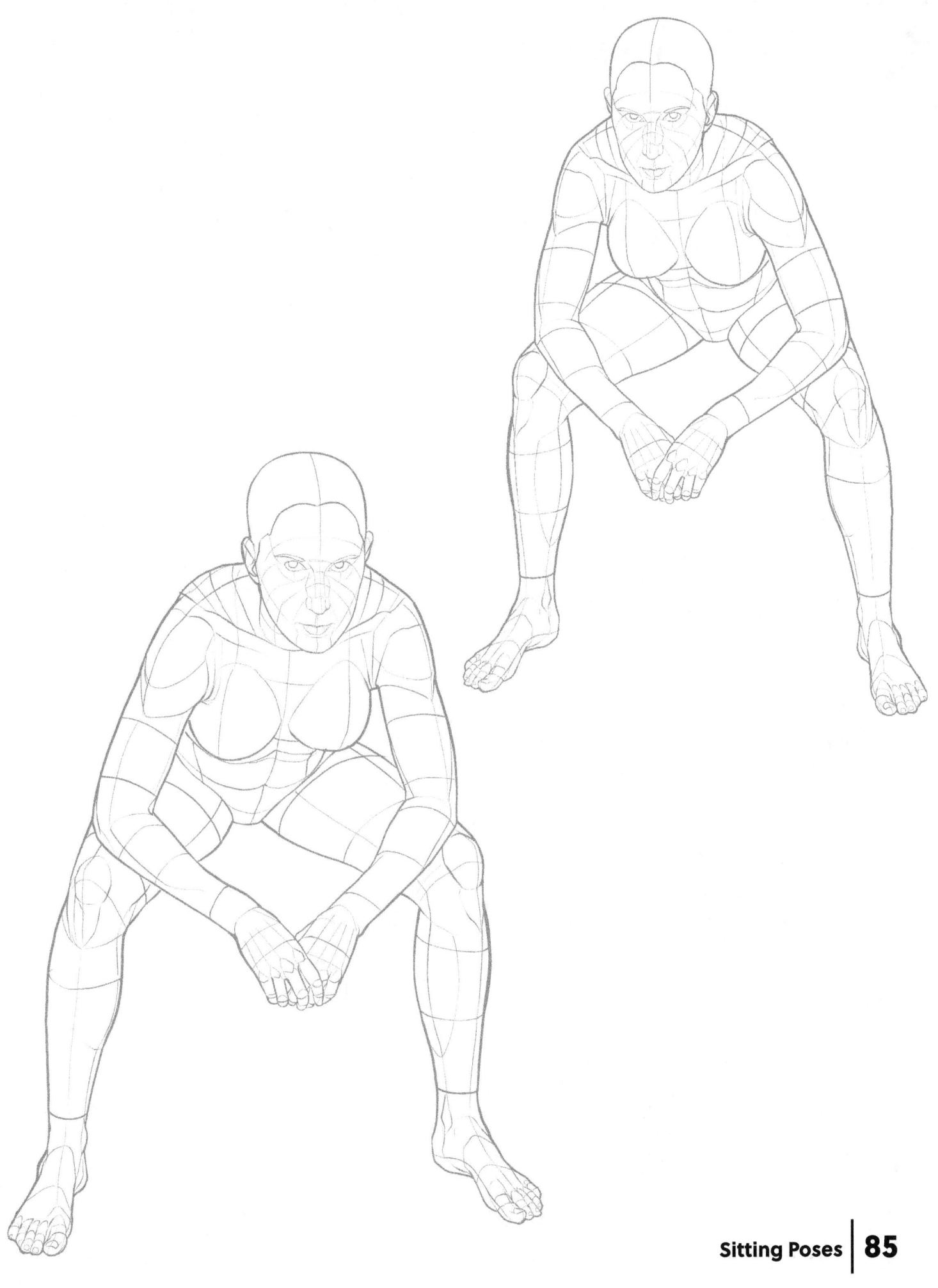

Sitting Poses

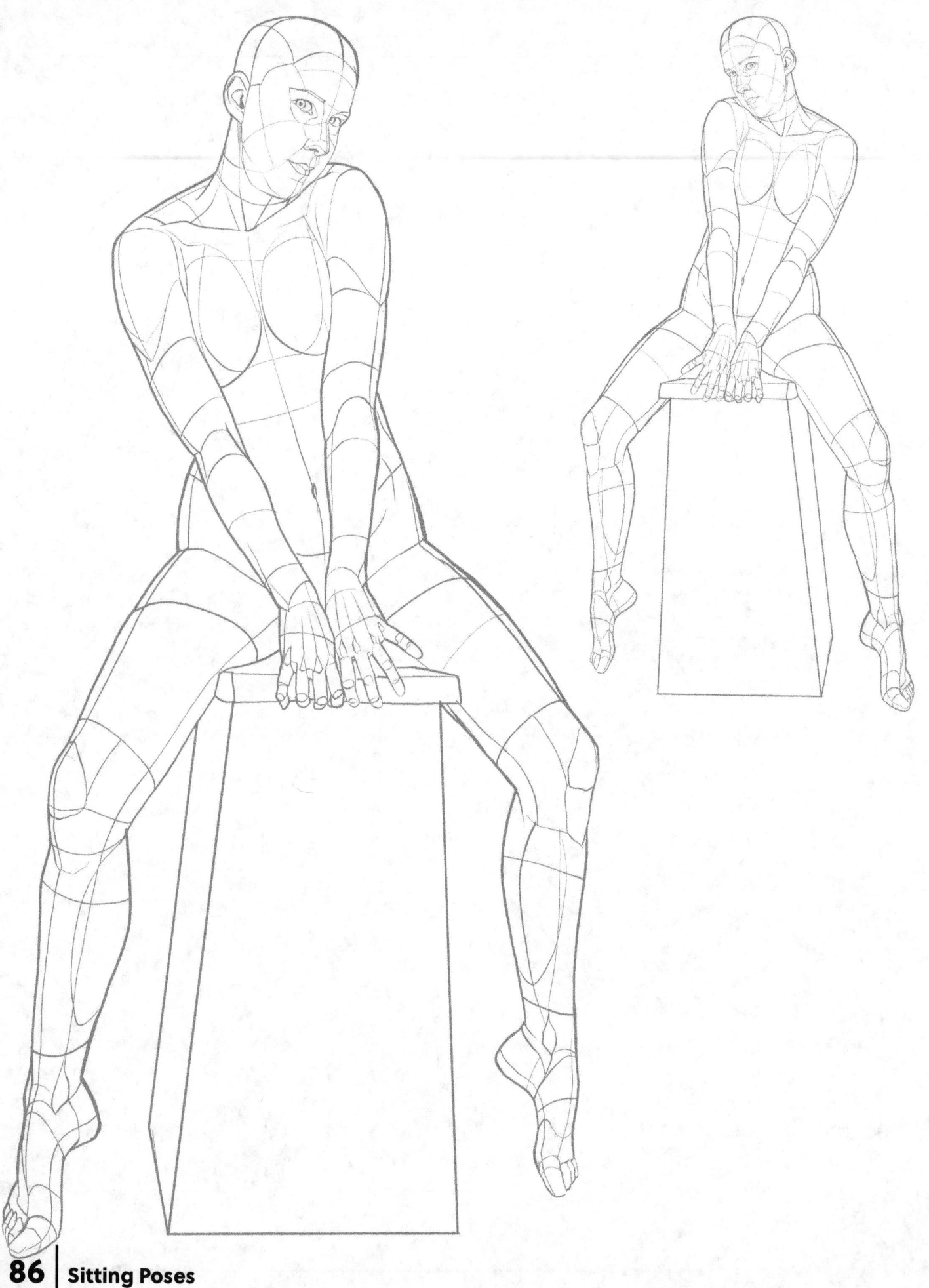

86 | Sitting Poses

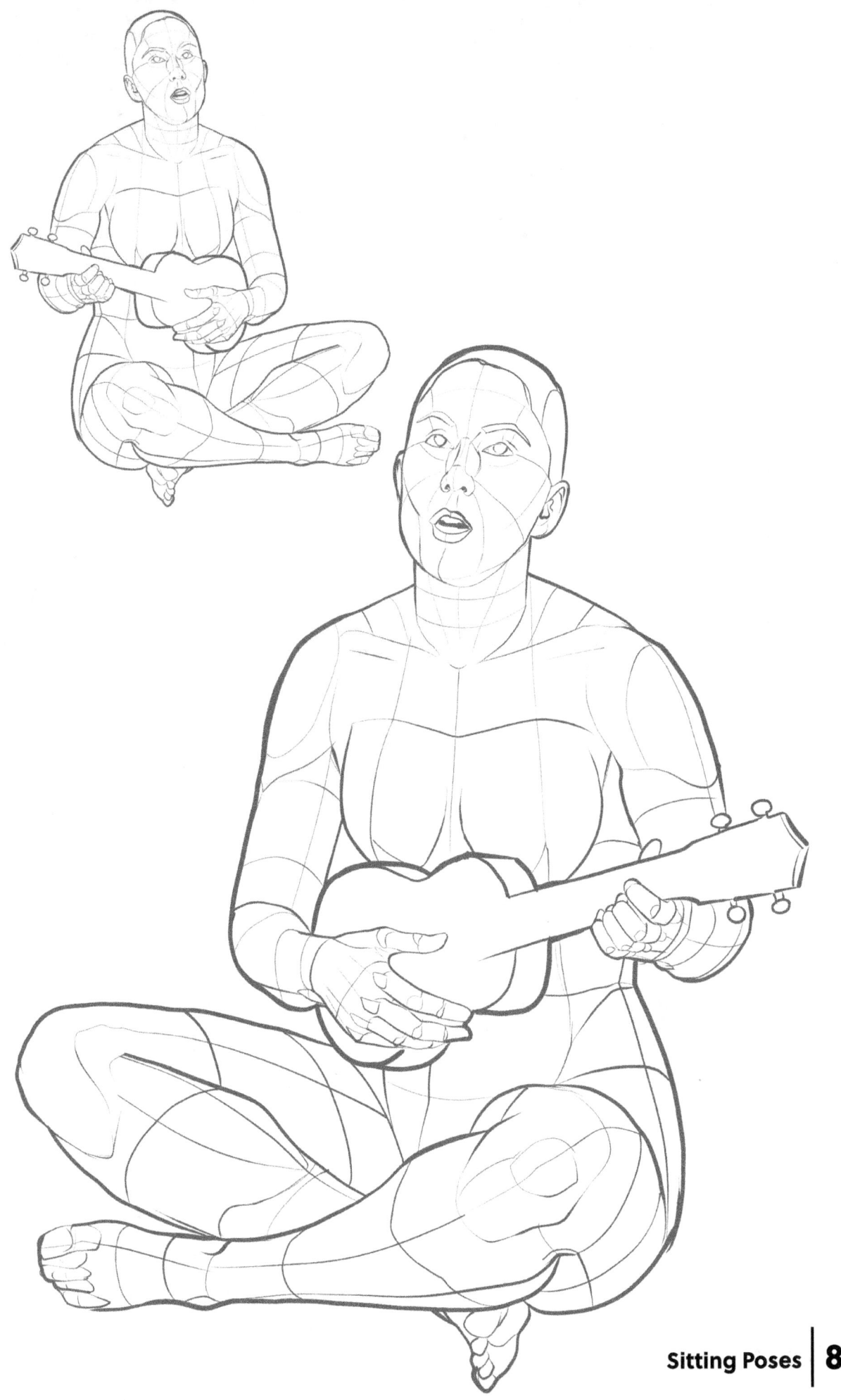

Sitting Poses | 87

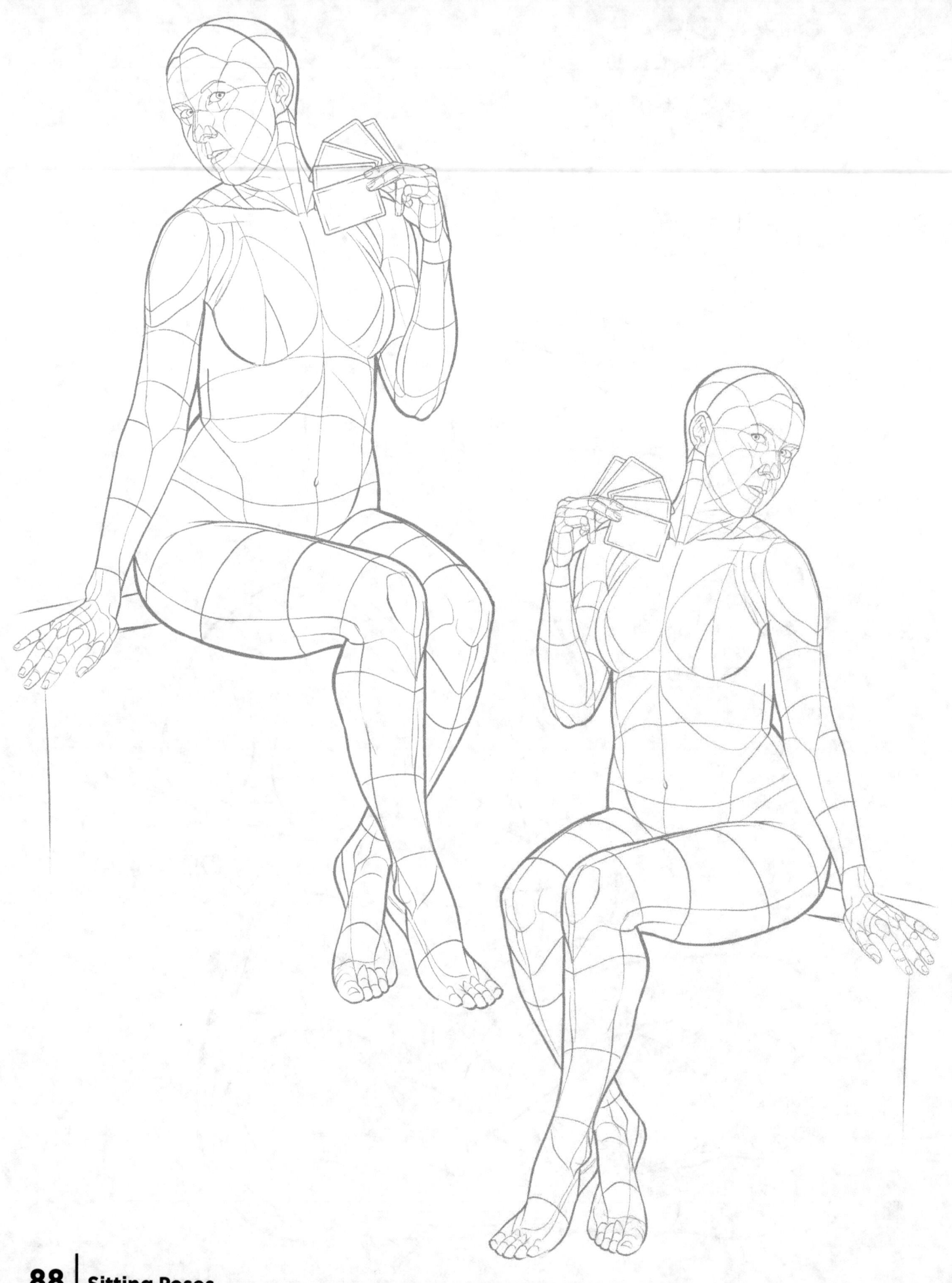

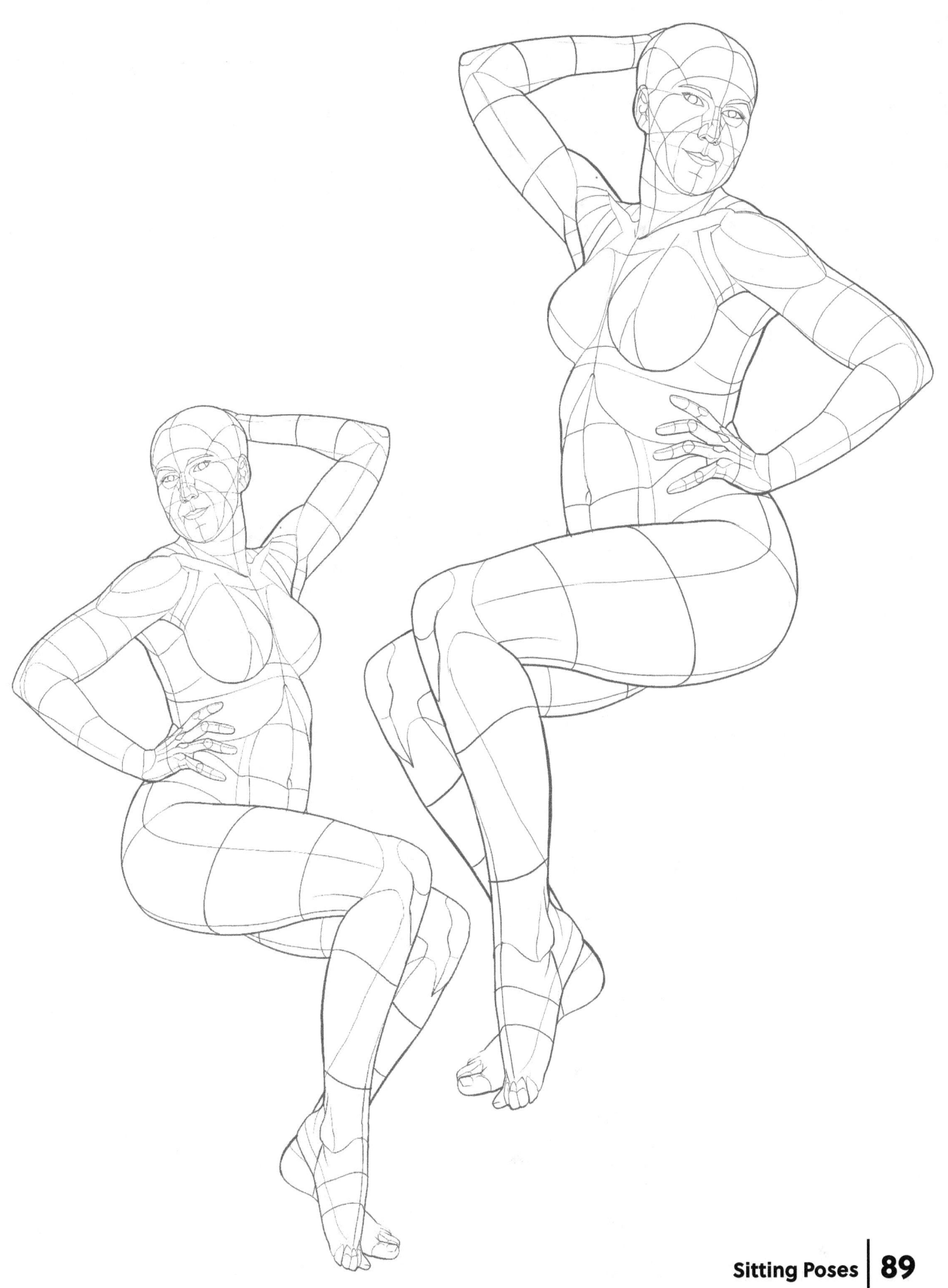

Sitting Poses

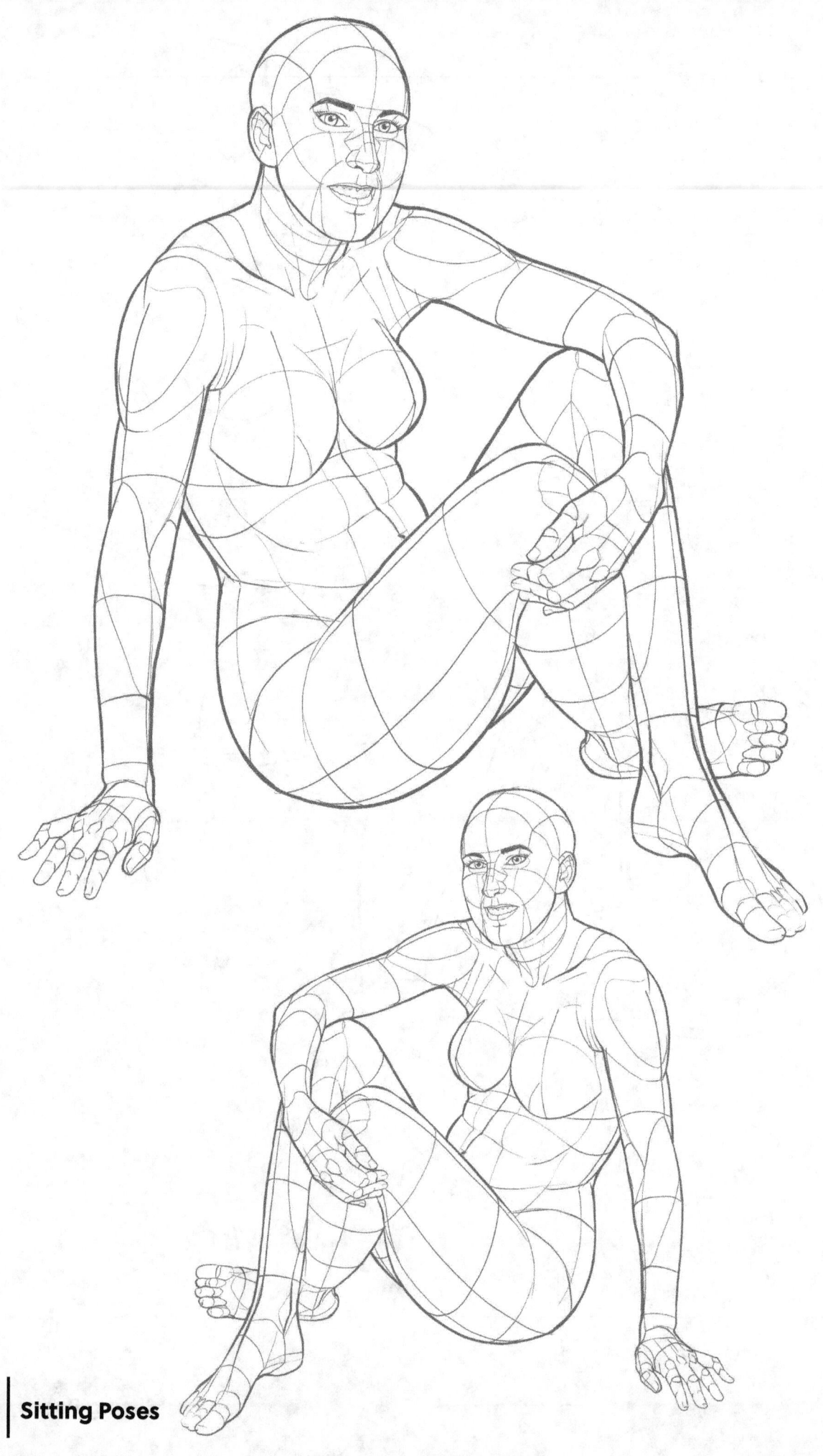

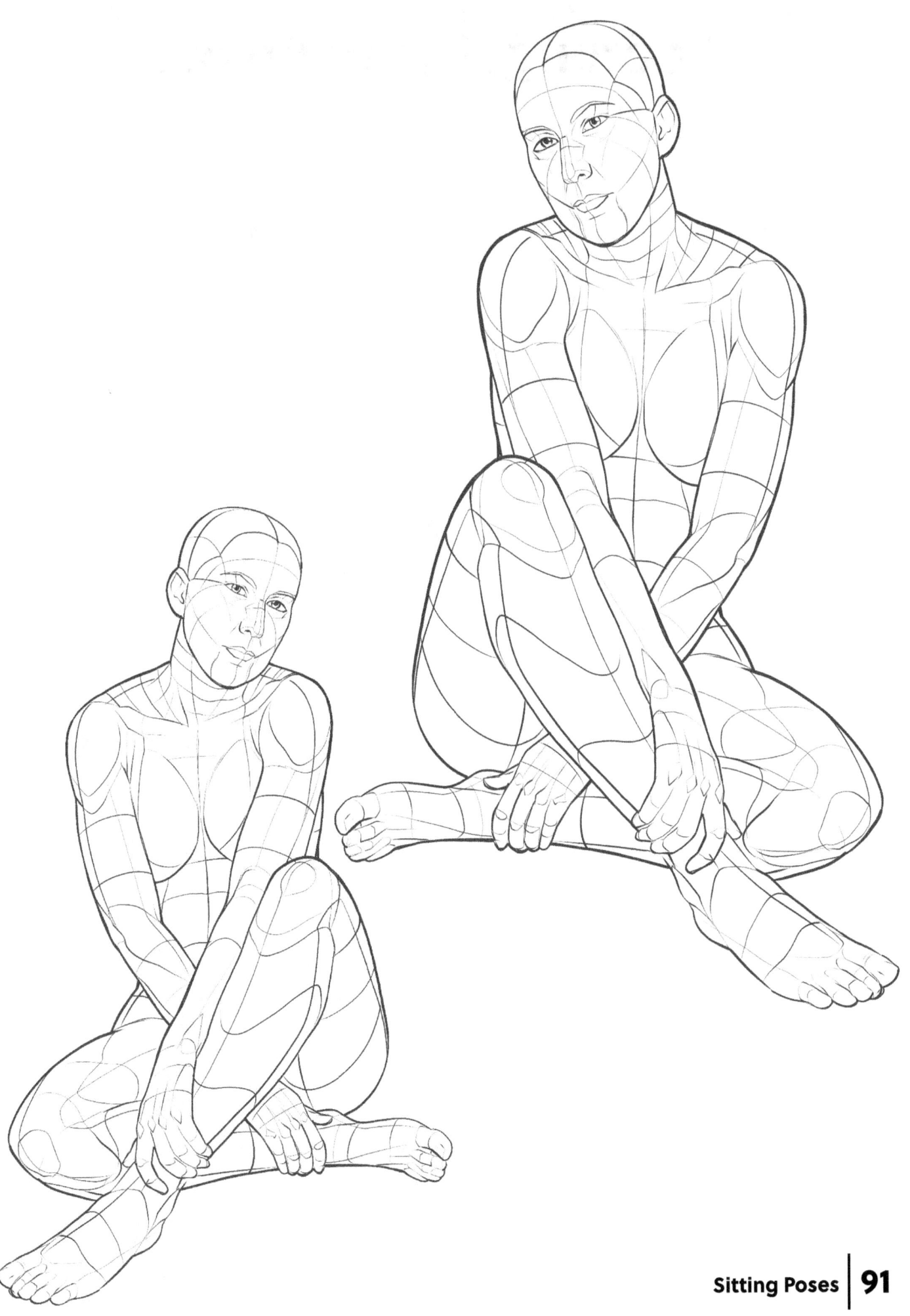

Sitting Poses | 91

Leaning/Lying Poses

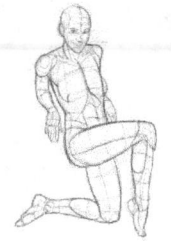

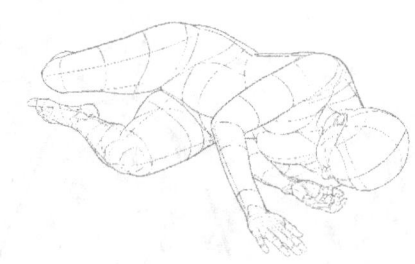

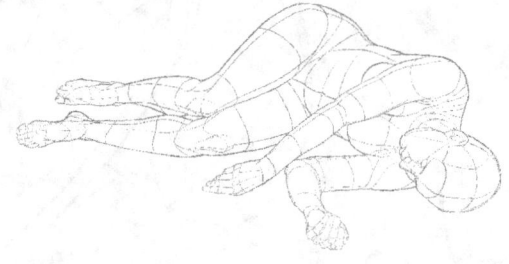

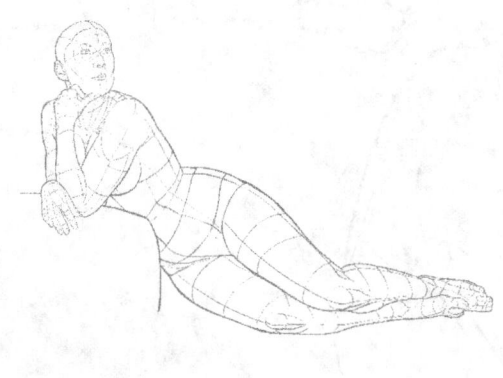

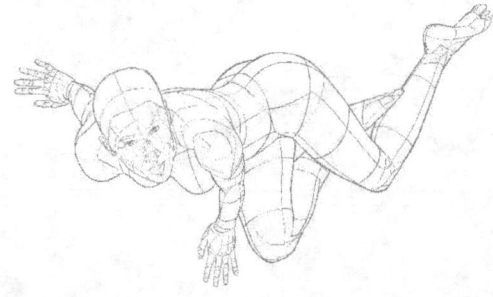

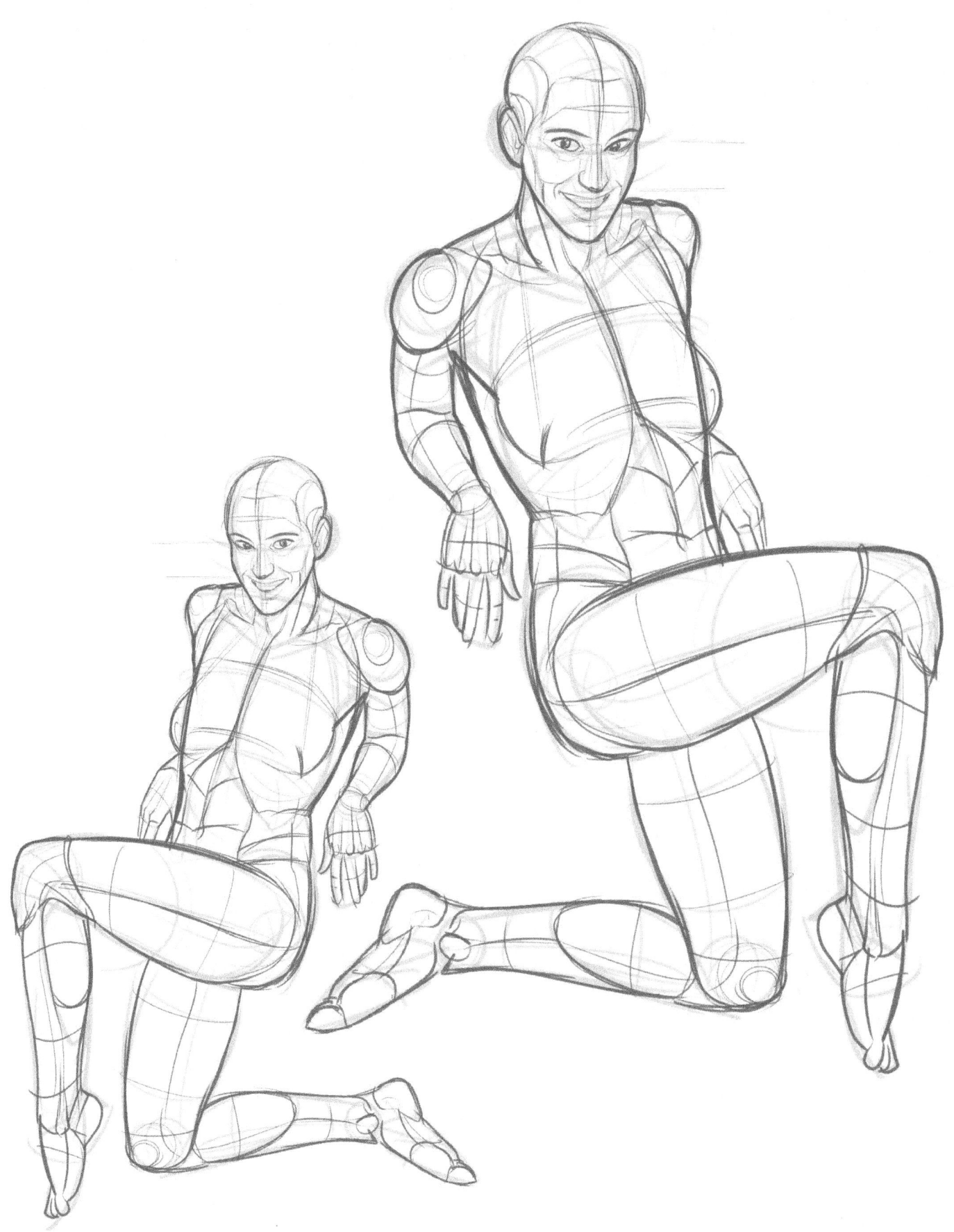

Leaning/Laying Poses | 93

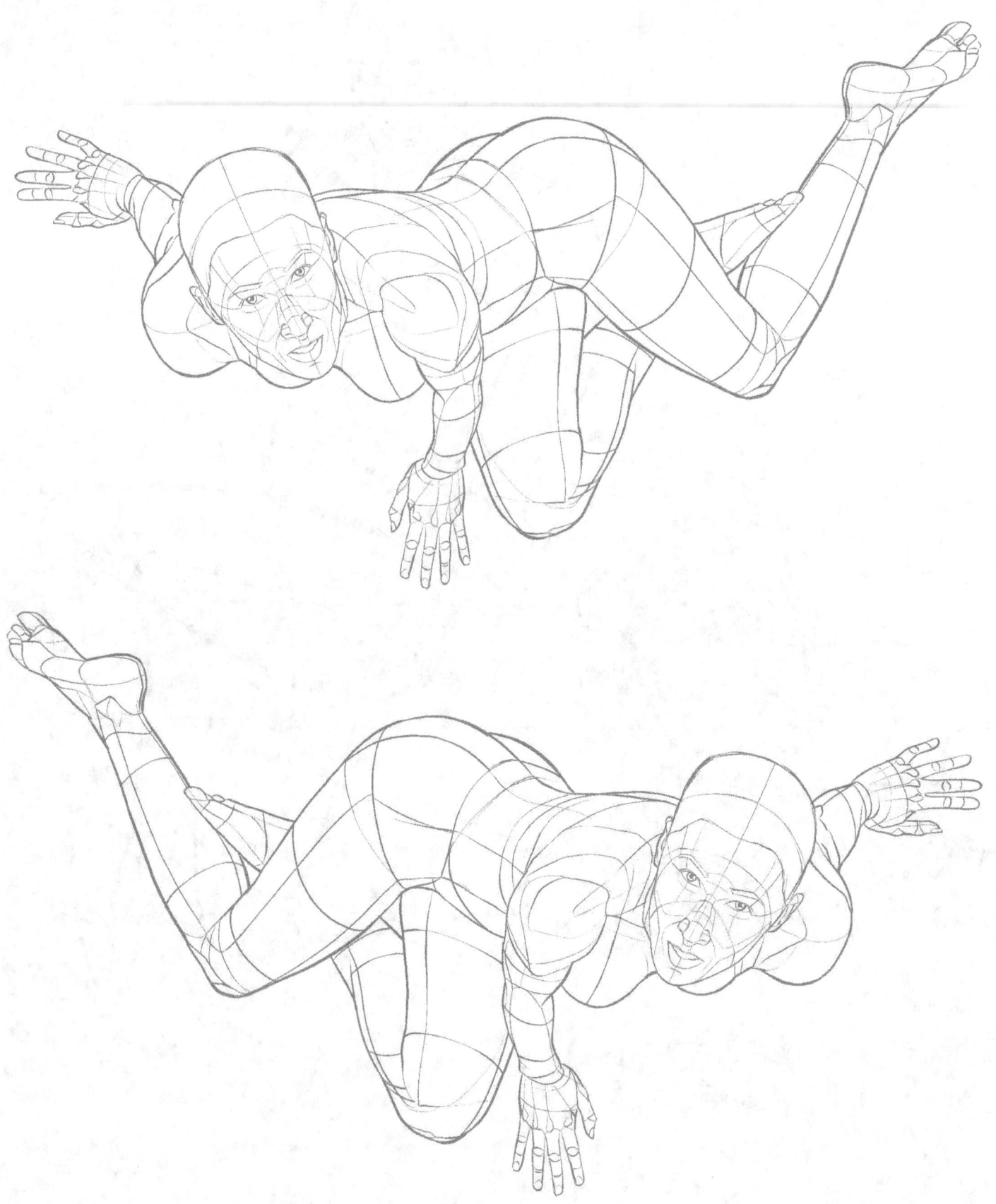

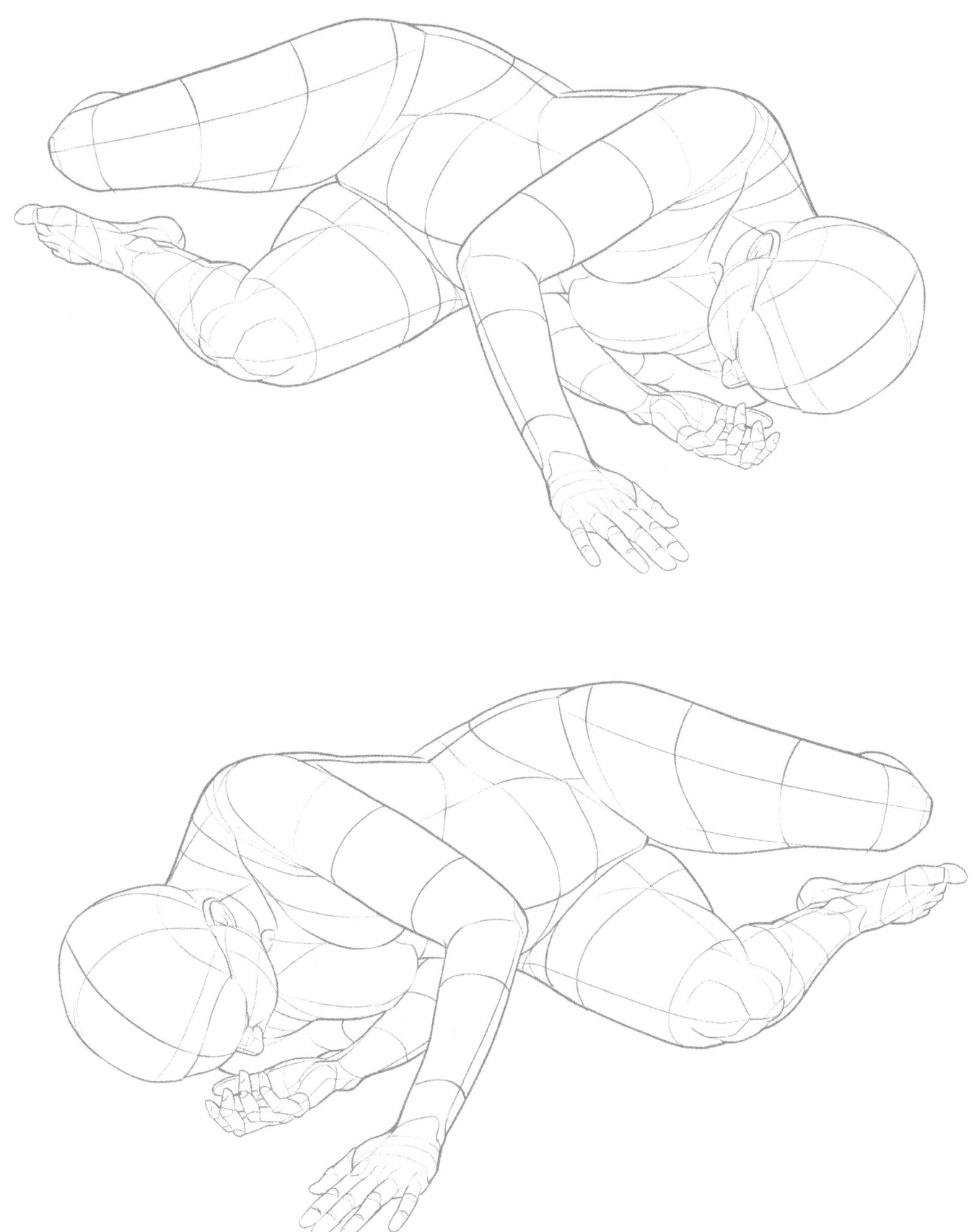

Leaning/Laying Poses | 95

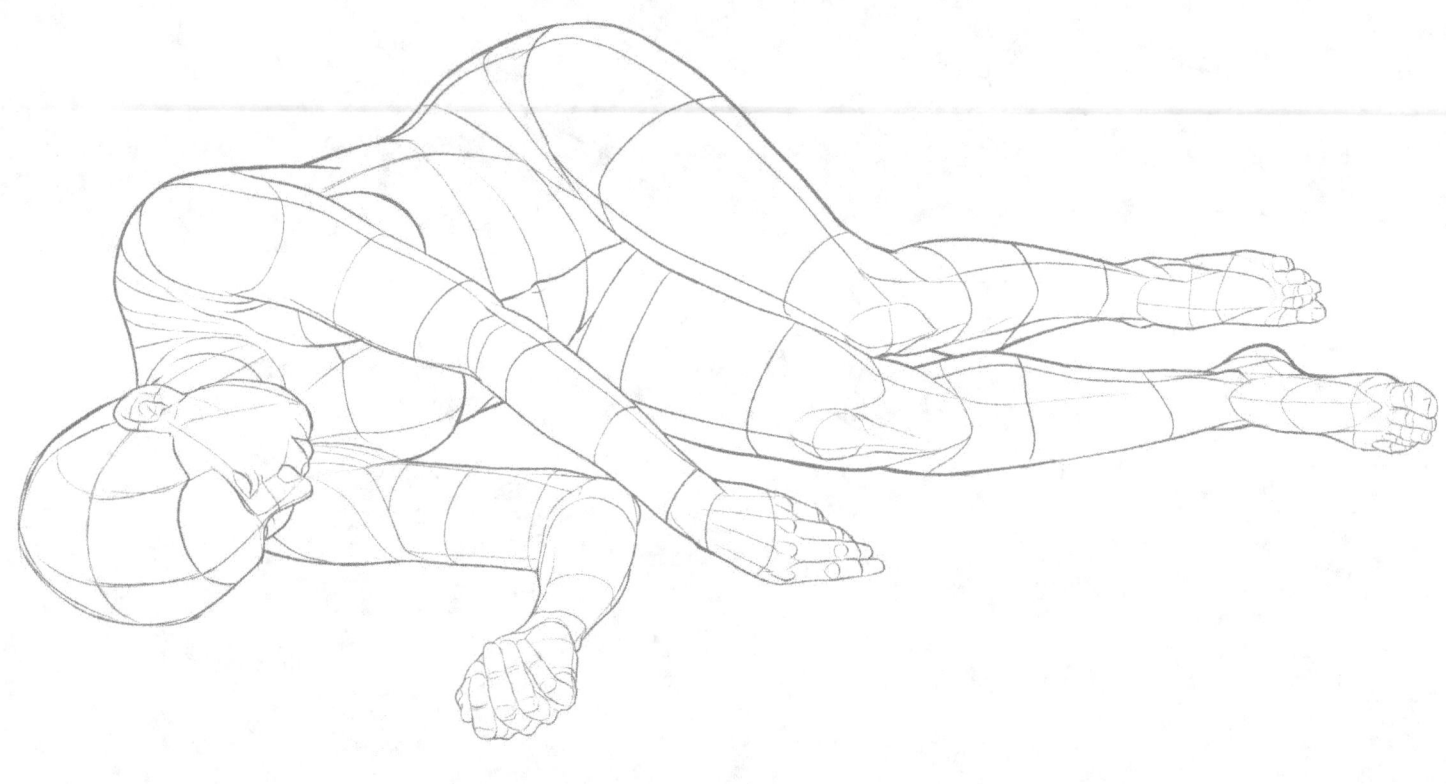
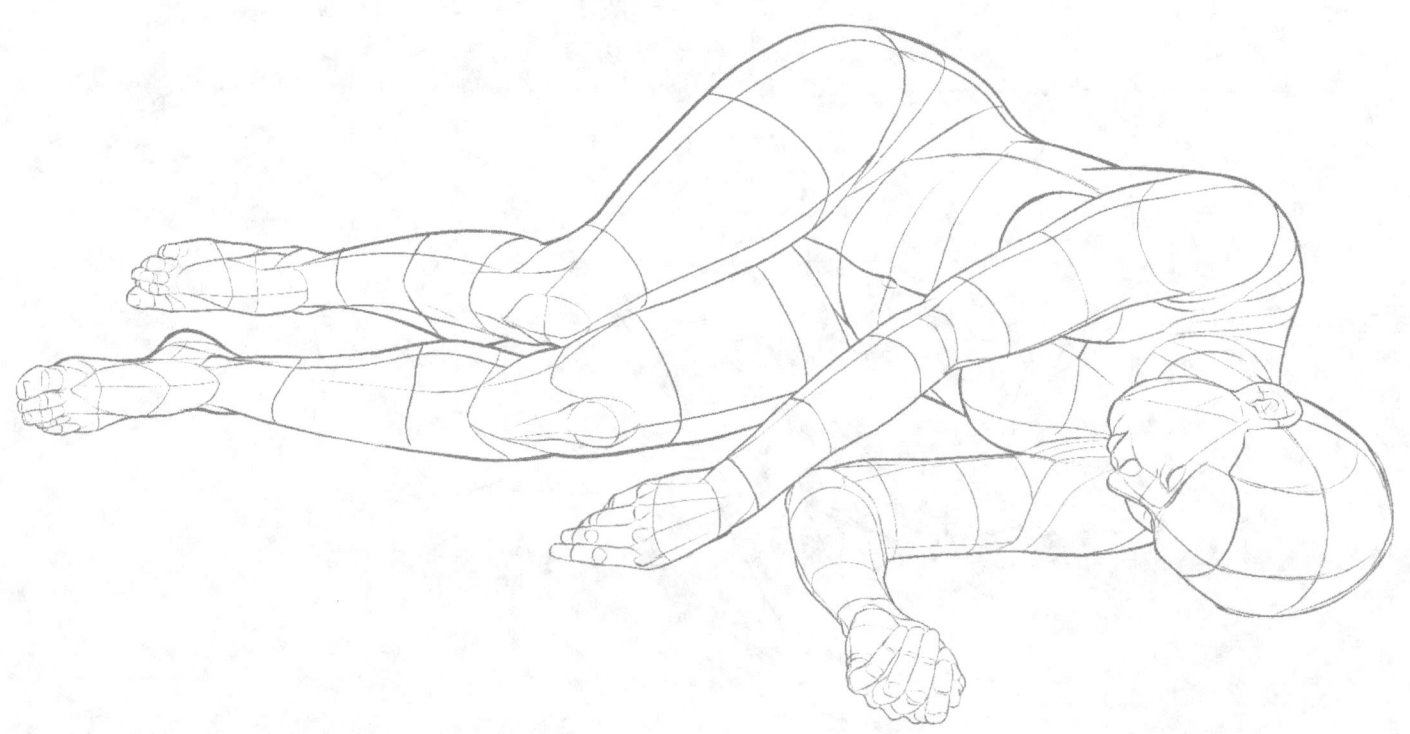

Leaning/Laying Poses

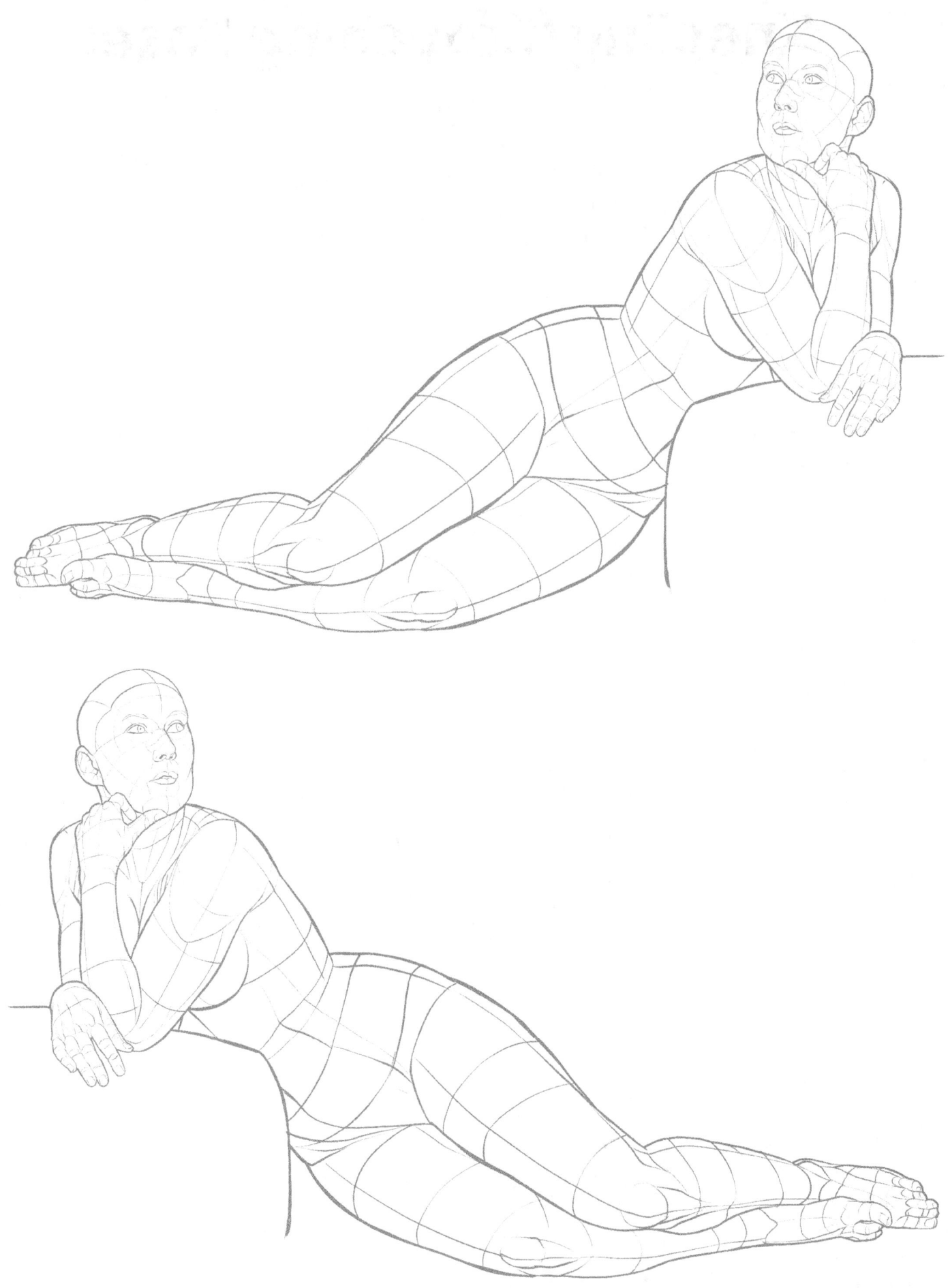

Leaning/Laying Poses | **97**

Kneeling/Crouching Poses

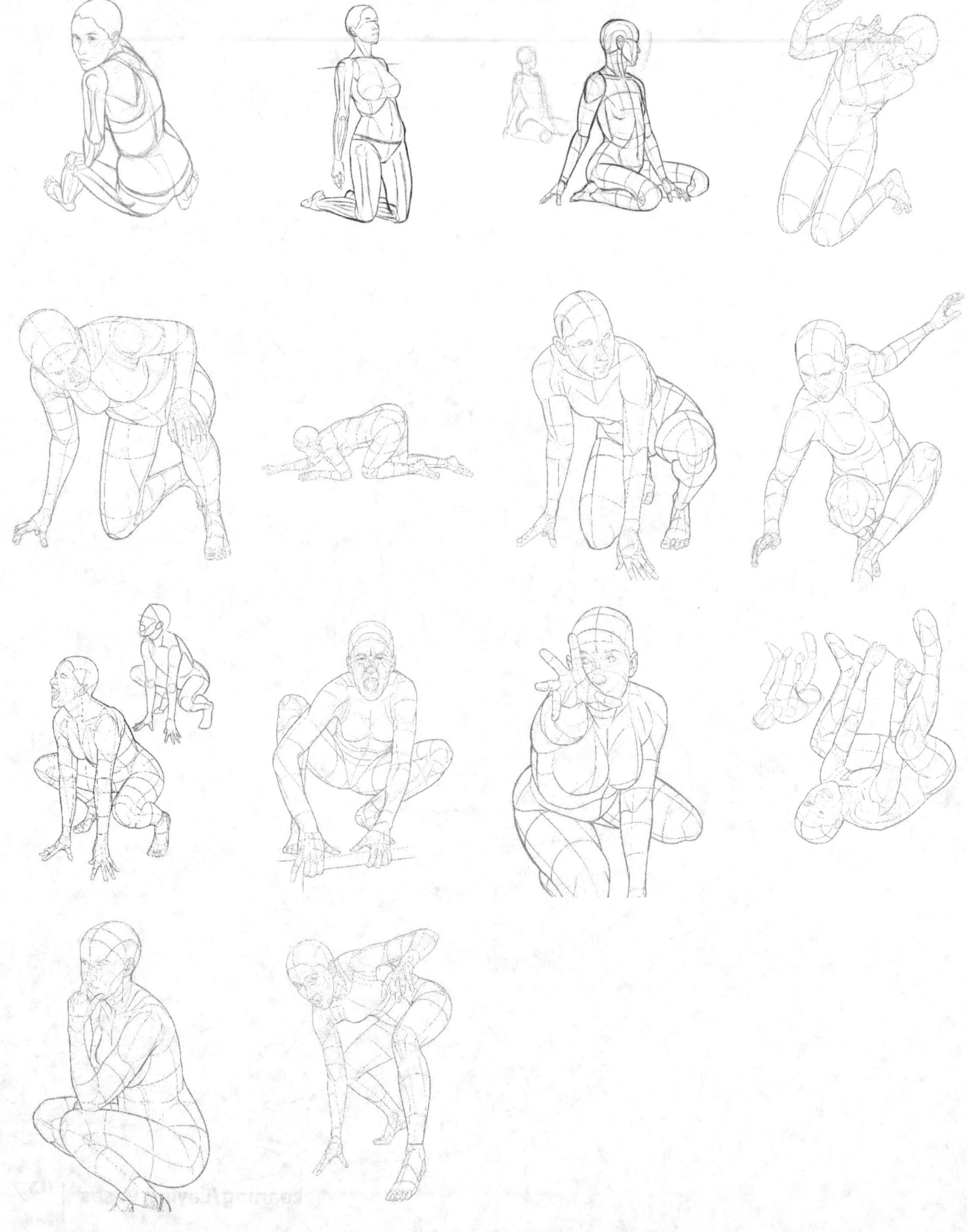

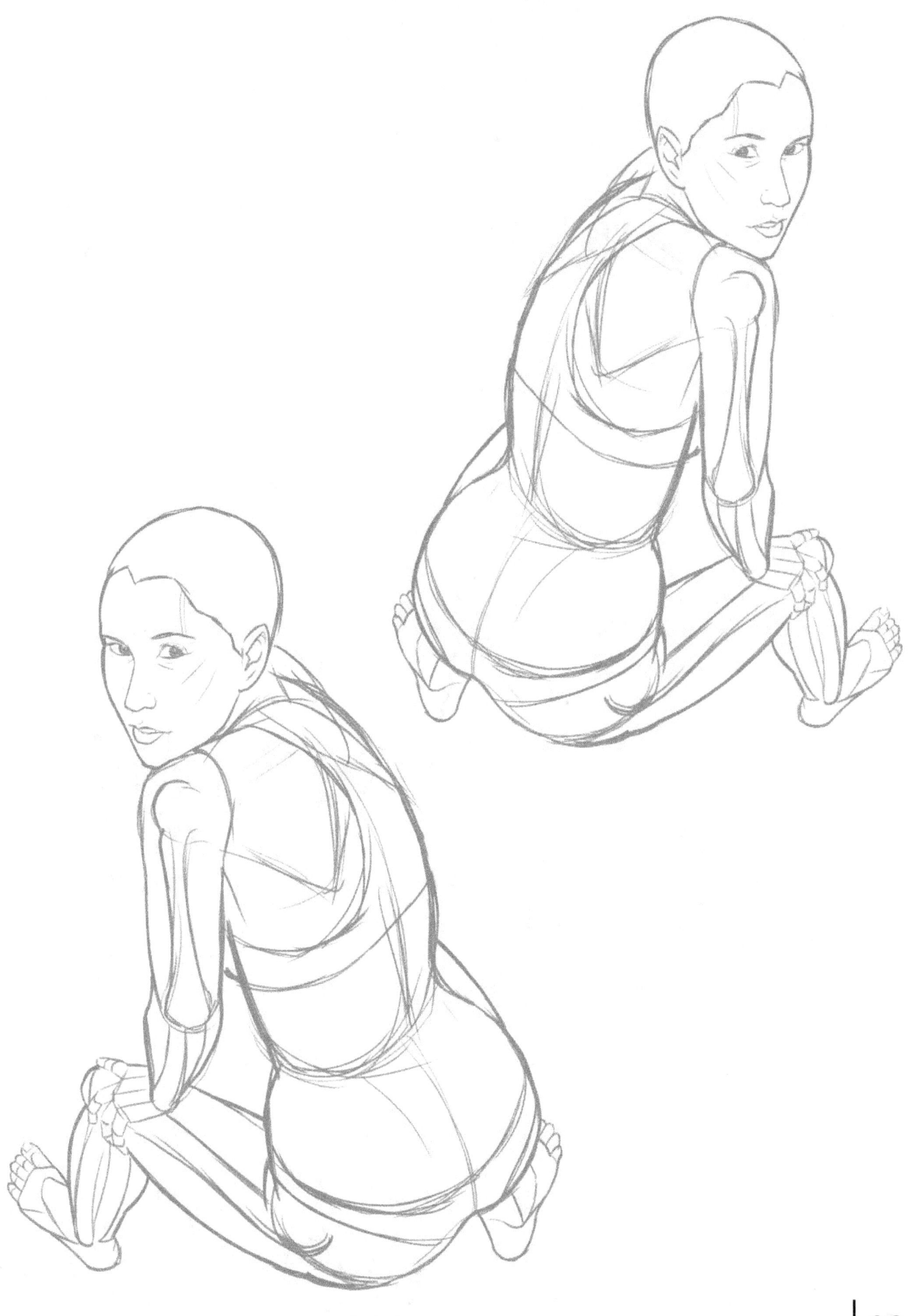

Kneeling/Crouching Poses

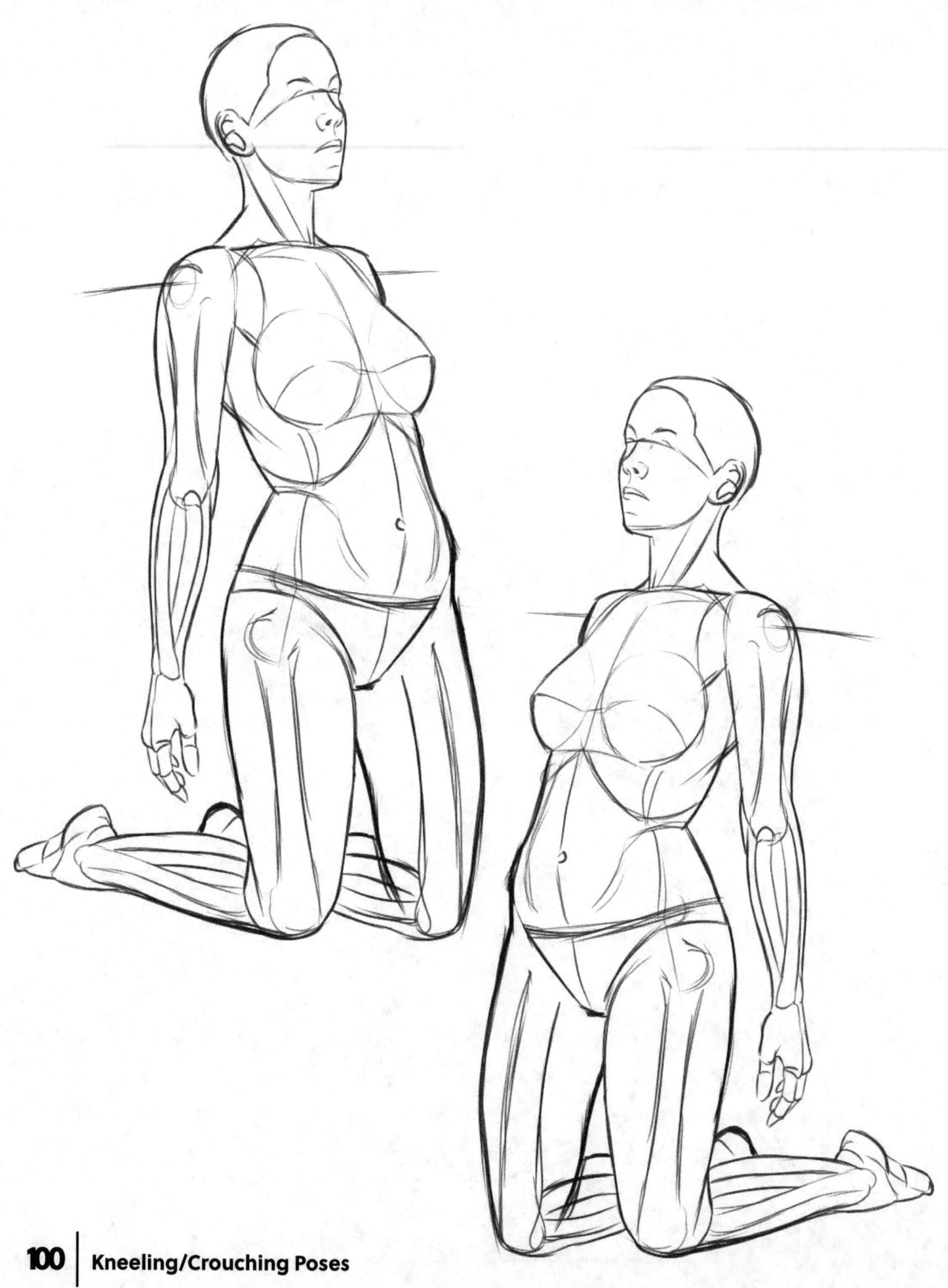

Kneeling/Crouching Poses

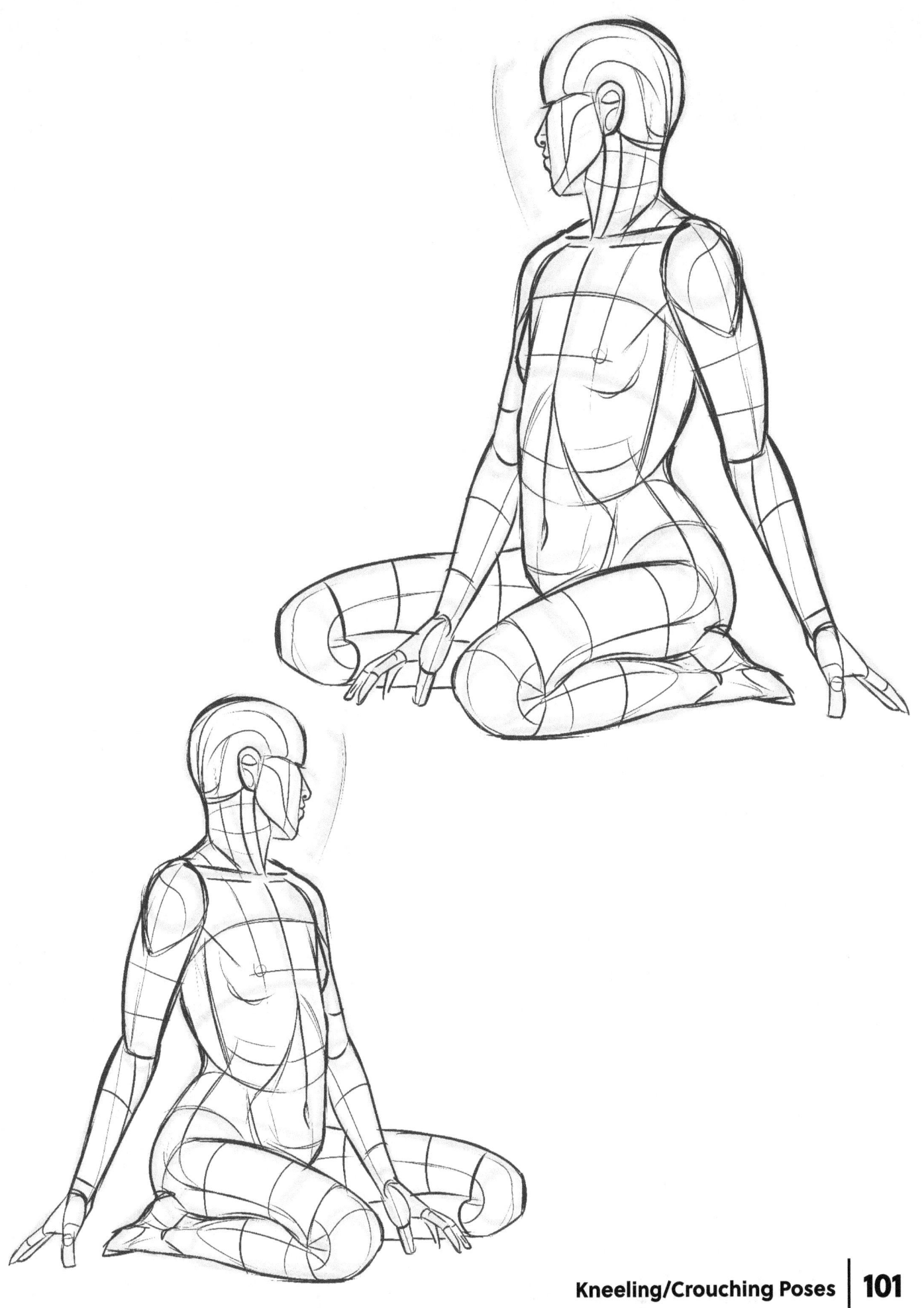

Kneeling/Crouching Poses | **101**

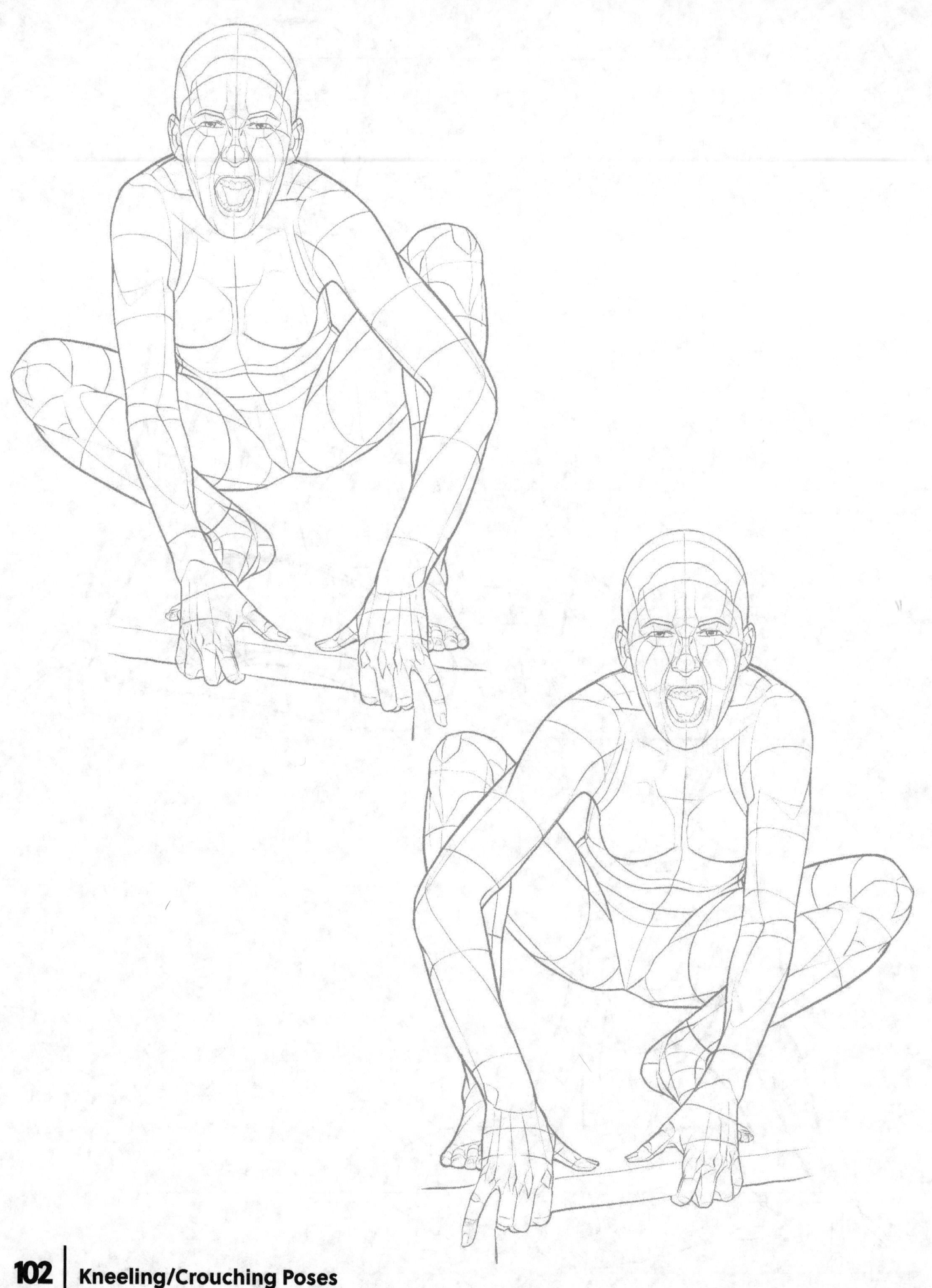

Kneeling/Crouching Poses

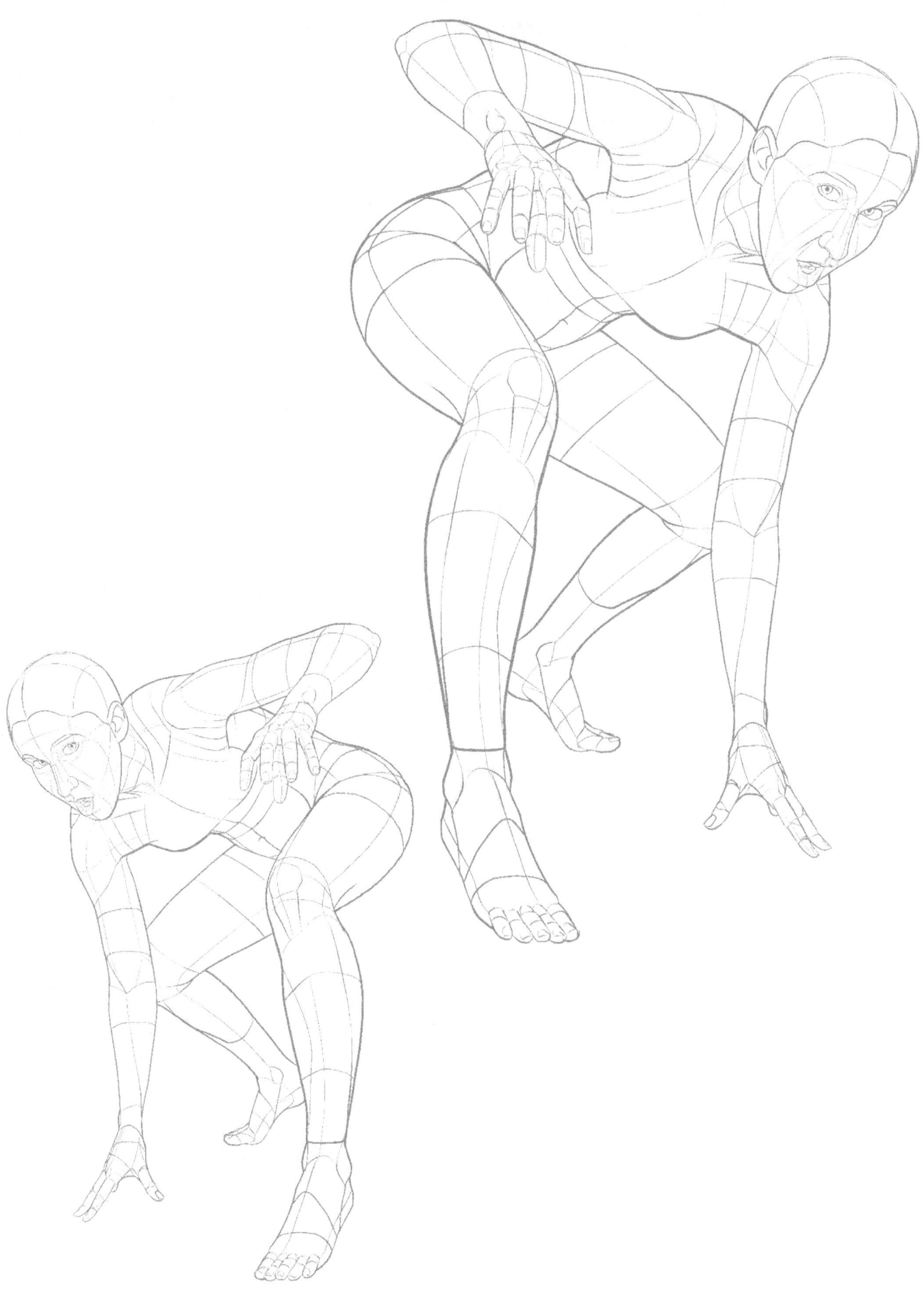

Kneeling/Crouching Poses | 103

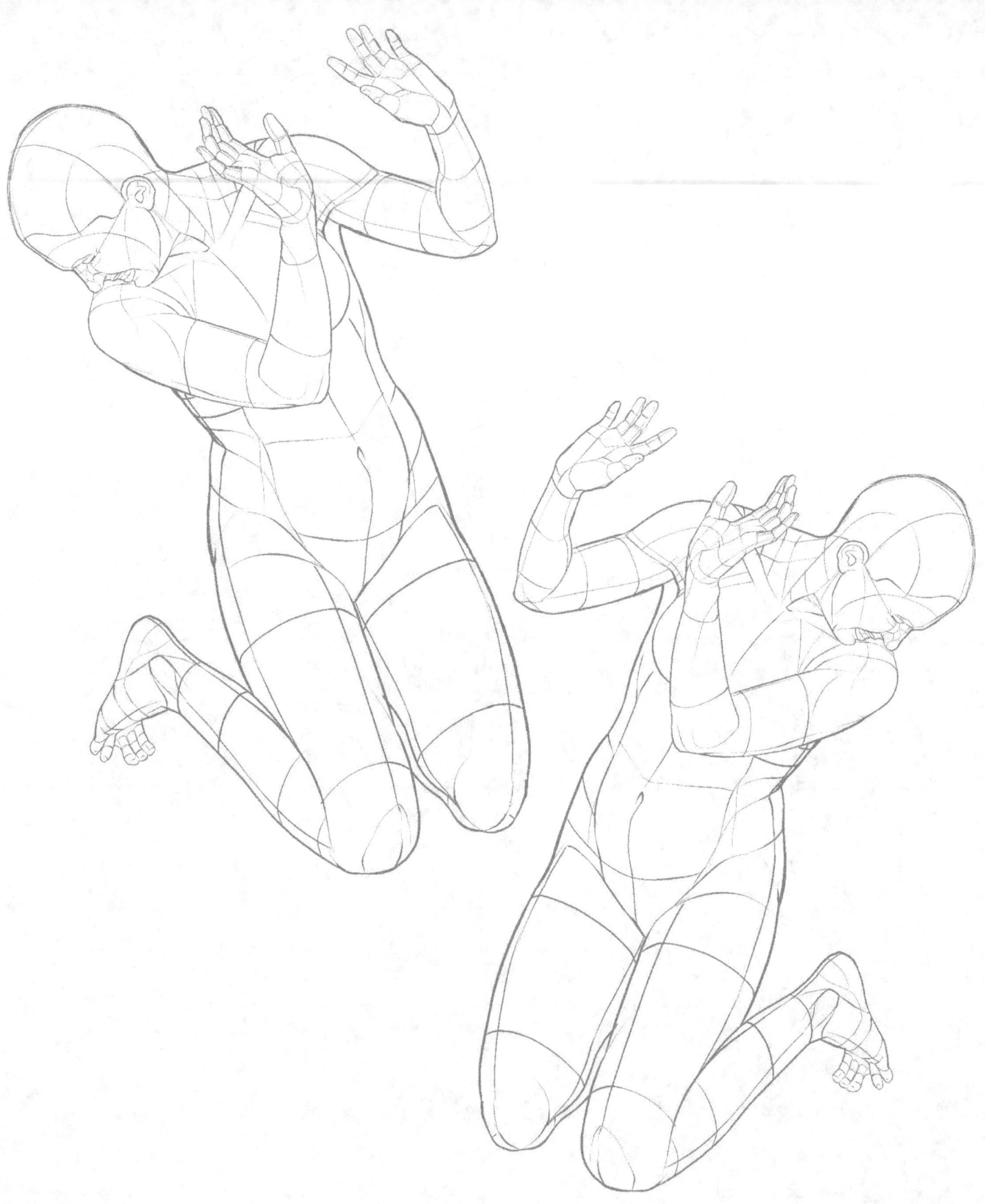

104 | **Kneeling/Crouching Poses**

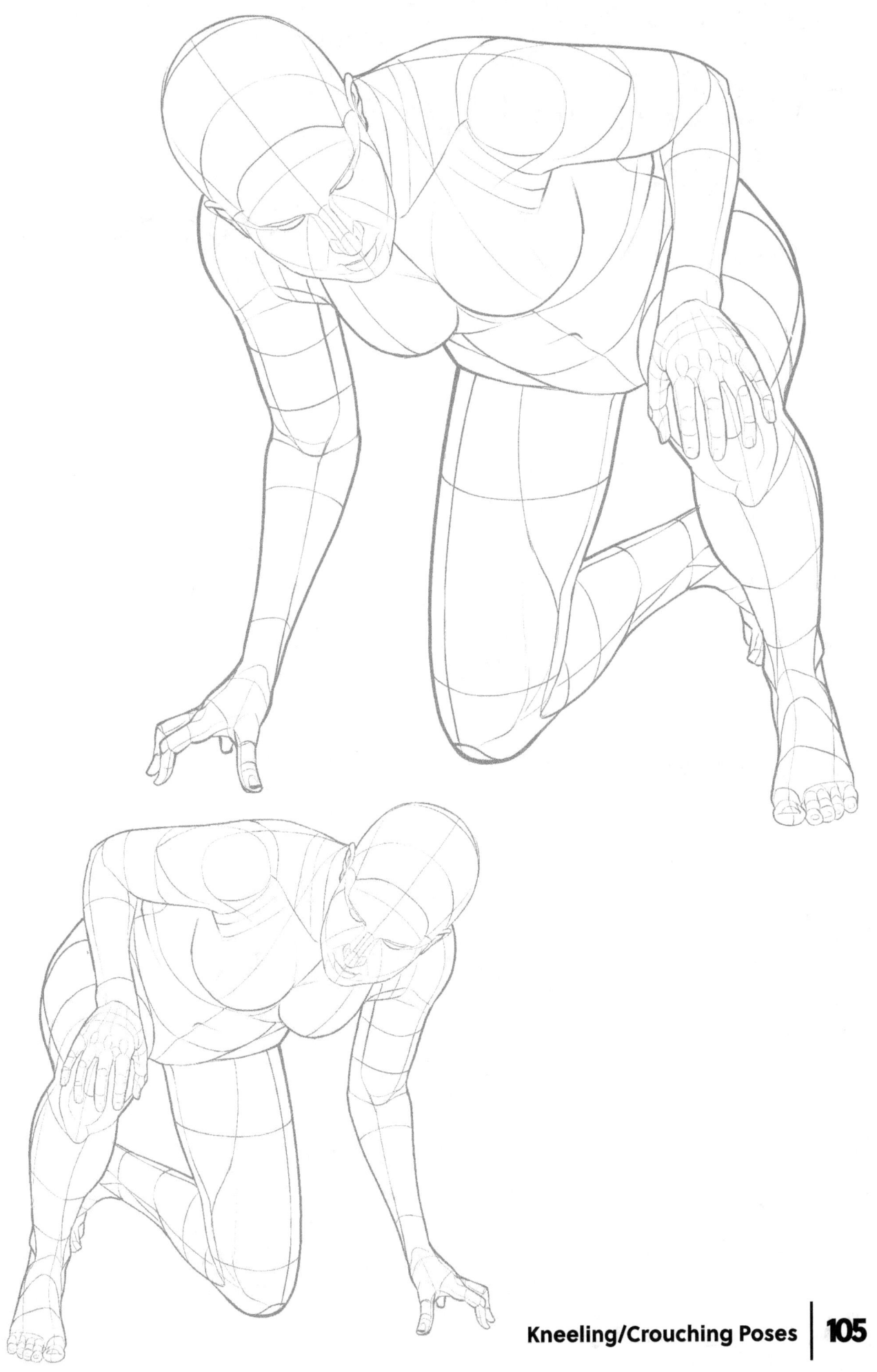

Kneeling/Crouching Poses

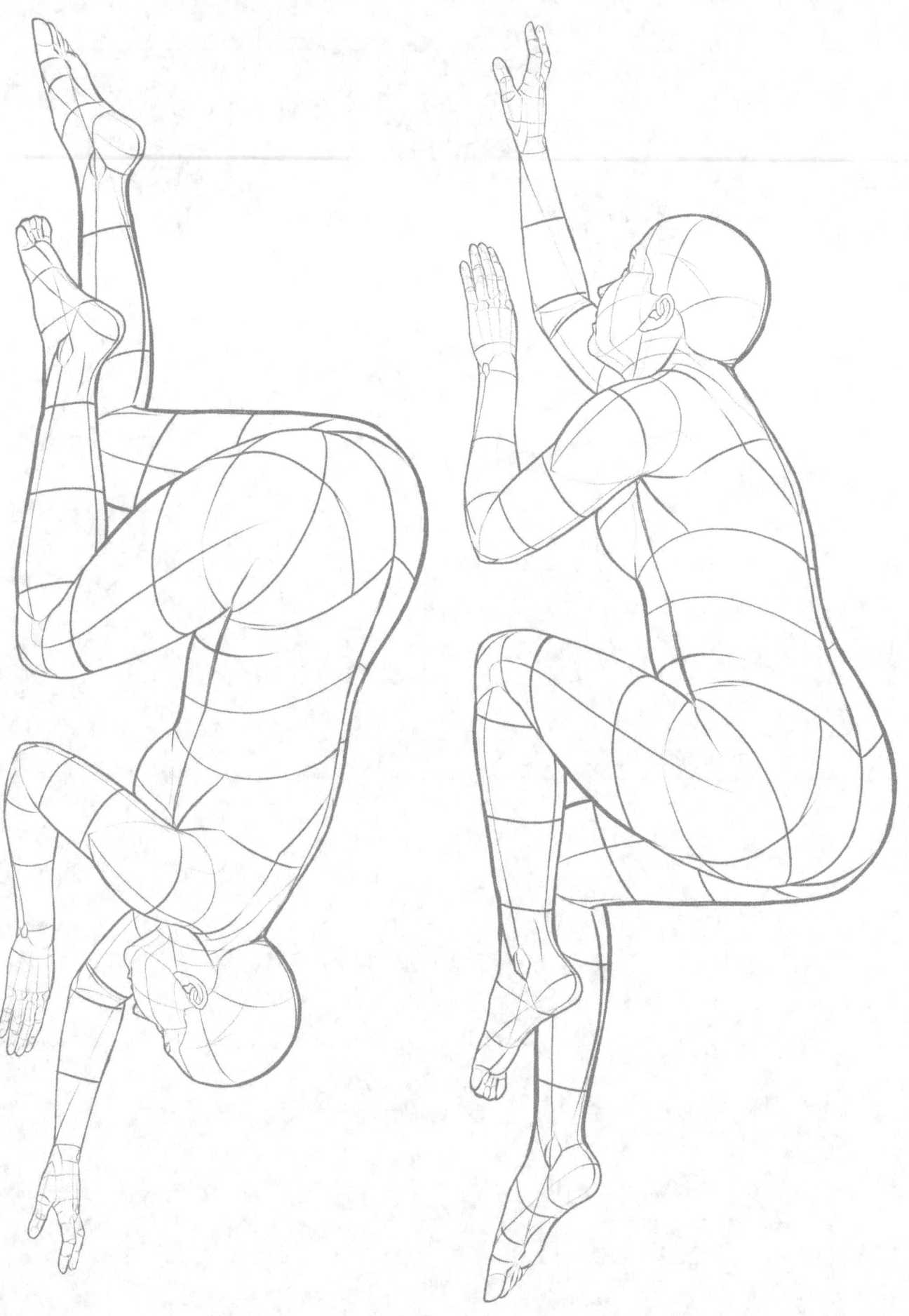

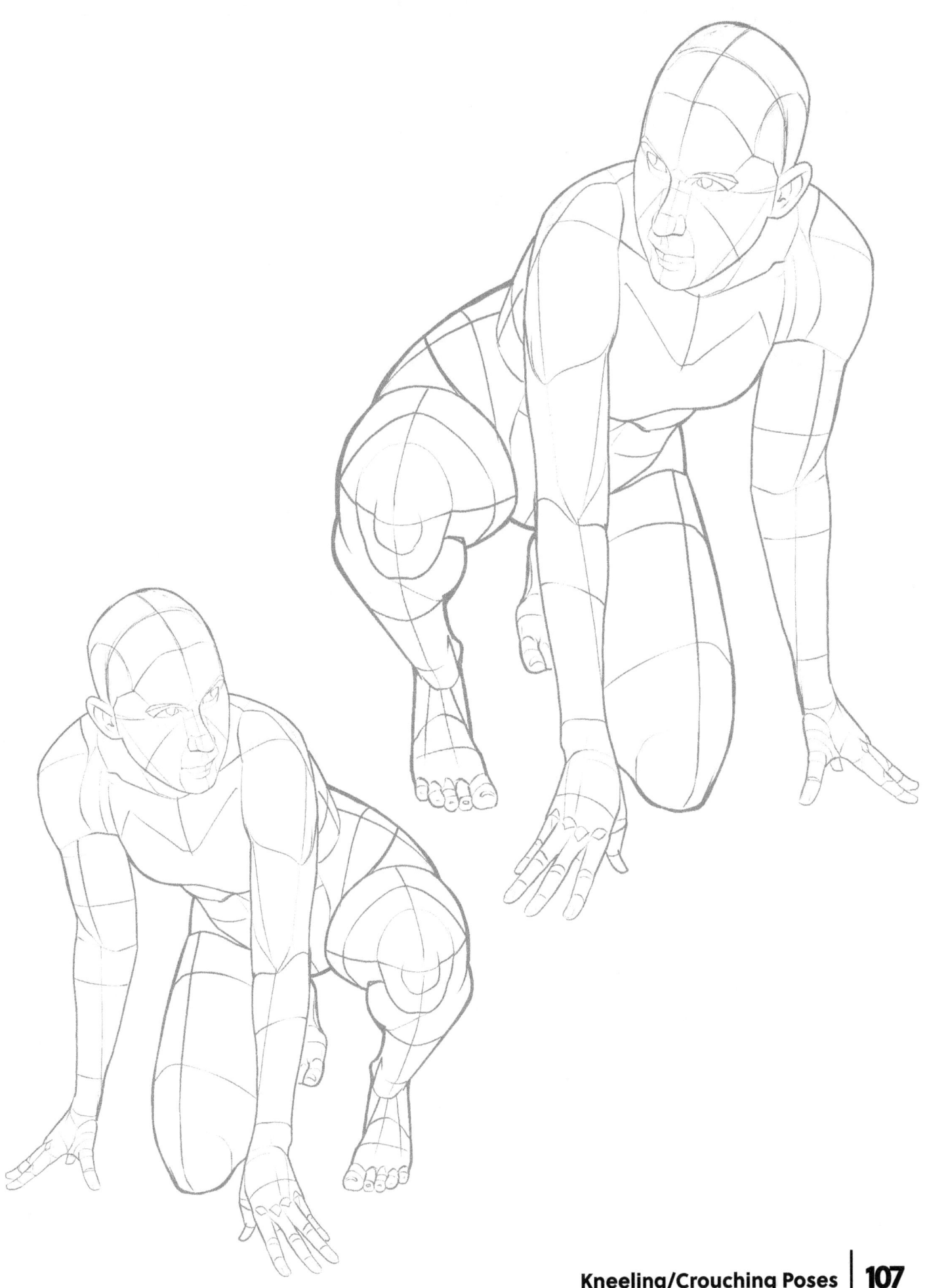

Kneeling/Crouching Poses | 107

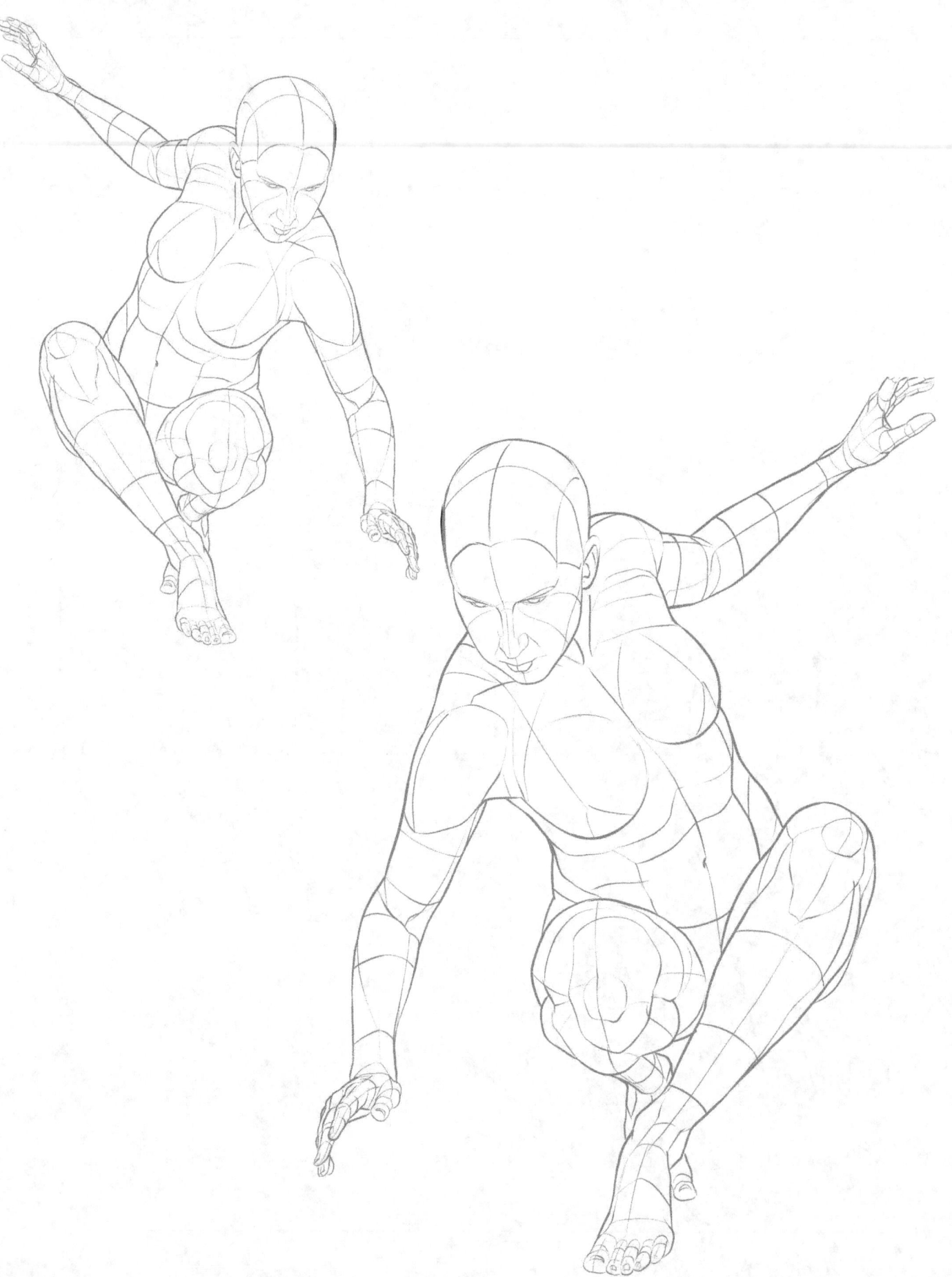

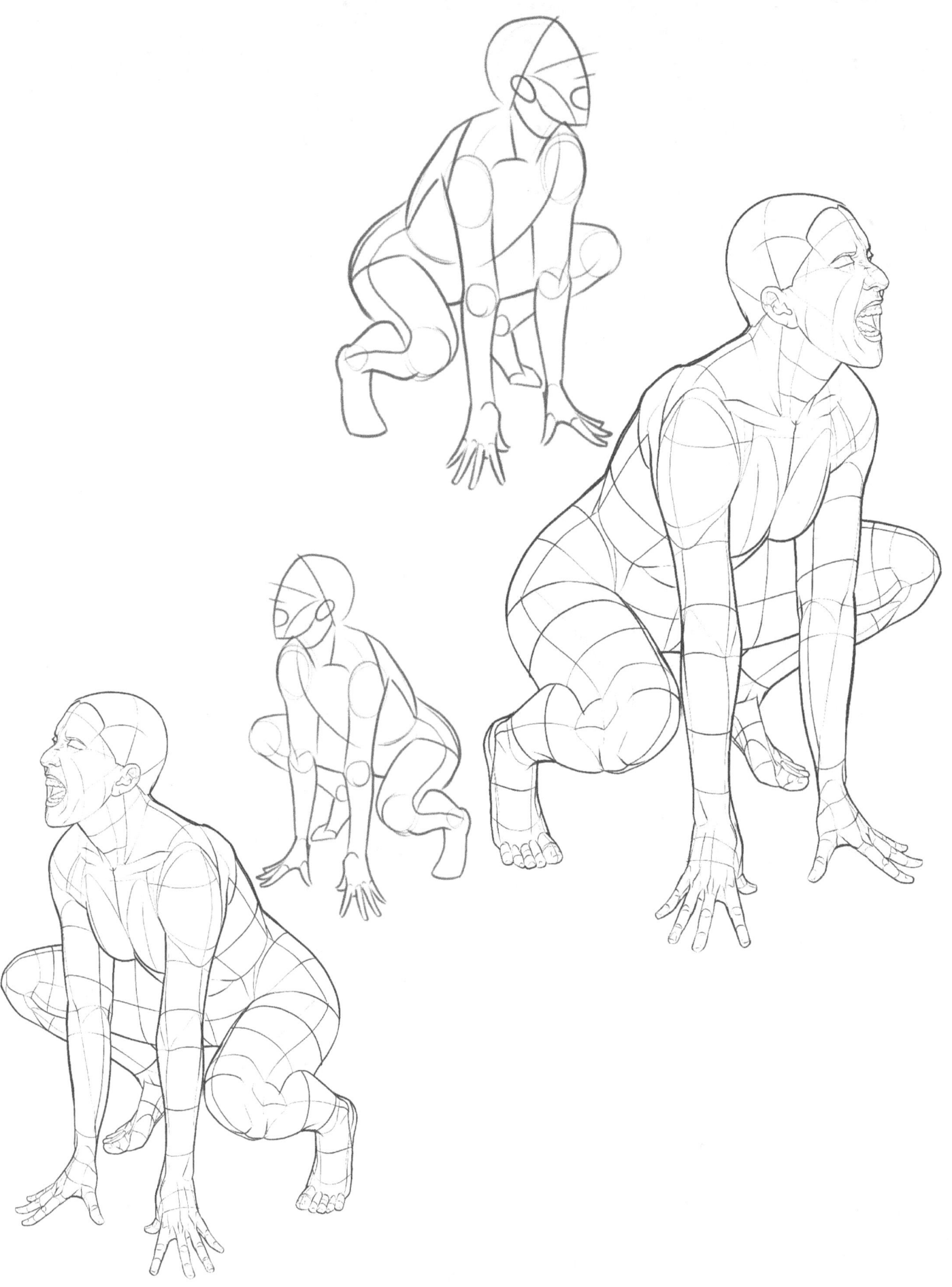

Kneeling/Crouching Poses | 109

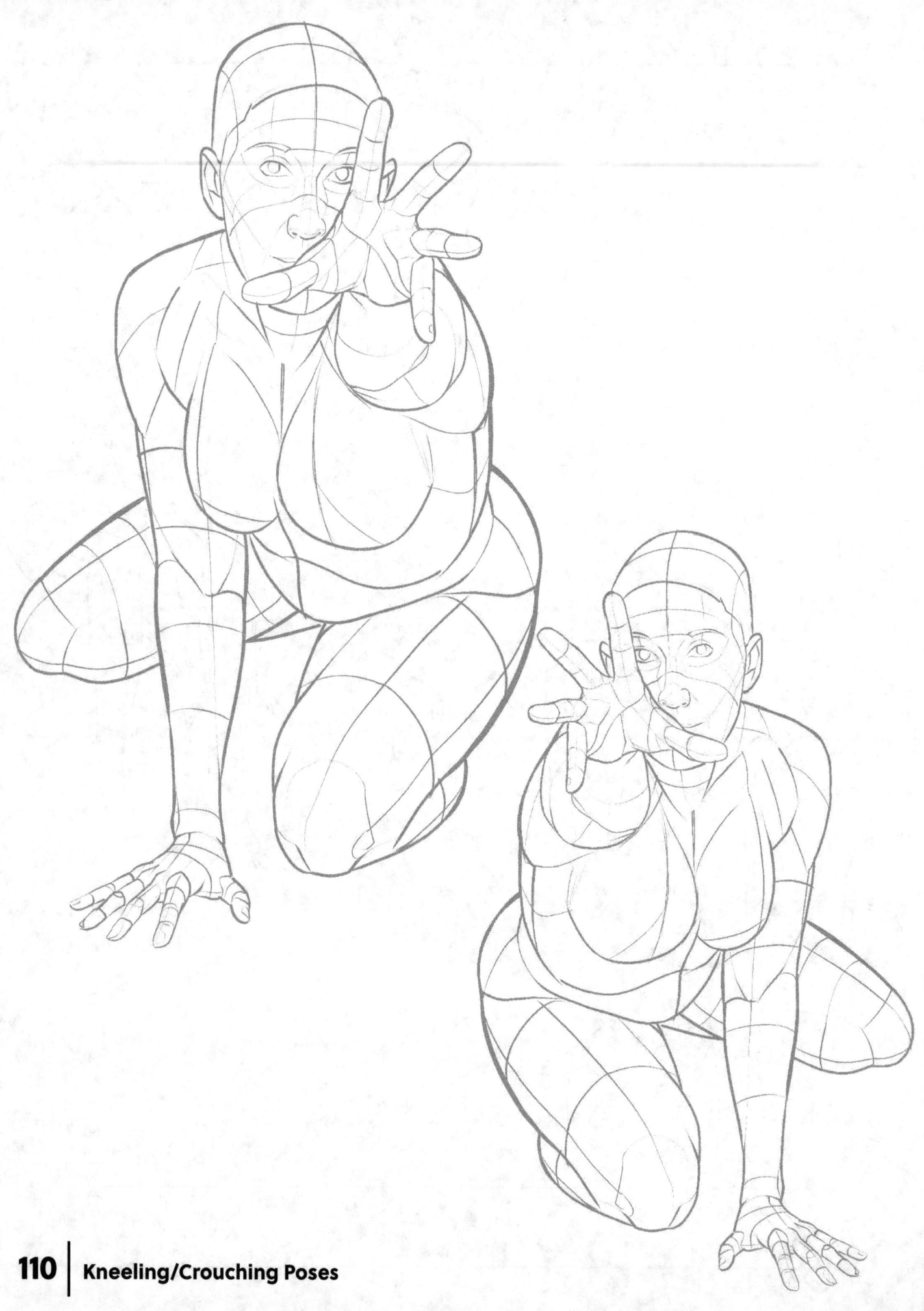

Kneeling/Crouching Poses

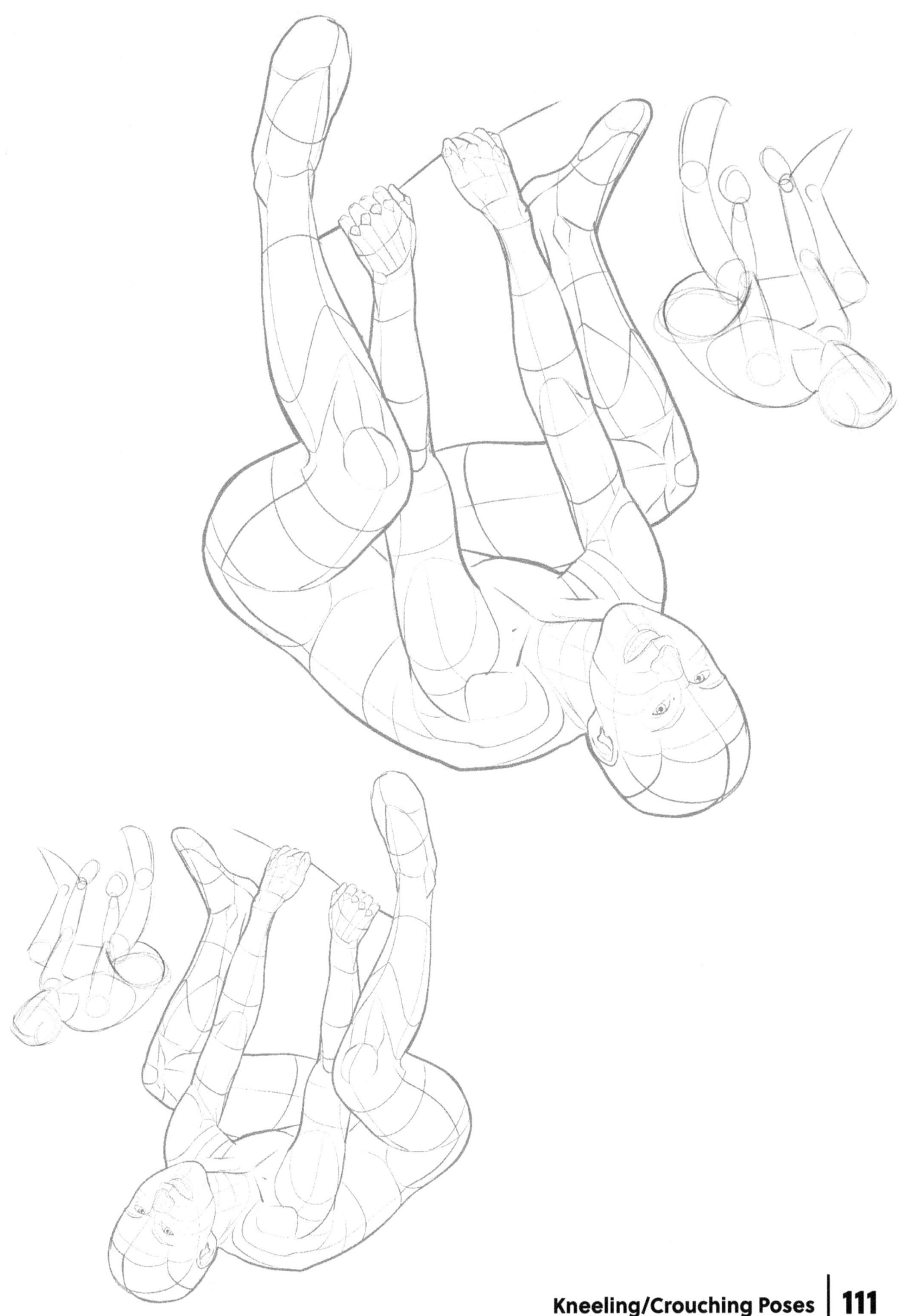

Kneeling/Crouching Poses | 111

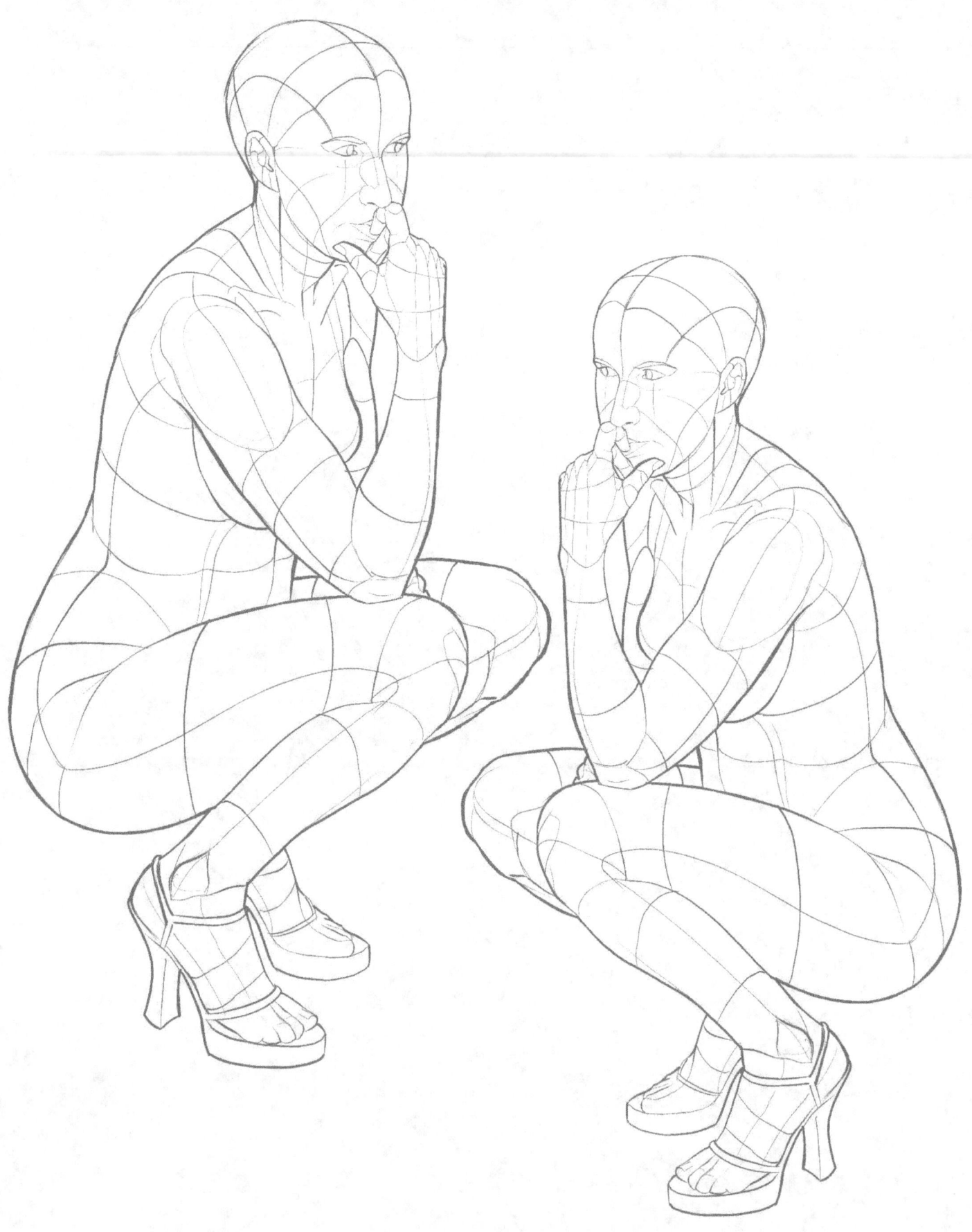

Magic Poses

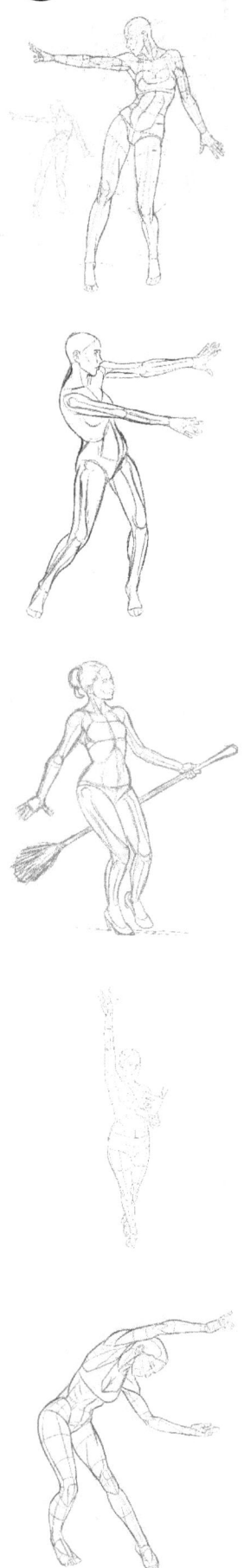

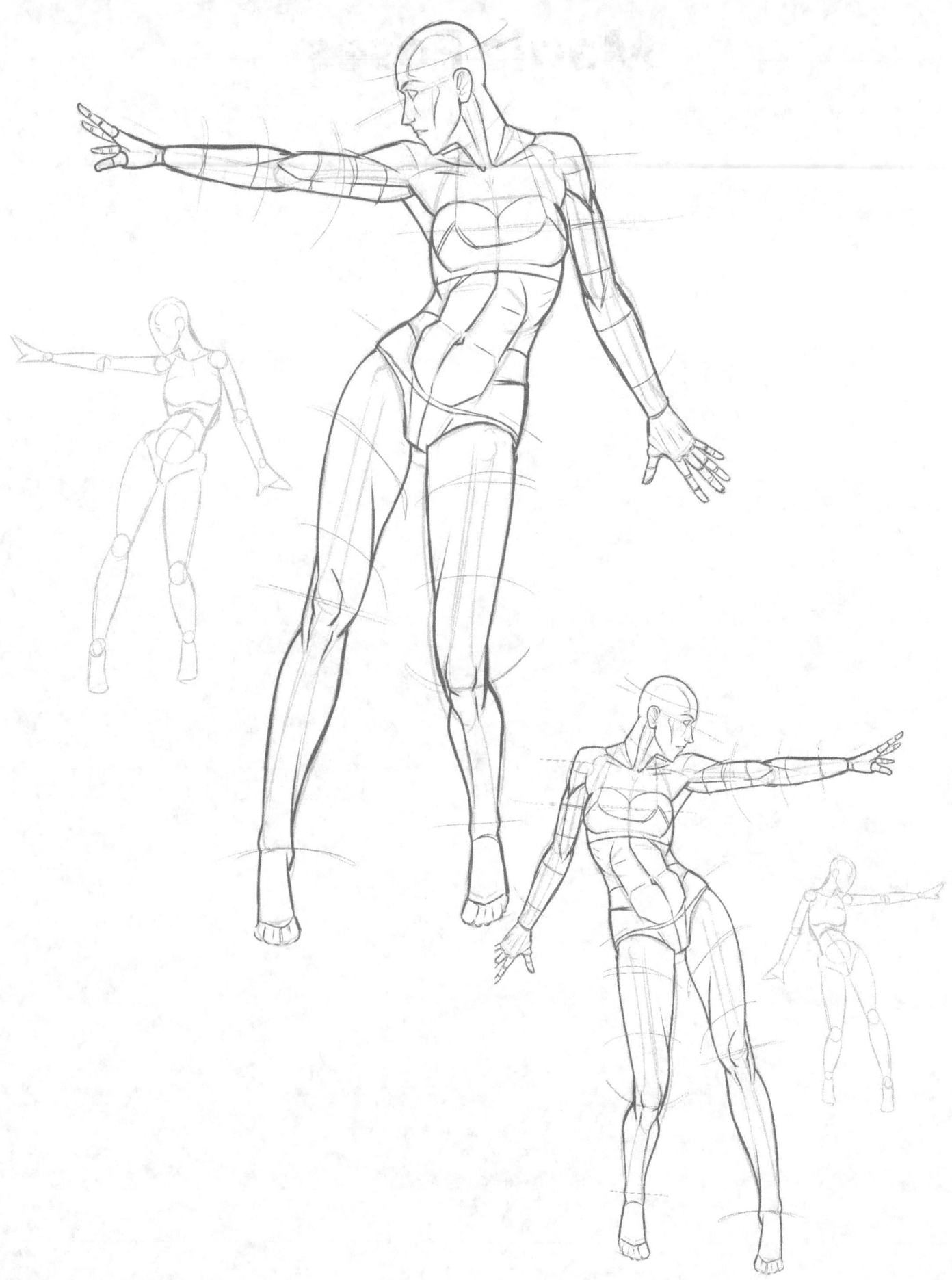

114 | **Magic Poses**

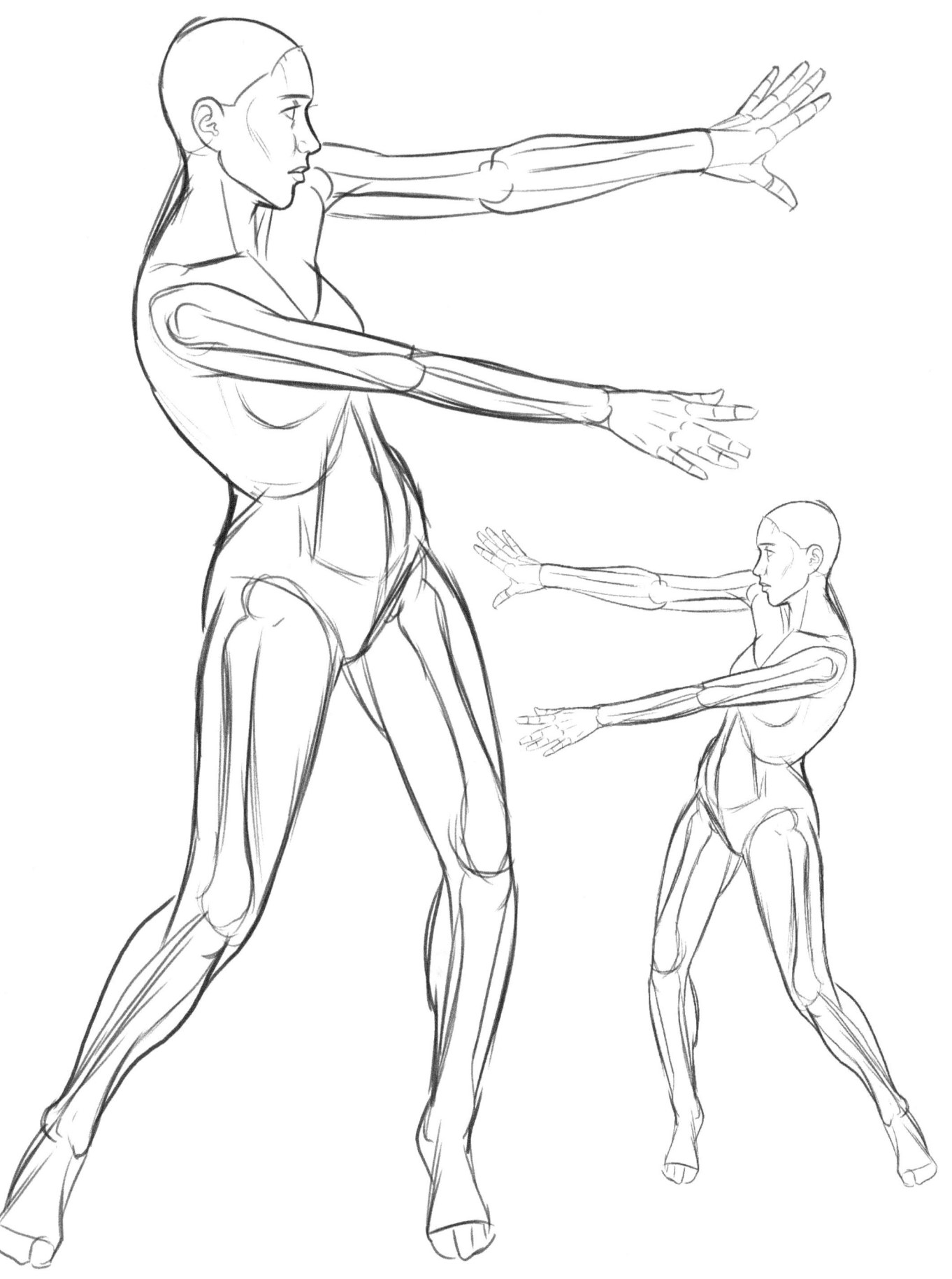

Magic Poses | 115

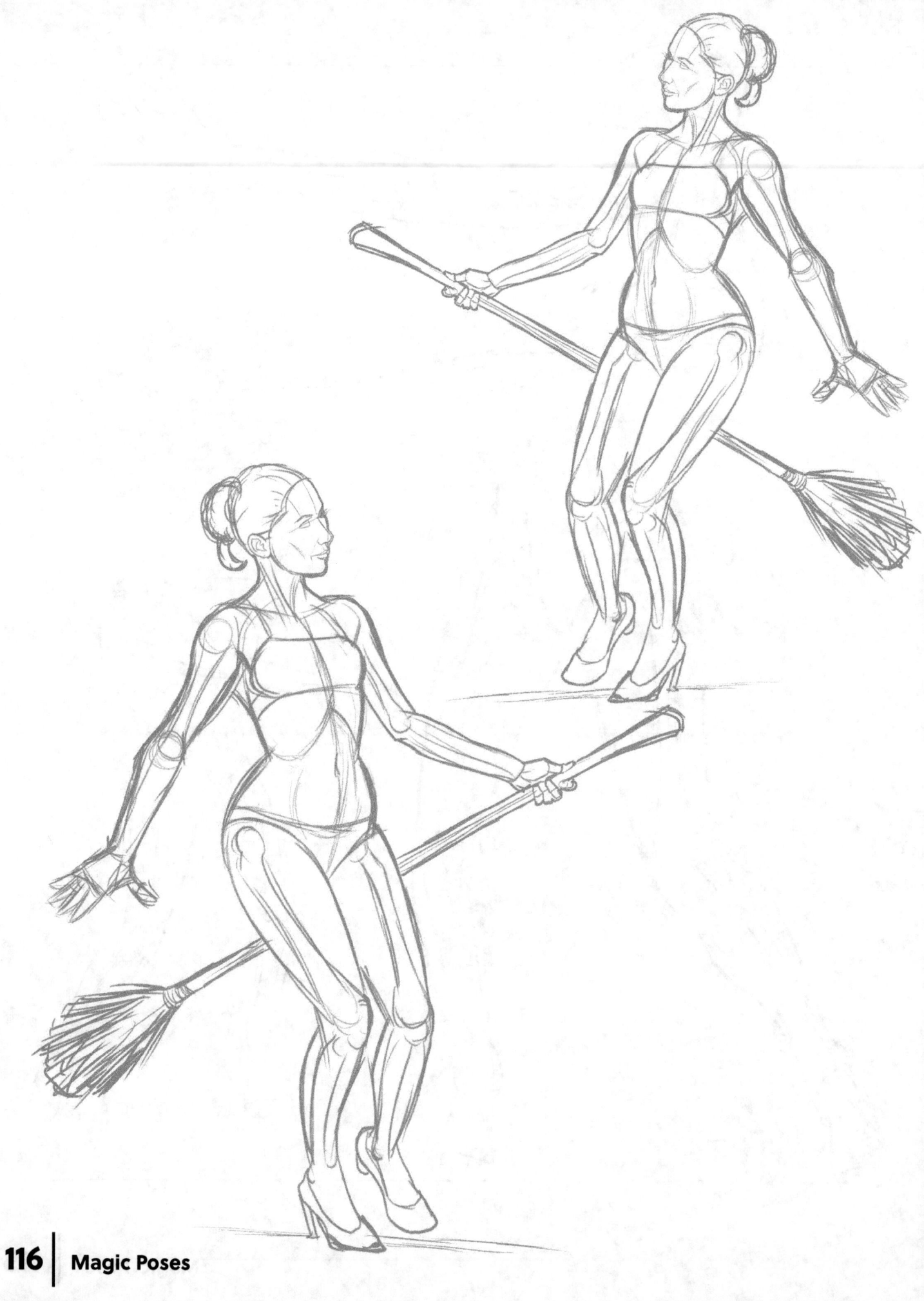

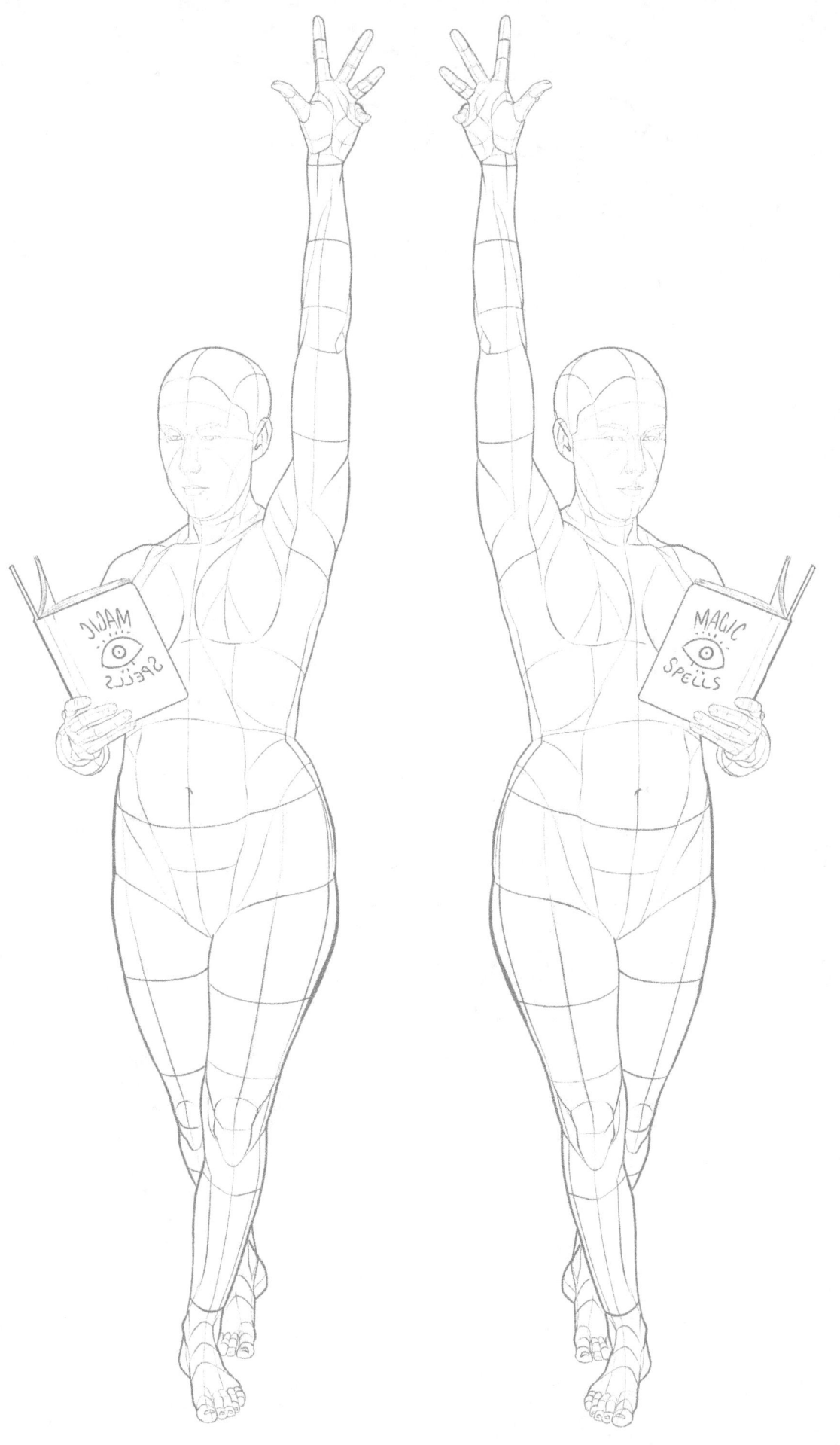

Magic Poses | 117

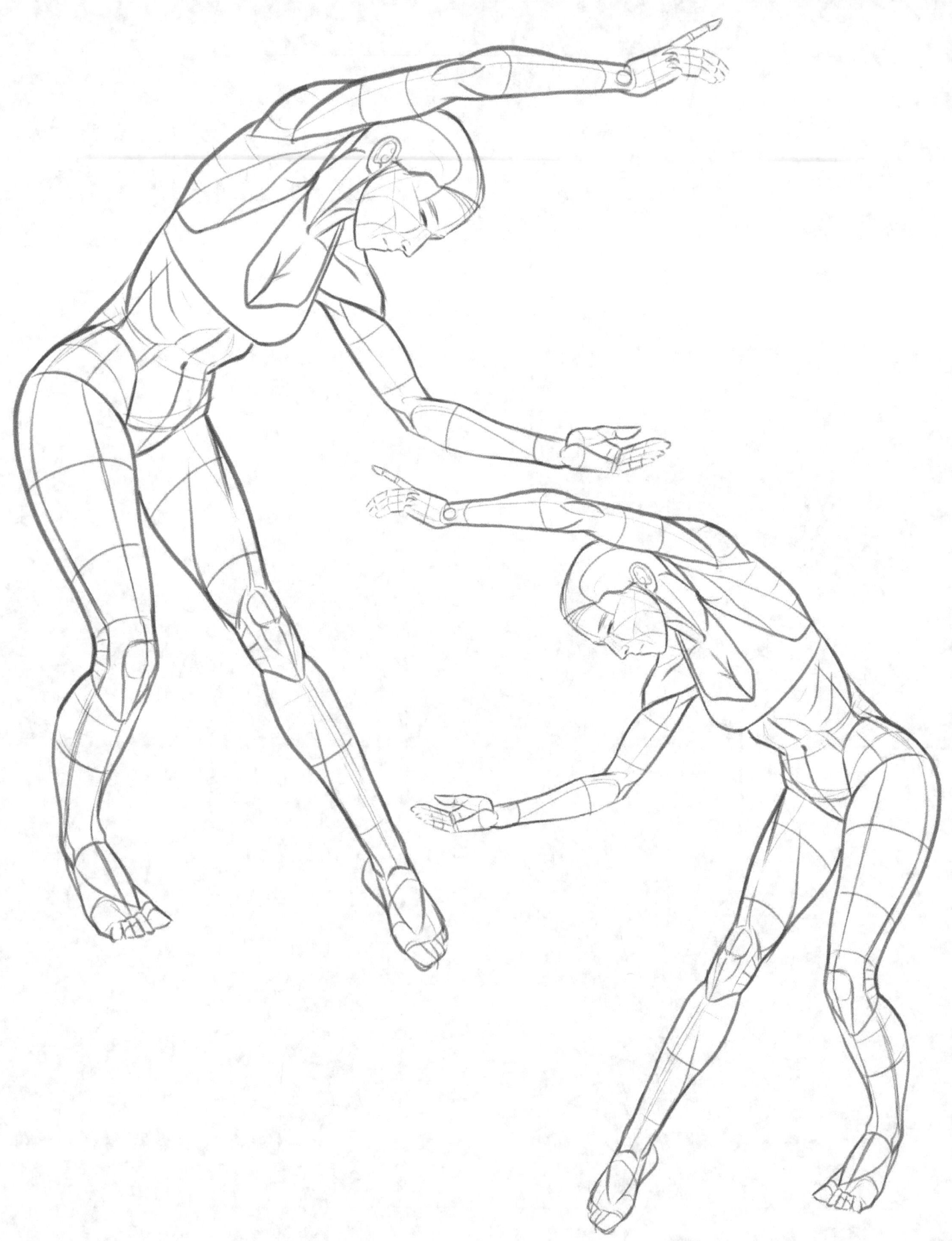

Leaping/Flying Poses

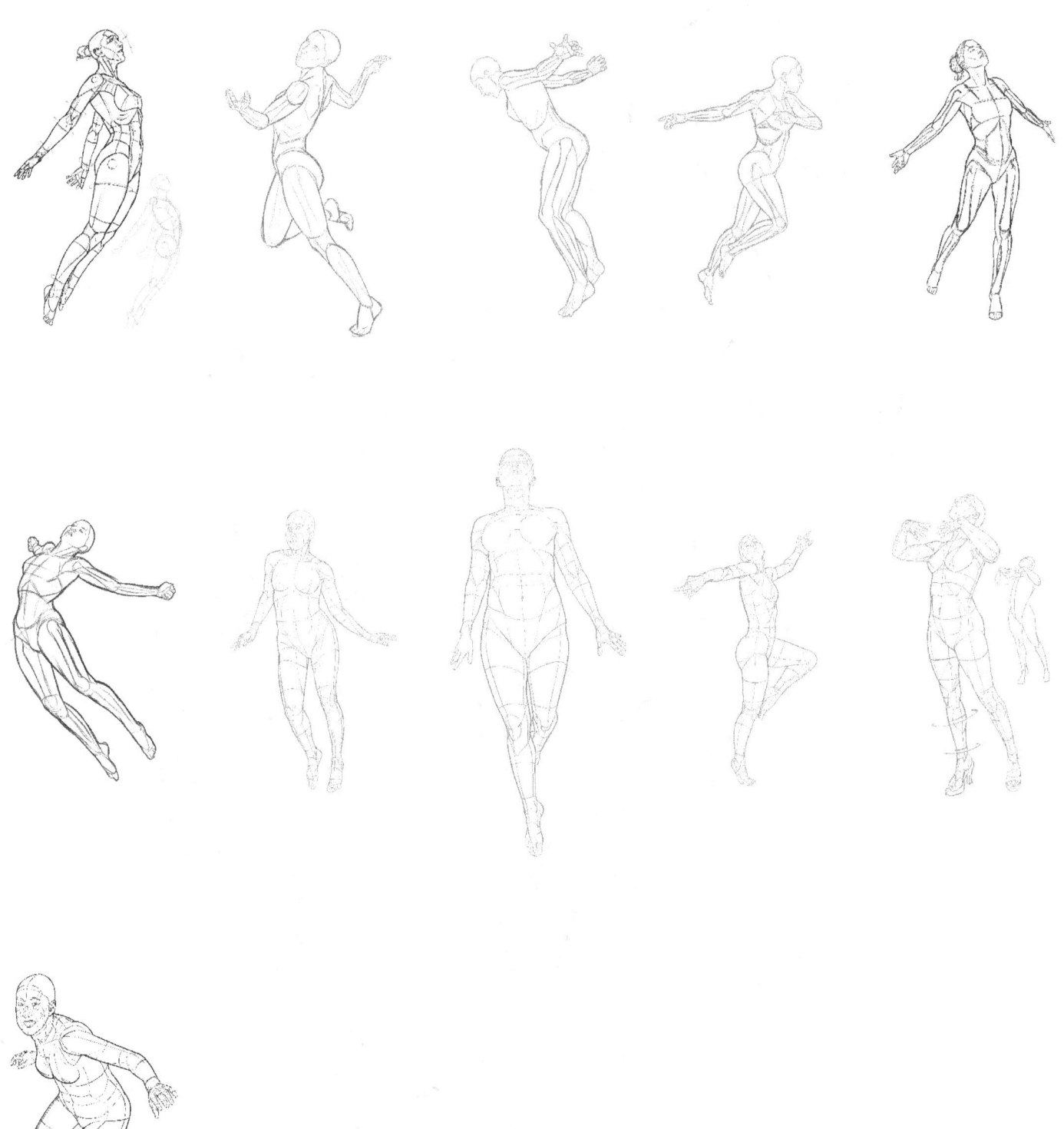

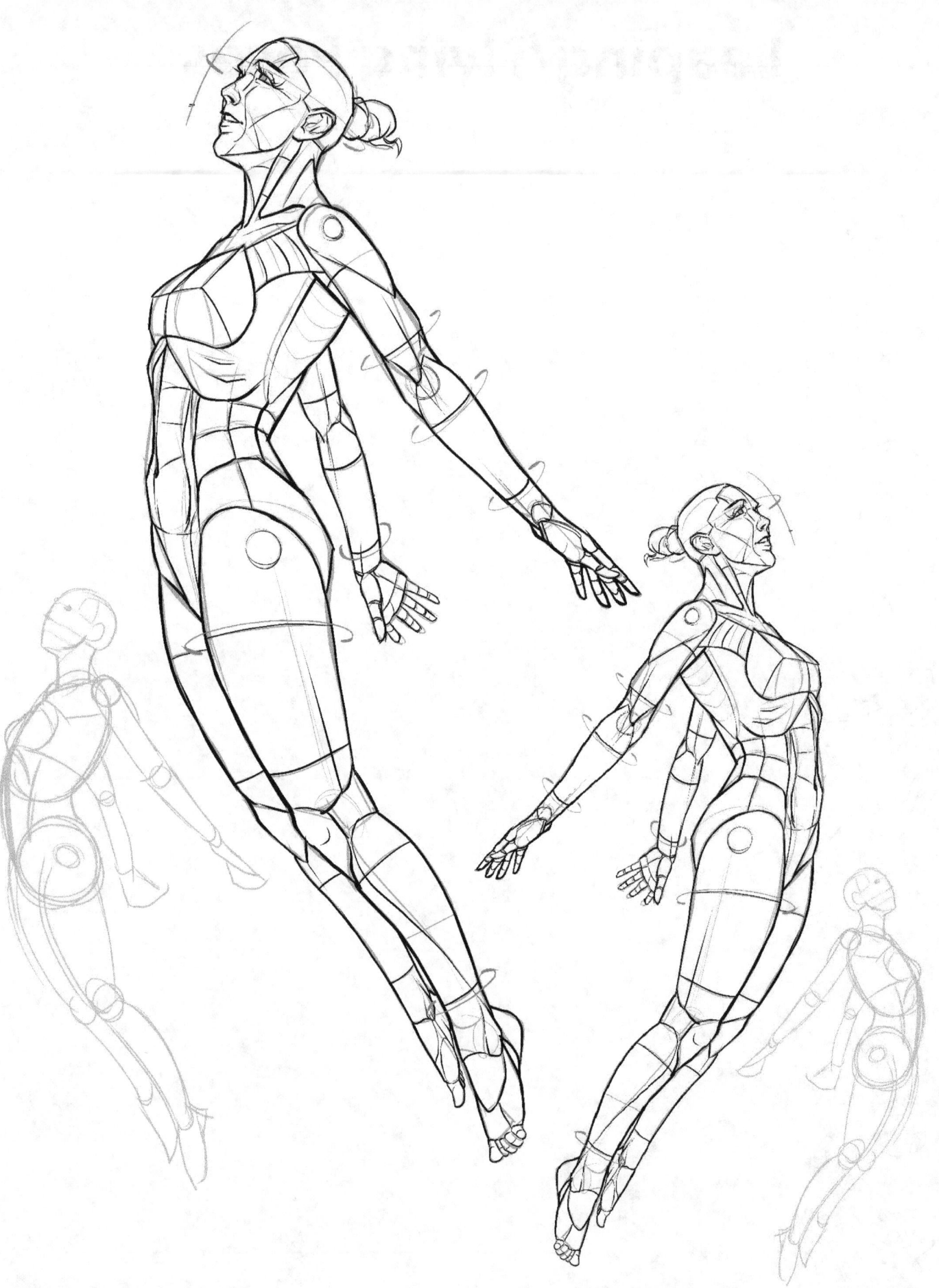

Leaping/Flying Poses

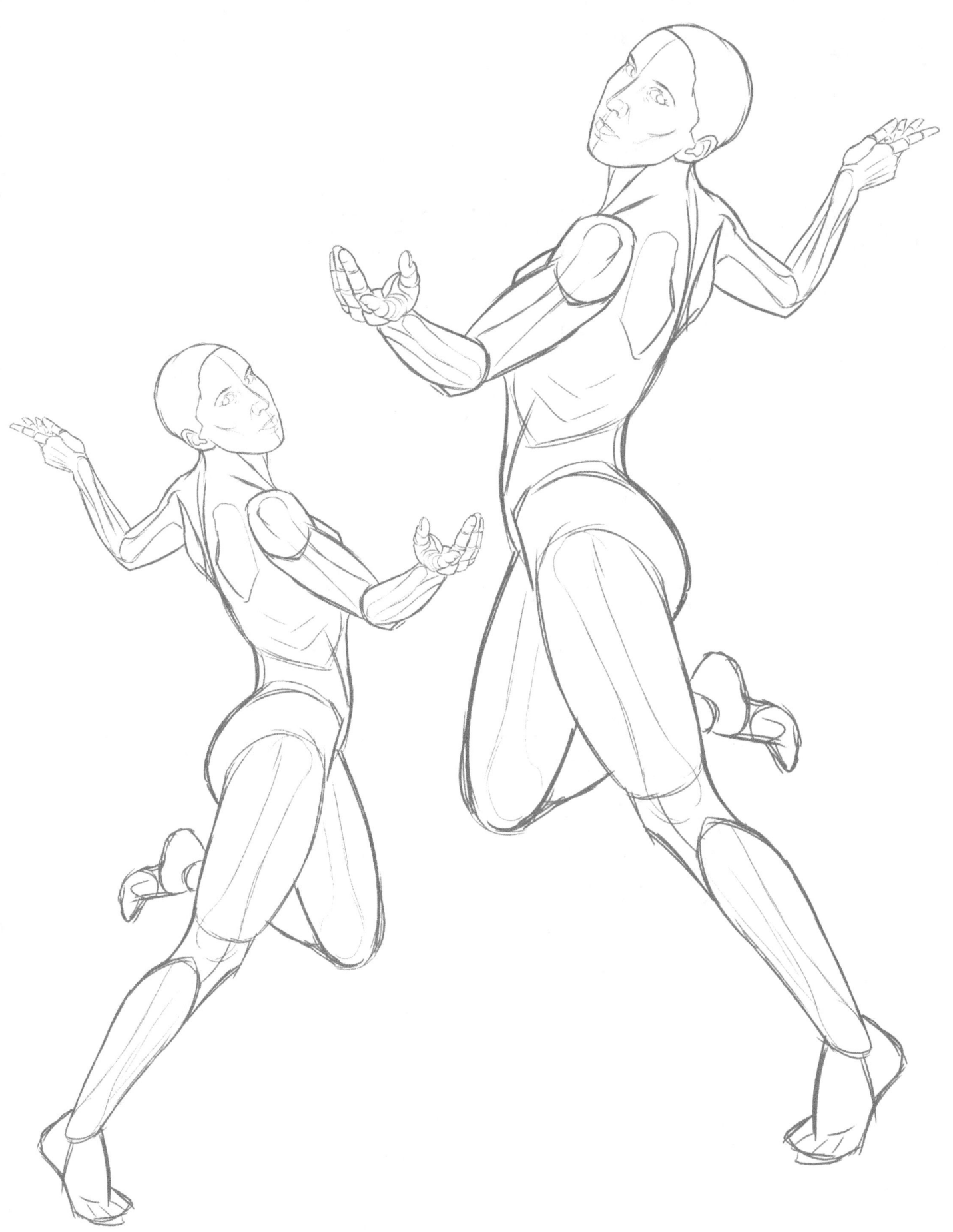

Leaping/Flying Poses | **121**

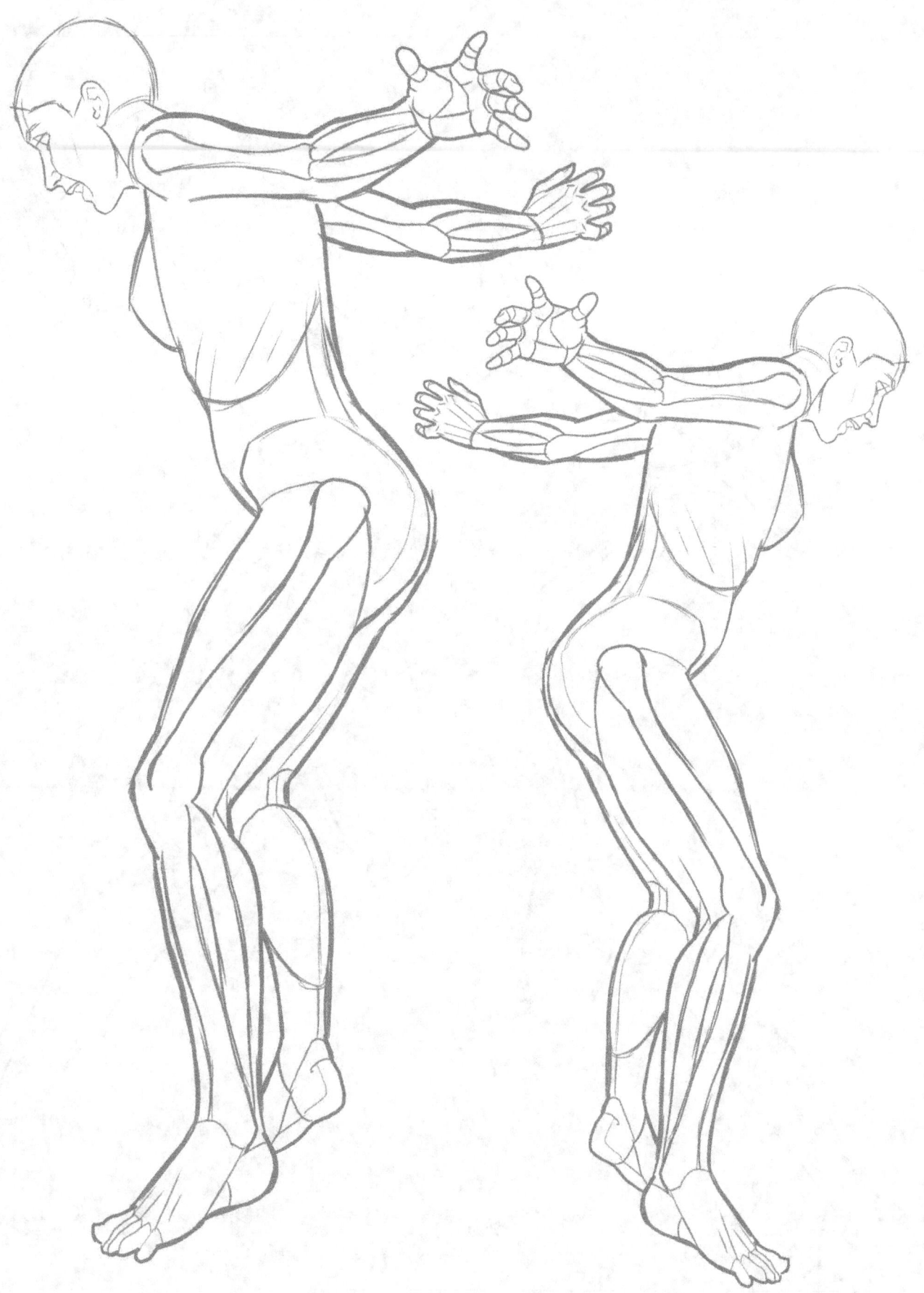

Leaping/Flying Poses

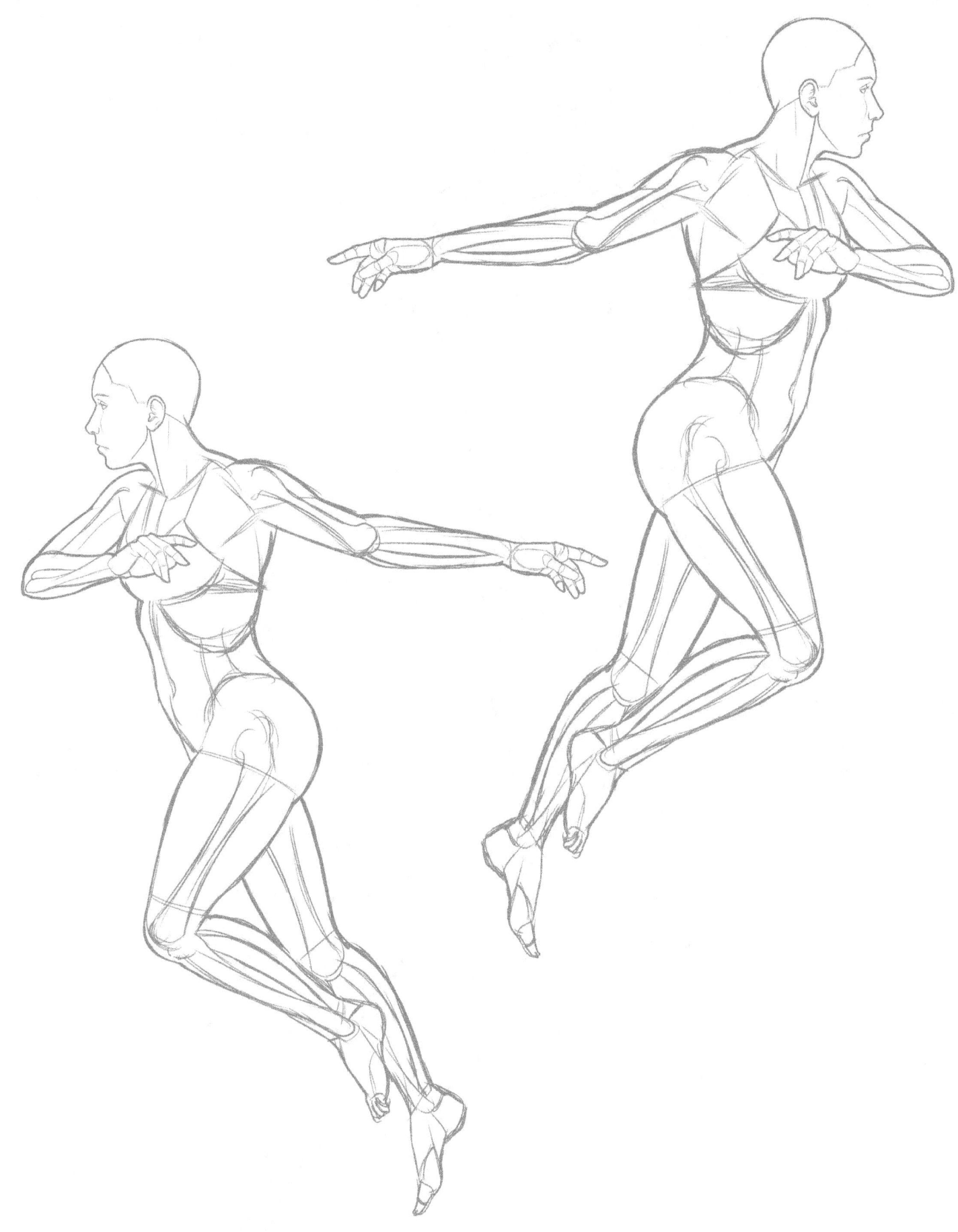

Leaping/Flying Poses

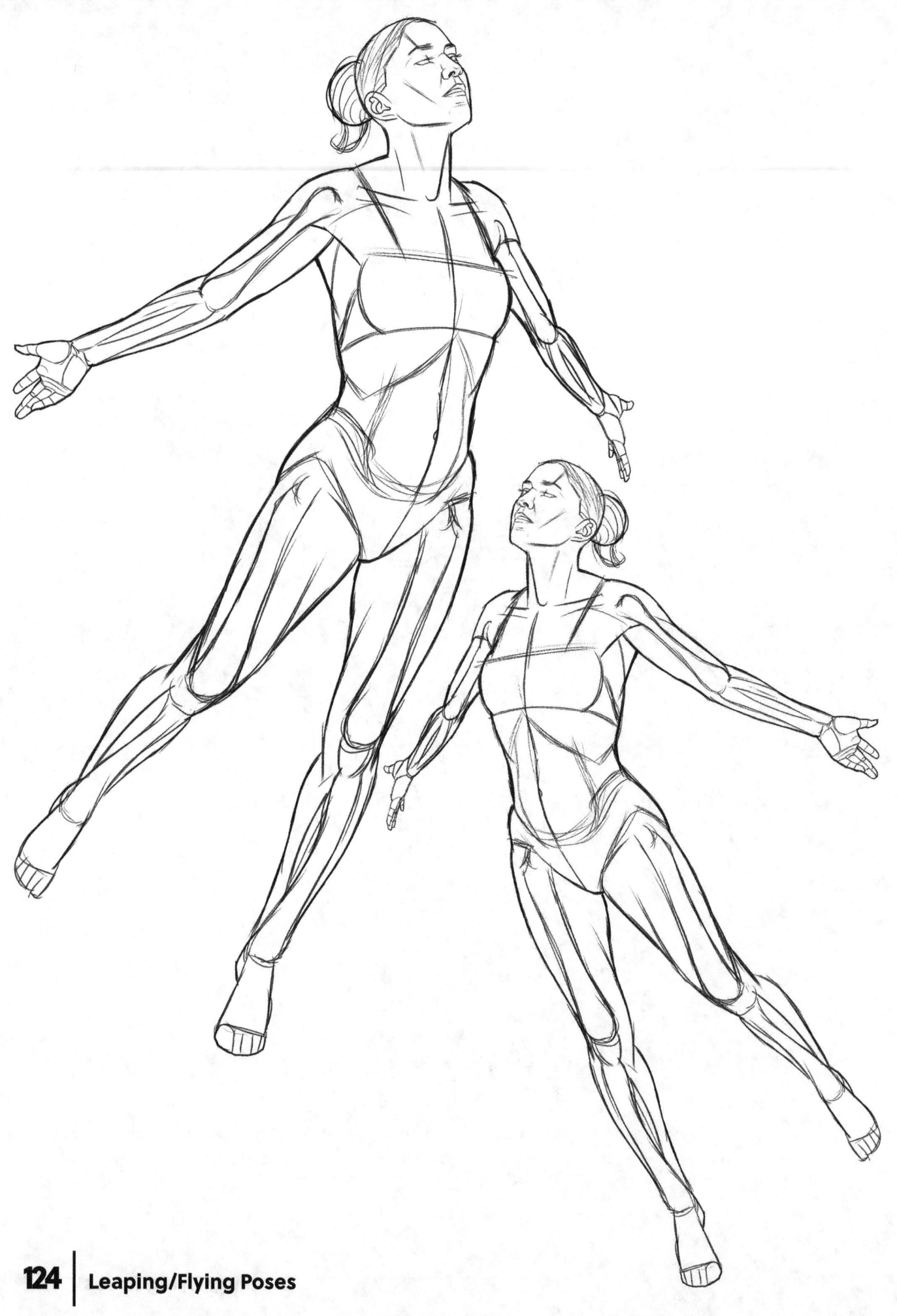

124 | Leaping/Flying Poses

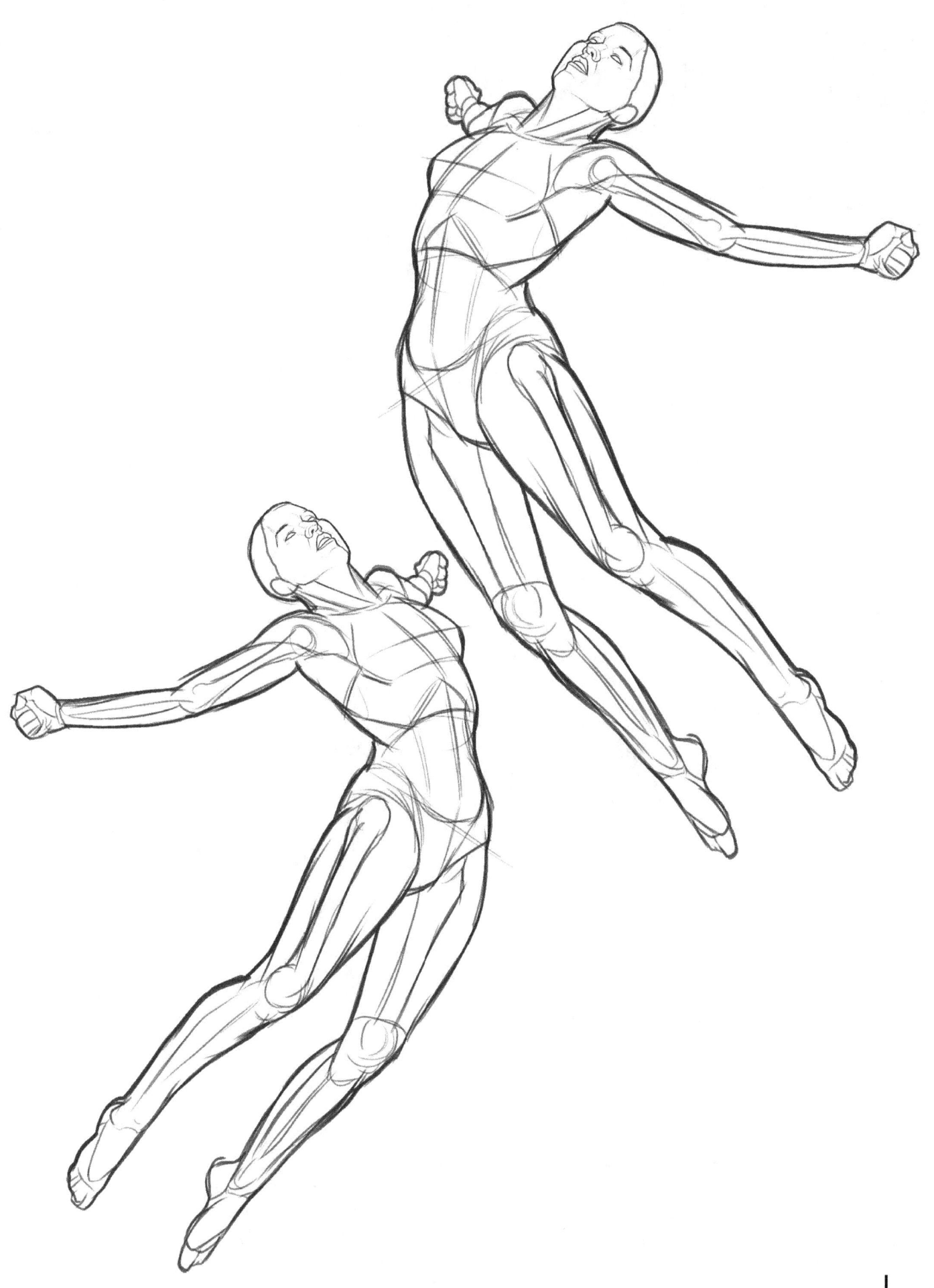

Leaping/Flying Poses | 125

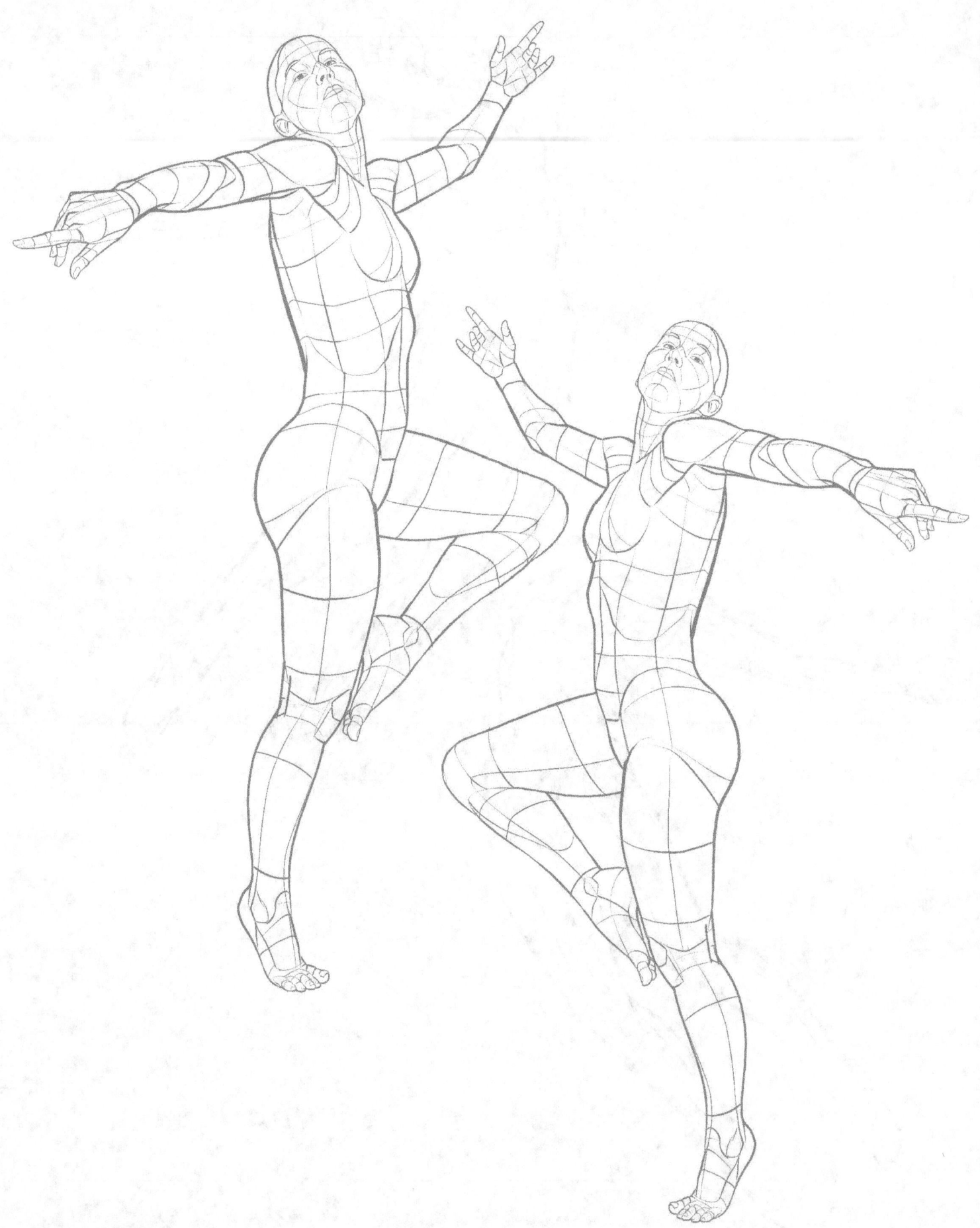

126 | Leaping/Flying Poses

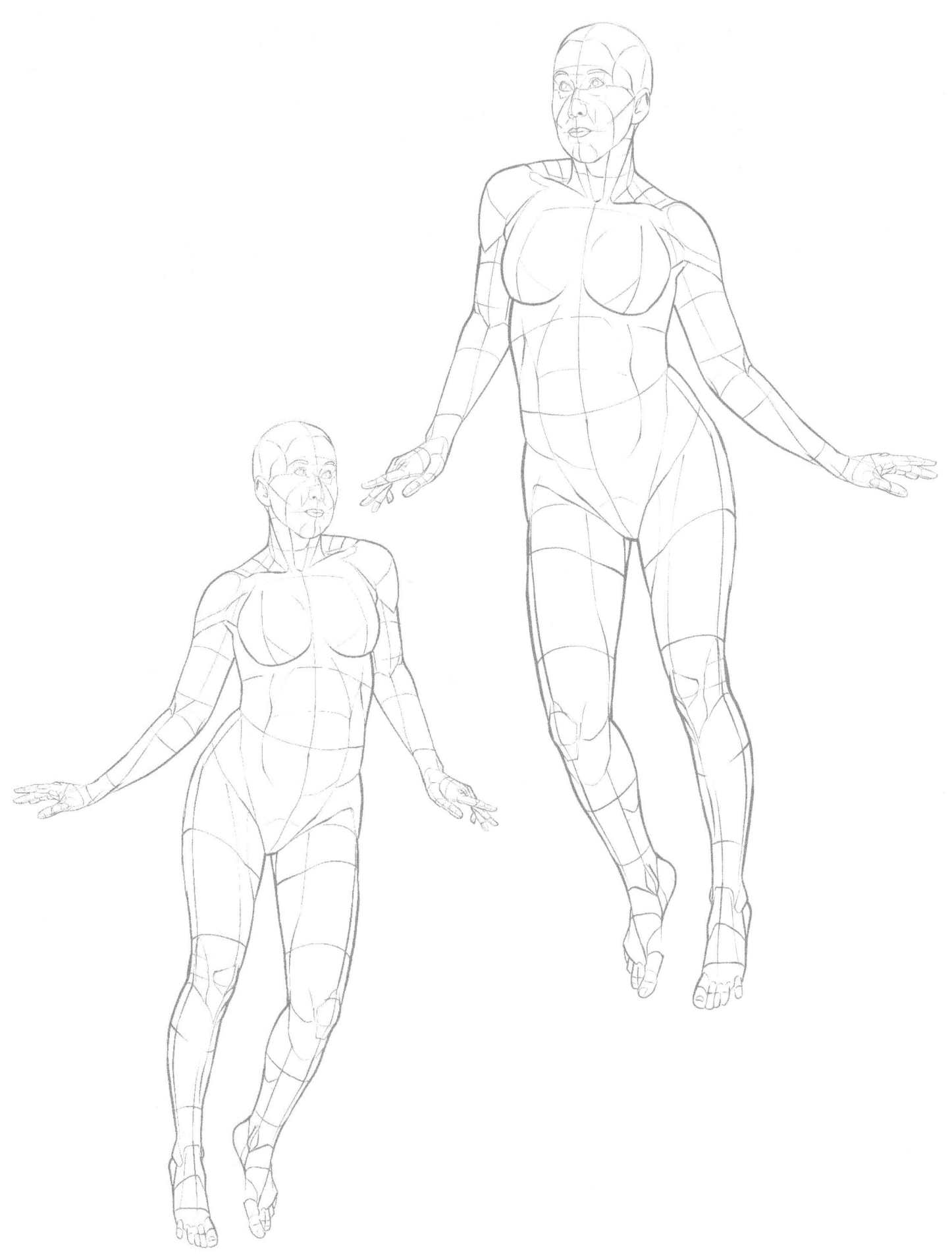

Leaping/Flying Poses

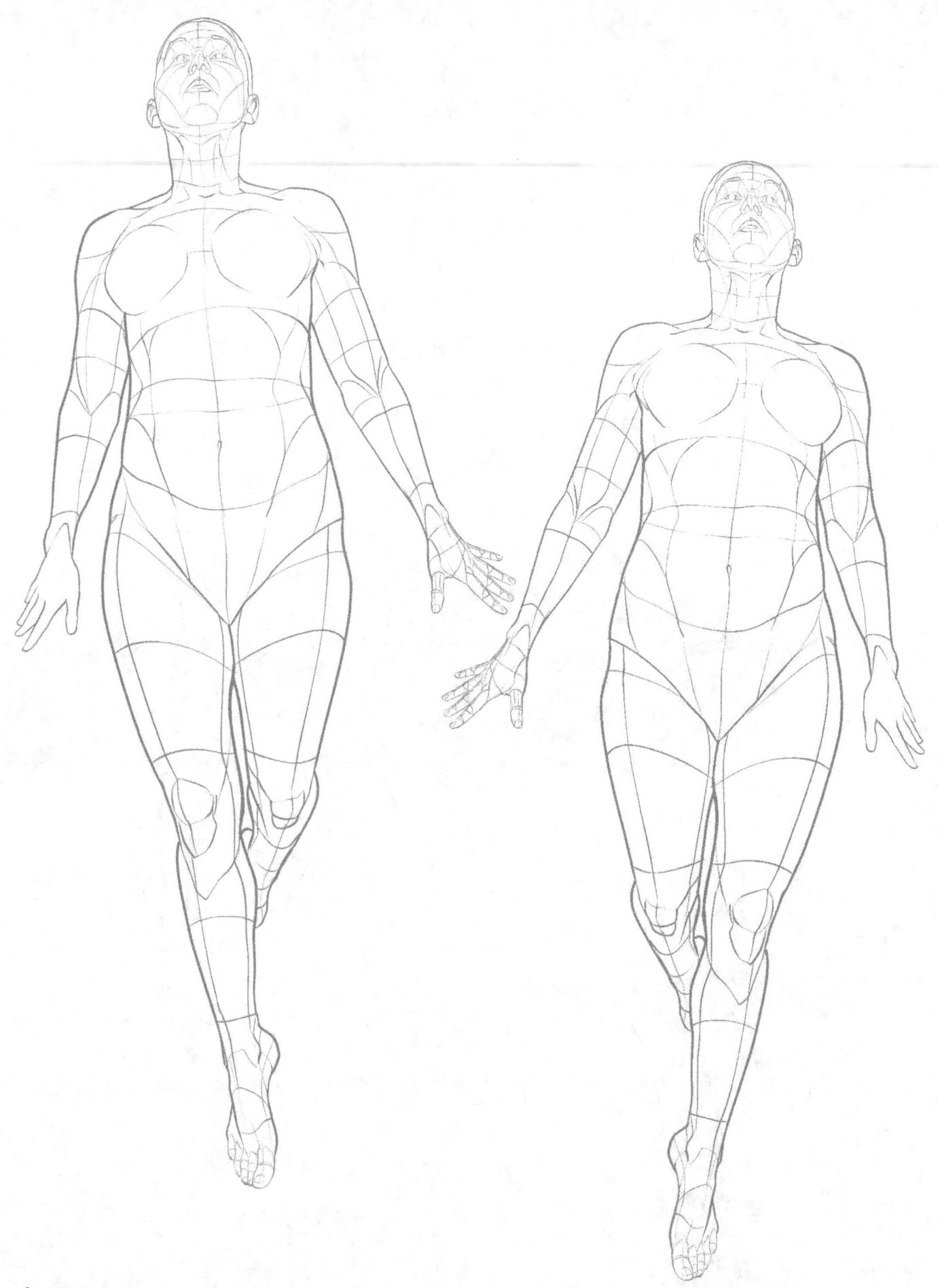

Leaping/Flying Poses

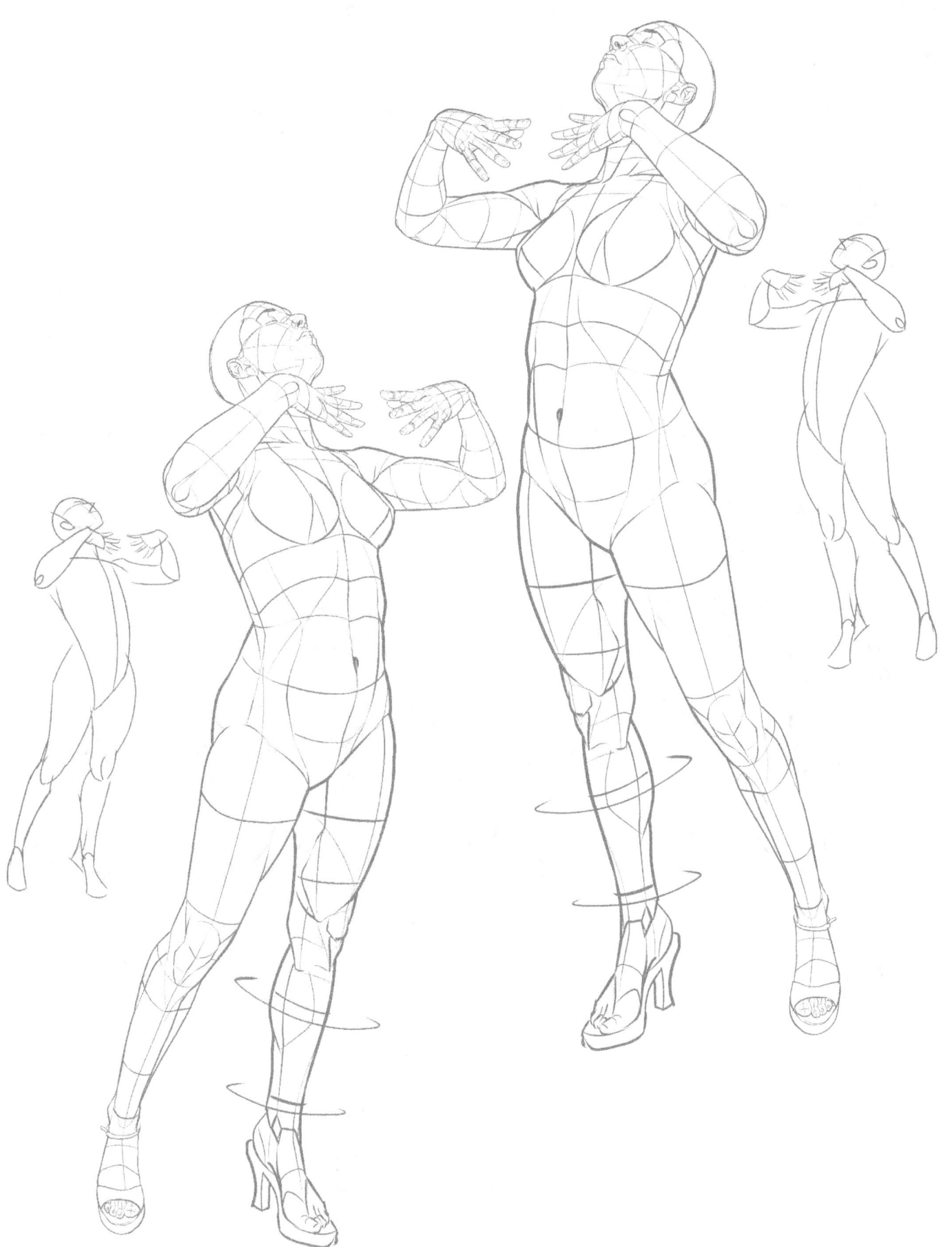

Leaping/Flying Poses

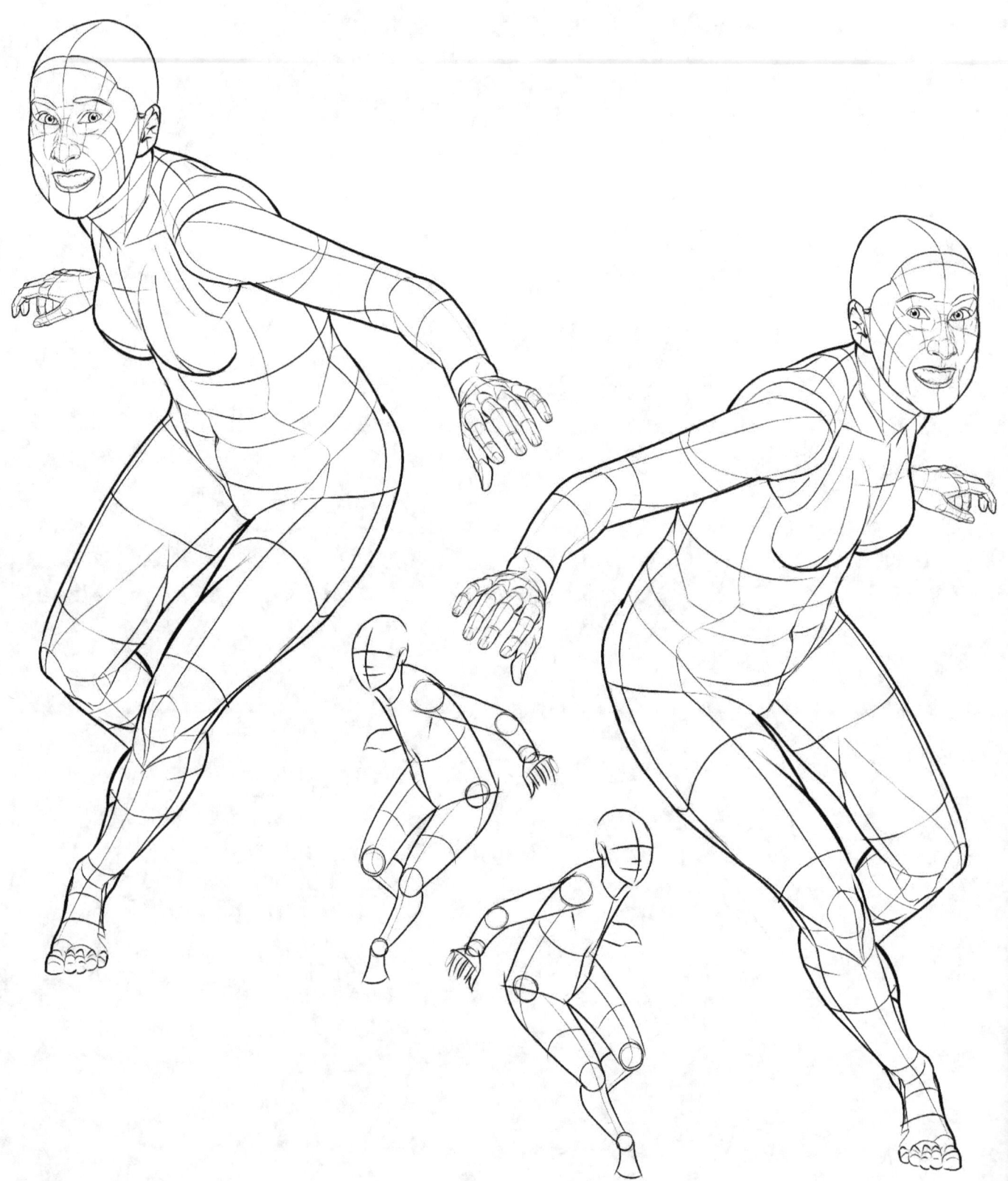

130 | Leaping/Flying Poses

Our Other Books

Our Poses For Artists book series includes hundreds of our original pose reference drawings in paperback, Kindle and ebook formats to help inspire your art. All five volumes are availableon our website POSEmuse.com

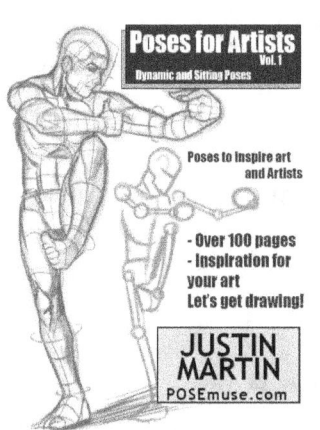

Volume 01
Dynamic and Sitting Poses

110 pages

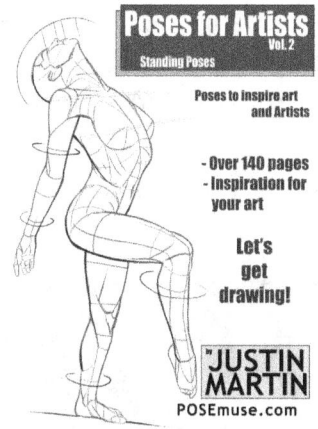

Volume 02
Standing Poses

140 pages

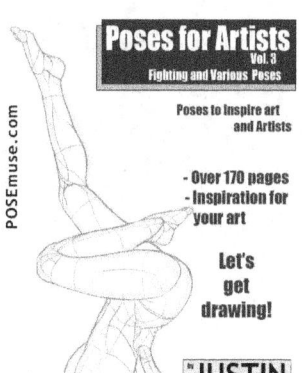

Volume 03
Fighting and Various Poses

180 pages

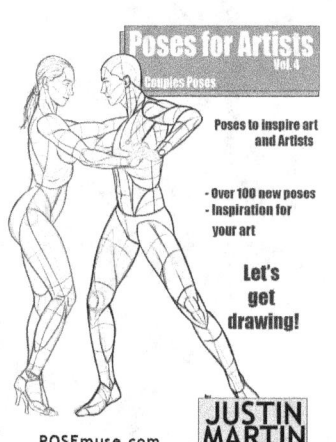

Volume 04
Couples Poses

110 pages

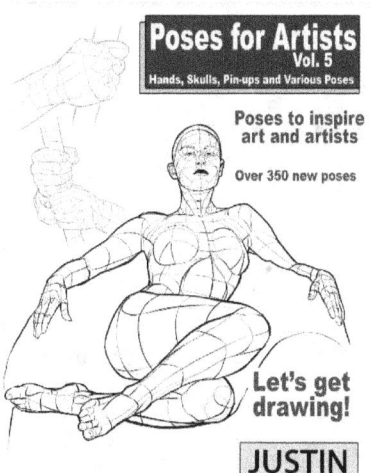

Volume 05
Hands, Skulls, Pin-ups and Various Poses

190 pages

Available in various formats including...
- Paperback Books
- E-books (pdf)
- Zip files of individual high res poses

Join us online:
Instagram: @posereference
Facebook Page: @posereference
Facebook Group: Reference for Artists
deviantart: @posemuse
Pinterest: posemusecom
Twitter: @poseref
Tumblr: @posereference

SenshiStock™ Pose Reference by Artists, for Artists

SenshiStock is a Creative Commons pose reference resource for artists. Its main gallery is located on deviantART.com as part of the wider Resources & Stock Image community there. The photos focus on models who are wearing form þtting, lightly colored clothing so an artist can see the pose clearly without nudity. This also allows all ages of artist access to the stock.

Sarah 'Sakky' Forde runs SenshiStock and she is the main model. She began making stock for her own pose reference material for her work as an artist and illustrator. You can view some of Sarah's artwork on deviantART as well.

This book is a collab between SenshStock and POSEmuse and we appreciate all she does

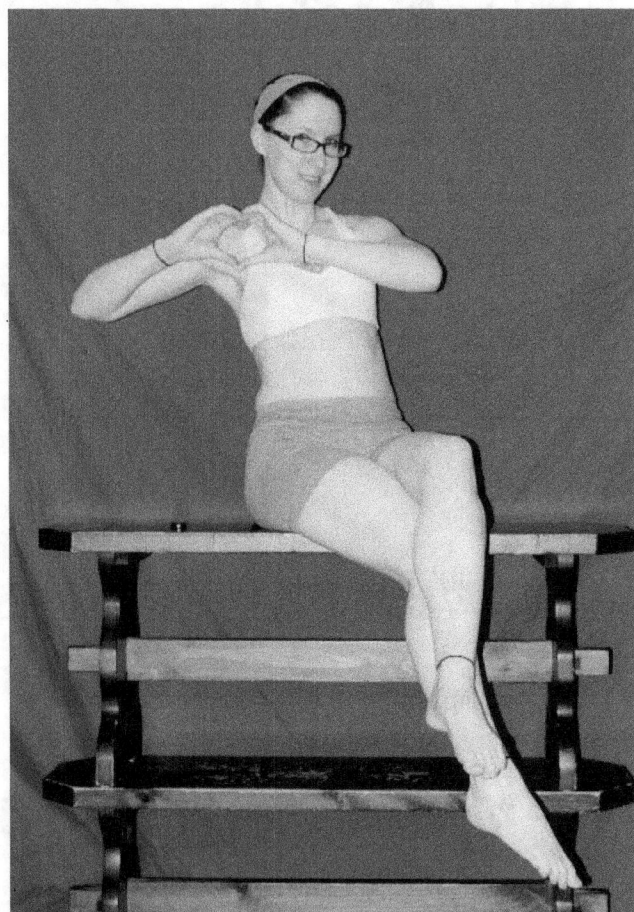
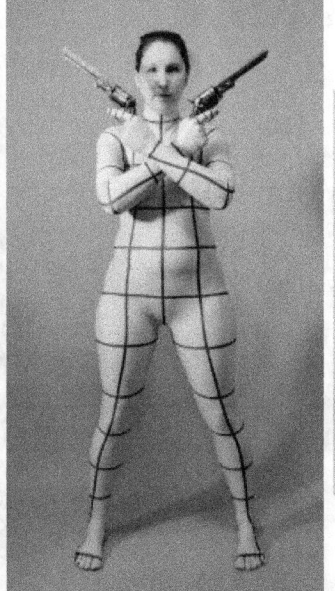
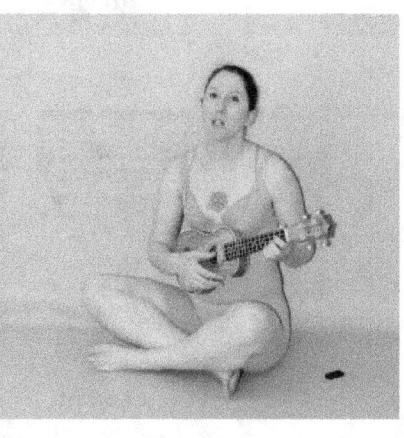
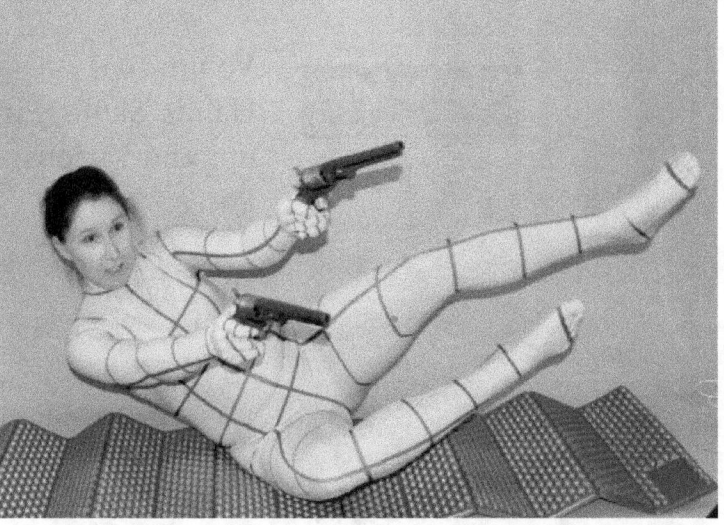

You can find SenshiStock online at:
SenshiStock.com
SenshiStock.deviantArt.com
Twitter: @SenshiStock
Facebook: SenshiStock
patreon.com/senshistock